FROM TEMPERAMENT TO CHARACTER

FROM TEMPERAMENT TO CHARACTER

ON BECOMING A VIRTUOUS LEADER

ALEXANDRE HAVARD

Edited by Anthony Salvia

 Scepter

Copyright © 2018 by Scepter Publishers, Inc.
info@scepterpublishers.org
www.scepterpublishers.org
800-322-8773
New York

Text and cover design by Rose Design

Graphic designer: Stanislav Volkov

Cover image: Michelangelo Buonarroti (1475–1564). Detail of Head in profile (1501–1504), marble. Photo Credit: Scala / Art Resource, NY.

Library of Congress Cataloging-in-Publication Data

 Names: Havard, Alexandre, author. | Salvia, Anthony T., editor.
Title: From temperament to character : on becoming a virtuous leader / Alexandre Havard ; edited by Anthony Salvia.
Other titles: Du tempérament au caractère. English.
Description: New York : Scepter Publishers, Inc., [2018]
Identifiers: LCCN 2018037964 | ISBN 9781594173370 (pbk. : alk. paper)
Subjects: LCSH: Character. | Virtues. | Temperament. | Leadership--Moral and ethical aspects.
Classification: LCC BJ1522 .H3813 2018 | DDC 170/.44--dc23
LC record available at https://lccn.loc.gov/2018037964

Printed in the United States of America

ISBN: 9781594173370

ABOUT THE AUTHOR

Alexandre Havard is the founder of the Virtuous Leadership System. His books *Virtuous Leadership* and *Created for Greatness* have been translated into twenty languages. A native of France and a graduate of one of its leading law schools, he is an attorney by profession and has practiced law in several European countries.

" There can be only one true Progress: the sum total of the spiritual progress made by individuals; the degree of self-perfection in the course of their lives. "

CONTENTS

FOREWORD

No ATTEMPT TO PRACTICE Virtuous Leadership can succeed without a basic understanding of temperament and character, which, together, constitute human personality. Temperament is our native predisposition to react in certain ways. Character is made up of virtues, which are moral habits, acquired through training. We are not born with character: it is something we build.

I have found Alexandre Havard's Virtuous Leadership approach to temperament and character to be convincing in its clarity and precision. Many people are familiar with the Myers-Briggs Type Indicator (MBTI), and in fact this is often the first thing people think of when they talk about temperament. Leaving aside doubts about the MBTI's validity and reliability that have surfaced in the scientific literature, its major difficulty is its failure to distinguish between temperament and character. It measures a mixture of both. The MBTI is useless from a self-development perspective: if you do not distinguish traits of character you have developed through the exercise of freedom from inborn traits of temperament, then you will not be able to distinguish what you can and must change from what you cannot and must not change. Experience shows us that in practice you will end up believing that everything in you is innate, and that nothing can change, and indeed must not change. The MBTI is interpreted, in practice, in a deterministic way. The same applies to the DiSC (Dominance, Influence, Steadiness, Conscientiousness) assessment, so popular in management circles.

Another popular approach to temperament is the Kiersey Temperament Sorter (KTS). This model makes no allowance for virtue and freedom. When Kiersey speaks of habits, he does not mean moral habits, but physiological habits developed in the interaction of temperament and environment. We understand why Kiersey claims it is impossible to change one's character. For him temperament *determines* character. Kiersey's determinism allows for no genuine science of character and virtue (an emergent and growing field in psychology), and denies any possibility of authentic human flourishing actually taking place.

In contrast to all of this, the *Virtuous Leadership* approach to the classical temperaments is founded on a more holistic and balanced understanding of human nature rooted in a long tradition and supported by the best of modern science, namely, that human personality is neither a product of conditioning (education and environment), nor a determinant strictly of instinct or biology, but is endowed with a profound capacity for free will and self-determination.

The latest and best psychological research validates what has been taught around the world throughout human history: that there are certain traits rooted in our common human nature that can be acquired by habit and constitute the very definition of what it means to be human, regardless of our temperament, gender, or culture. It is these habits of excellence, which, together, allow us to flourish and lead good, fruitful lives.

The *Virtuous Leadership* approach to temperament affirms the legitimate diversity of our physiological and psychological makeup, and proposes that temperament, rightly understood, undergirds the efforts of all persons to flourish and achieve excellence. It recognizes that temperament does not determine goals (much less outcomes), but instead gives shape and color to the efforts of human beings to flourish through mastering the habits of excellence. In doing so, the habits of excellence—the virtues—become second-nature to us, part and parcel of our very selves. And thus, we ascend from temperament to character, and are no longer slaves to our natural inclinations but have achieved self-mastery in true human freedom.

CAMERON THOMPSON, PhD
MINNEAPOLIS, MINNESOTA, USA

PREFACE

LEADERSHIP CAN ONLY BE VIRTUOUS or it is not leadership. When the Ancient Greeks wrote about leadership, they described their leaders' character and virtues. They could not imagine such a thing as "value-free leadership." Leadership has been conceived from the very beginning as a moral activity. We should be humble enough to listen to these heralds of modern civilization, and magnanimous enough to let ourselves be inspired by the great humanistic tradition.

And we should be intelligent enough to acknowledge the contribution of Judeo-Christian thought, which purifies, reinforces, and elevates the heritage of the Ancient Greeks.

This book is a systematic presentation of the things you need to know and do in order to become a virtuous leader. To begin with, you need to know yourself well.

This book is about self-knowledge, self-improvement, and self-realization. It is highly practical.

ALEXANDRE HAVARD

1

TEMPERAMENT AND CHARACTER

HUMAN PERSONALITY IS MADE up of temperament and character.

Temperament is given to us by nature. It is the pattern of inclinations and reactions that proceed from the physiological constitution of an individual. It is our native predisposition to react in certain ways.

Temperament may be choleric, melancholic, sanguine, or phlegmatic. We are born with our temperament and we cannot change it: we die with the qualities and defects of our temperament.

On the foundation of temperament, we build character. Character is made up of virtues. The most important virtues are prudence, courage, self-mastery, justice, magnanimity, and humility. Virtues are moral habits, acquired through training. We are not born with character; it is something we build.

The word "character" is derived from the Ancient Greek word "charaktêr," referring to a mark impressed upon a coin. The virtues *stamp* character on our temperament so that temperament ceases to dominate us.

Through character we compensate for the weakness of our temperament. We are often tempted to do what "comes naturally" even if it leads us to do things that are far from excellent. Character impels us to resist this temptation and do the right thing. Cholerics, for instance, are naturally inclined to pride and anger. They can overcome these defects by developing the virtues of humility and self-mastery. Their initial reaction to things and events, which is physiological, will be followed by a second one, which is spiritual.

The four temperaments are characterized as follows:

The choleric temperament is marked by quick, *intense*, and sustained reactivity.

The melancholic temperament is marked by slow, *deep*, and sustained reactivity.

The sanguine temperament is marked by quick, *spontaneous*, and ephemeral reactivity.

The phlegmatic temperament is marked by slow, *restrained*, and ephemeral reactivity.

- Cholerics are *intense: they are action-oriented.*
- Melancholics are *deep: they are idea-oriented.*
- Sanguines are *spontaneous: they are people-oriented.*
- Phlegmatics are *restrained: they are peace-oriented.*

Children may inherit the different temperaments of their parents. It may happen that in one person two temperaments are so mixed that both

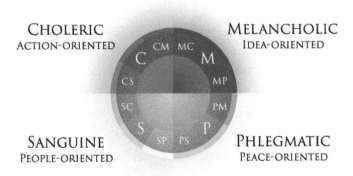

Graphic 1: The Four Temperaments

are equally strong. However, with the passage of time one of the four temperaments will manifest itself as the predominant one.

In Russia and Portugal, the dominant temperament is the melancholic, in Spain, the choleric, in Italy, the sanguine, and in Finland, the phlegmatic. In many countries there is no dominant temperament (in the U.S. and France, for instance).

We must not confuse culture with temperament. U.S. culture, including the American Dream, meets the needs of choleric people. Contemporary global culture with the development of social media meets the needs of sanguine people. But this does not mean that the majority of American citizens are choleric or that the majority of the earth's population are sanguine.

Our temperament inclines us in one direction or another: the choleric person is more inclined to accomplish things than to demonstrate sensitivity to other people, the melancholic is more inclined to contemplate ideas and experiences than to take action; the sanguine is more inclined to communicate with people than to carry out his or her many projects to perfection; the phlegmatic is more inclined to pragmatic analysis than to dreams of great endeavors.

Our physiological inclinations can be balanced by virtue: cholerics need to practice humility (to care for people); melancholics need to practice audacity (to take action); sanguines need to practice endurance (to finish the job); phlegmatics need to practice magnanimity (to dream of great things). We do not all climb the same slope toward the summit of perfection. The slope depends on our temperament.

The spheres of the physiological and the spiritual have to be clearly differentiated. Physiological toughness, for instance, is not courage, although it can help us to practice courage. Physiological apathy is not laziness, although it may facilitate laziness. Two extreme tendencies must definitely be avoided: one is to deny character, the other is to deny temperament. The first error can be called "biologism," the second "voluntarism."

Biologism denies the spirit, character, and virtue. It interprets human actions from the exclusive point of view of biology. In fact, to use temperament as an excuse for bad behavior means to deny freedom, responsibility, and personal dignity.

Voluntarists deny temperament and its natural inclinations. They interpret human actions from the exclusive point of view of the will (Latin: *voluntas*). As a result, they confuse physiological tendencies with spiritual defects. In the choleric's tireless and effective action they see pride; in the melancholic's creative self-absorption they see egoism, cowardice, and escapism; in the sanguine's *joie de vivre* they see a lack of self-mastery; in the phlegmatic, they see laziness.

Voluntarists' conception of excellence is uniform—they see it, unconsciously, from the perspective of their own temperament. They often accuse those who speak about temperament of "putting people into boxes," but they themselves have already put the whole of humanity into a "box"—a box of their own making, which is in fact a spiritual jail for those who share another temperament. Never choose a mentor or spiritual director among the voluntarists!

▶ **Exercise:** Go back and read pages 2 and 3. See where you fall on the temperament compass. This is not a test of your moral character, but of your physiological temperament. It is a test of your initial, spontaneous reaction to external stimuli.

2

THE VIRTUES OF CHARACTER

CHARACTER IS MADE UP OF VIRTUES. The most fundamental virtues are prudence, courage, self-mastery, justice, magnanimity, and humility. Prudence, courage, self-mastery and justice are the *foundation* of leadership, whereas magnanimity and humility constitute the *essence* of leadership.

PRUDENCE: MAKING RIGHT DECISIONS

Prudence enables us to perceive situations in all their complexity (or simplicity, as the case may be) and make decisions in accordance with this perception. Prudent decision-making consists of two things: deliberation and decision.

Deliberation	Decision
Embrace reality.	Do not expect certainty where it cannot exist.
Do not lie to yourself.	Overcome your fear of mistakes.
Seek advice.	Enact decisions with dispatch.

Prudence requires a keen mind capable of confronting reality straight on. Prudence is not the same thing as cunning (achieving your ends by deceit or evasion) or even cleverness (having sharp intelligence). It is about making the right decisions.

Right decisions correspond to the reality of things (the concrete situation) and of human beings (their dignity). If, instead of making decisions that correspond to the facts, you bend the facts to serve your own interests and satisfy your passions, you will never be able to practice prudence.

In order to make right decisions, you need sincerity (you must live by the truth), perspicacity (you must possess keenness of mental perception), diligence (you must take time to study reality), humility (you must ask for advice), and boldness (you must be capable of taking risks).

If you lack prudence, you will make, as a rule, either no decisions or the wrong ones. Without prudence, your path toward leadership will be closed.

George Washington was a prudent soldier. During the American War of Independence, he confronted reality and correctly assessed the situation: he was outnumbered, outgunned, and out-generaled. He decided to transform the conventional war he was fighting, involving pitched battles, into a guerrilla war. Had he thought and acted less prudently, American history might have turned out differently.

St. Teresa of Calcutta was a prudent nun. Her mission was to be a mother to the poorest of the world's poor, to share their interior desolation, to demonstrate to the entire world the infinite love of God for each and every person. "A beautiful death," she said, "is for people who lived like animals to die like angels—loved and wanted." To fulfill that mission, she founded "The Missionaries of Charity" in 1950. Soon thereafter, many people in her circle tried to pressure her into using decision-making criteria proper to philanthropic organizations. Teresa resisted. She was prudent—and courageous—enough to confront reality head on: "We are a religious order, not a philanthropy!" Within a few decades, the organization she founded became one of the leading religious congregations in the Catholic Church.

Aleksandr Suvorov, the commander-in-chief of the Imperial Russian Army in the eighteenth century, was a prudent soldier. He did not like preconceived ideas. His words, "Achieve victory not by numbers, but by knowing how," were revolutionary. His daring disregard of the military theories then current was astonishing. His way of waging wars based on speed and mobility was absolutely new. "To surprise the enemy is to defeat him, he said. . . . Judgment of eye, speed and attack are the basis of victory. . . . Swiftness and impact are the soul of genuine warfare. A good solution *now* is better than a perfect solution tomorrow."[1] When it was necessary to plan a battle, he reached deep within himself and made precise, complex, strategic plans in conditions of uncertainty. During actual battles, he made decisions in a flash, quickly choosing among options that had been worked out earlier. He was always up to the situation, took the initiative, and foisted his plan of action on his opponents. Suvorov was excellent at both deliberation and decision. He must surely be considered one of the greatest military commanders of all time. He is one of the few generals in history who never lost a battle.

1. Aleksandr Suvorov, *Nauka potbezdat'* (Moscow: Eksmo, 2011), p. 150.

He remained undefeated in more than sixty large battles, always while being at a numerical disadvantage. One of the most educated people of his time, Suvorov was described by several of his contemporaries as one of the most extraordinary men of the century. In a letter Lord Nelson wrote to Suvorov, we read: "I am being overwhelmed with honors, but I was today found worthy of the greatest of them all: I was told that I was like you. I am proud that, with so little to my credit, I resemble so great a man."[2]

Abraham Lincoln was prudent. He listened to different points of view. He created a climate in which cabinet members were free to disagree without fear of retribution. At the same time, he knew when to stop the discussion and make a final decision.

The *Pharisees* in the Gospel are often held up as an example of imprudence. Instead of thinking rationally: "This man was blind and now he sees, so Jesus Christ, who cured him, must be a saint," they brutally distorted reality under the power of passion (hatred and envy) and interest (power and money): "Jesus Christ is a sinner, and as

---

2. *YourDictionary*, s.v. "Aleksandr-vasilievich-suvorov," accessed April 19, 2018, *http://biography.yourdictionary.com/aleksandr-vasilievich-suvorov*.

sinners cannot perform miracles, clearly, the man who was born blind was never really blind." The pharisaical spirit, with its contempt for reality, looms as a constant threat even now. The abortion debate is a good example. Modern genetics affirm what every woman who has ever been pregnant knows, namely that a human being is a human being from the moment of conception. Abortion, therefore, is never justified. And yet many countries consider the destruction of innocent human life "progressive." From the point of view of prudence, the problem is not that abortion is not punished by the law (that is a political decision), but that the means of social communication make it the standard of liberty, democracy, progress, and human rights. When one tramples on science, to even talk about prudence seems like an aberration.

▶ **Self-examination:** Identify your enemy. What is it? Is it your indifference to truth and reality? Or is it your obsessive desire for certainty?

COURAGE: RUNNING RISKS AND STAYING THE COURSE

Courage has two dimensions: boldness (audacity) and endurance (fortitude). The courageous run risks and stay the course. While their endurance—their penchant for staying the course—makes them predictable, their audacity makes them unpredictable. Boldness generates creativity.

Boldness	Endurance
Learn to run risks.	Persist in the face of obstacles.
Check that your goals and means are just.	Make sure that your perseverance is not pig-headedness but principled steadfastness.

Courage requires a strong will. But courage is not the same thing as toughness. Courage is a moral virtue. A terrorist may be tough but cannot be courageous. Courage is directed toward the realization of just goals with the use of just means. People are courageous only if their goals and means are just: if they respect the basic principles of human nature and the dignity of the human person.

Endurance is about persistence and faithfulness. Faithful people are time-tested. They stick to their principled decisions, although circumstances and situations change, sometimes radically. Faithful people do not let themselves be manipulated by novelty. They are stable souls in an unstable world.

If you lack courage, you will not be able to practice what you preach. You will hesitate to act, and, when finally you do, sooner or later you will collapse under pressure. People who trusted you because you seemed to be prudent will not trust you anymore. Without courage, you have no future as a leader.

Herb Kelleher, the co-founder and former CEO of the U.S. company Southwest Airlines, was courageous. For him, the higher calling was to make air travel affordable for everyone, to open up the skies, to give ordinary people the chance to go places and do things they had only dreamed of doing. In 1971, everybody in Texas was telling him that they thought he was crazy to create Southwest Airlines. Kelleher needed boldness to buck popular opinion. He was also patient and persistent. There were airline monopolies in Texas, which Kelleher consciously sought to destroy for the good of the flying public. The monopolists were incensed. They brought legal action against Kelleher, tying him up in thirty-one judicial and administrative proceedings over a period of four years in an effort to impede competition. They did not succeed. After September 11, 2001, Kelleher maintained the course he had set for his company and did not compromise his principles in the face of unprecedented difficulty. This is endurance.

With his discovery in 1958 of the cause of Down's Syndrome, *Jérôme Lejeune* became world-famous and was touted as a possible recipient of the Nobel Prize. But then this happened on October 1, 1969: Jérôme was in San Francisco to receive the William Allan Prize of the American Society for Human Genetics. The day before he was to receive the prize, he learned to his stupefaction that a slight majority of the geneticists gathered in San Francisco were convinced that it is a decent and charitable thing to do to screen babies in the uterus for chromosomal abnormalities in order to kill them before birth. It almost seemed they were awarding Jérôme the Prize for having facilitated such screenings. Jérôme was shocked by the pro-death agenda of his colleagues. He faced a choice: either stifle the truth about the inception of human life in order to further his career, or speak the truth and be crucified. He chose the second option. He knew the words he was about to speak would be well understood by his colleagues because they would be based on scientifically verifiable facts and raw data, not on faith or morality. He knew that they would never forgive him for forcing them to face facts, and for exposing their mendacity. He knew they would make him pay for the rest of his days. Honors, prizes, emoluments, the Nobel Prize in Medicine . . . all of that was finished. Here is what Jérôme said: "Modern genetics demonstrate that at the very moment the ovum is fertilized by the sperm, all of the genetic information that defines the resulting individual is already inscribed in its entirety in the first cell. No new genetic information enters into an egg at any stage after its initial fertilization. Thus, genetic science postulates that a human being could not be a human being if not first conceived as a human being. Abortion is a tremendous crime."[3] By insisting on upholding scientific truth and the larger moral truth that flowed from it, Lejeune flew in the face of the spirit of the times, the revolutionary spirit of May 1968. He no longer received invitations

---

3. Anne Bernet, *Jérôme Lejeune* (Paris: Presses de la Renaissance, 2004); Jérôme Lejeune, "Child, Family, State: Scientific Progress and Human Rights," Address to a conference of Bulevardi Foorumi, April 1990, Helsinki.

to international conferences on genetics. Funding for his research was canceled. He was forced to disband his laboratory and research team. He found himself in the prime of life with no collaborators, no funding, not even an office. He was dropped by his friends, excoriated by the press, and made into a social pariah. He accepted this state of affairs with serenity and with the joy of knowing he had stood up to evil. He died on Easter Sunday, 1994, after a brief but agonizing illness that began on Wednesday of Holy Week. This is endurance.

Aleksandr Solzhenitsyn was courageous. He bore unflinching witness to truth, and did so under a totalitarian regime sworn to his destruction. The nation's foremost writer, he suffered imprisonment and forced exile from his homeland. Solzhenitsyn's reputation was high at home and abroad as long as he limited himself to criticizing Stalin, as in such early works as *One Day in the Life of Ivan Denisovich*. This suited the purposes of the Soviet leader Khrushchev, who was conducting a campaign against Stalin's personality cult. It also suited many Western intellectuals, who admired the October Revolution but felt that Stalin had betrayed it. In subsequent works, Solzhenitsyn made it clear that he opposed not only Stalin, but Lenin and the

October Revolution. He even rejected the February Revolution. Thus, he earned the undying enmity not only of the Soviet regime, but also of the legions of Western intellectuals—many his erstwhile supporters—who were broadly sympathetic to the revolutionary cause and its secularizing aims. Once disgorged into Western exile, he faced incomprehension and derision for his failure to pay obeisance to secular materialism. His growing army of detractors, unable to allow the legitimacy of a worldview that contradicted their own, soon made him out to be an enemy of all freedom and progress. Solzhenitsyn remained utterly unfazed. This is endurance.

Pyotr Stolypin was courageous. He served as prime minister of Russia under the last Tsar, Nicholas II. His agricultural reform program, which consisted of giving the Russian peasantry a stake in the economic system, provoked the bitter opposition of the Socialists, who had no desire to see the Tsar carry out a reform to benefit the very constituency whose disaffection they sought to exploit. No less opposed were the powerful landowners, who feared an empowered peasantry would put an end to a centuries-old social system that was the source of their power. Eleven terrorist attempts on his life failed to deter Stolypin from his efforts to reform

Russian agriculture. He remained true to his conscience, his mission, and his people. Hours after a terrorist bomb exploded during a reception at his home, killing twenty-seven people and injuring thirty-two, including two of his children, Stolypin, though barely recovered from the blast, repaired to his study to work on his reform proposal far into the night. With Russia on the brink of catastrophe, he understood that his duty as head of government was to drive through a sweeping reform of Russian life. For Stolypin, the good of the nation outweighed his personal sorrow: in the terrorist attack, his fourteen-year-old daughter Natasha was left disabled for life. He knew that the only way to keep himself and his family out of harm's way was to resign his office, but he had no intention of acquiescing to terror. He wrote in his testament, "Bury me where I will be killed." Stolypin was alone in his struggle, but he never gave up. He carried on with his mission until he was assassinated in September 1911 by Dmitri Bogrov, a shadowy figure with links both to revolutionary terrorists and the Tsarist secret police. This is endurance.

▶ **Self-examination:** Identify your enemy. Is it your fear of mistakes? Or is it your lack of constancy and endurance?

SELF-MASTERY: DIRECTING PASSIONS

Good passions contribute to good actions; evil passions contribute to evil actions. Self-mastery subdues our evil passions. It also energizes our good passions and directs them to the fulfillment of the mission at hand.

Subduing evil passions	Energizing noble passions
Control impure desires and feelings (envy, greed, lust, etc.).	Embrace noble desires and feelings (love, a noble enthusiasm, contrition, forgiveness).
Manage anger.	Allow righteous wrath.

Self-mastery is *mastery* of the heart. It is the capacity to say "yes" to what makes us grow, and "no" to what debases us. Intemperance is a mark of impotence and the inability to take effective action; it is the agony of a heart incapable of affirming itself in the depth of its being.

Self-mastery requires first of all humility: you need to acknowledge that you have evil passions. If you are convinced that natural inclinations are good because they are natural, then why would you practice self-mastery? In fact, not everything that "comes naturally" is a good thing. Envy, greed, and lust are evil realities. You need to accept the truth about yourself and be vigilant in the preservation of your personal dignity. The fact is, human nature was wounded near the dawn of human history, and we are all subject to giving in to unworthy inclinations, whether natural or unnatural.

Self-mastery opens up a space in your heart for greatness and service—for virtuous leadership. If you are obsessed with your image, power, pleasures, and possessions, you will probably lose all sense of mission and all capacity for serving others. There will be no real place for others in your heart and mind.

Self-mastery is not only about subduing your evil passions. It is also about energizing your noble ones. You need to strive for the good not only with your will, but also with your heart, which is to say, with your feelings. Eastern nirvana, stoic apathy, platonic spiritualism, religious puritanism and Kantian moralism fail to grasp human nature in the richness of its totality. People who fear passion—or at least do not perceive its ontological and existential value—and who, for instance, in the face of injustice, suppress their righteous wrath instead of giving it free rein, cannot achieve human excellence. In this regard, Christianity dealt a mortal blow to deviant spiritualism in all its various guises: Jesus Christ, the God made flesh, does not hide his fear, his tears, his anger, his pity, his joy, his compassion, and his love.

Martin Luther King preached nonviolence, but like many authentic leaders, he exhibited, in the face of injustice, the righteous wrath that impels us to action. King tells us that meekness is a mistake and a sin when wrath is required by justice and common sense. In 1963, he wrote from his cell in the Birmingham jail: "When you have seen vicious mobs lynch your mothers and fathers at will and drown your sisters and brothers at whim; when you have seen hate-filled policemen curse, kick and even kill your black brothers and sisters; when you see the vast majority of your twenty million Negro brothers smothering in an airtight cage of poverty in the midst of an affluent society; . . . When you are forever fighting a degenerating sense of 'nobodiness'—then you will understand why we find it difficult to wait."[4] This is righteous wrath.

Aleksandr Solzhenitsyn exhibited righteous wrath in front of injustice: "I will publish everything! Tell all I know! Touch off the explosive

---

4. Martin Luther King, Jr., "Letter from Birmingham Jail," *Liberation: An Independent Monthly*, 8, no. 4 (1963): 10–16, 23.

charge that had been piling up since I first saw the box cells of the Lubyanka, through all those winter work parades in the Steplag; for those who had been stifled, shot, starved or frozen to death."[5]

▶ **Self-examination:** Identify your enemy. Is it your lack of noble passion? Or is it rather your uncontrolled evil passion?

---

5. Aleksandr Solzhenitsyn, *The Oak and the Calf* (New York: Harper and Row, 1975), p. 292.

JUSTICE: GIVING EACH ONE HIS DUE

We give others their due when we practice the virtues of interpersonal communion (truthfulness and love) and promote the common good through the faithful fulfillment of our professional, social, and family responsibilities.

Communion	Common good
Pursue truthfulness, sincerity, and simplicity.	Employ industriousness.
Cultivate empathy, friendship, and cheerfulness.	Embrace domesticity.
Promote love and mercy.	Promote citizenship.

Justice is more than a legal or political concept; it is a personal virtue, a quality of character.

Justice requires prudence: you need to have a keen mind capable of identifying what is due the other. To have a keen mind means first of all to have a vision of the transcendent dignity of the human being. If not, you will give people not what is due them as people, but what is due chimpanzees.

Justice requires courage: you need to be strong-willed to be determined to give others their due.

Justice cannot be achieved without love. Precisely because humans are personal beings, you cannot give them their due except by loving them.

If you lack justice, you will be serving yourself, not others. Your path to leadership will be closed.

Abraham Lincoln was a just man. As early as the 1850s, a time when most American political rhetoric focused on the sanctity of the Constitution, he upheld the Declaration of Independence as the foundation of American moral and political values. The Declaration's emphasis on freedom and equality for all, in contrast to the Constitution's tolerance of slavery, shifted the debate. Lincoln understood that the common good is concerned with *all men*. Like Lincoln, those who seek to abolish abortion—one of the worst moral evils ever to be inflicted on mankind—also practice justice.

Jérôme Lejeune, the French geneticist, was a just man. He was a hard worker (at thirty-eight, he became France's youngest professor of medicine and held the country's first chair in fundamental genetics). He was an exemplary husband and father. He strove for the common good of humanity. He took care of thousands of children with Down's syndrome and helped thousands of parents to love their children affected by this genetic disorder. His discoveries in genetics led him to understand and affirm the unconditional dignity of the human being from the moment of conception. He said: "You are not obliged to accept science. You could say: 'Well, we prefer to be ignorant, we refuse absolutely any novelty and any discovery.' It's a point of view. I should say, it's a 'politically correct' point of view in some countries, but it's an obscurantist point of view, and science abhors obscurantism."[6] Lejeune gave his due to the world of science. He gave his family, his country, the whole of humanity their due. He gave millions of unborn children who are sacrificed every year in abortion clinics all over the world their due. Lejeune was sincere, simple, convincing. He did not fight against people, but against wrong ideas. He was such a good communicator (he possessed the virtues of interpersonal communion) that pro-abortion activists were terrified whenever they heard him speak in public debates. More than everything else, Lejeune was a just man: he gave God and people their due.

Peter Drucker explained better than anyone else the meaning of justice in business: "It is management's public responsibility to *make* whatever

---

6. Jérôme Lejeune, "Child, Family, State."

is genuinely in the public good *become* the enterprise's own self-interest. . . . Every leading group must, on the contrary, be able to claim that the public good determines its own interests. This assertion is the only legitimate basis for leadership; to make it reality is the first duty of the leaders."[7] A practical application of this principle is investing in social and cultural development, not merely in activities likely to rake in lots of cash.

▶ **Self-examination:** Identify your enemy. Is it your failure to practice the virtues of interpersonal communion? Or is it your indifference to the common good?

---

7. Peter F. Drucker, *The Practice of Management* (New York: Routledge, 2007), p. 339.

MAGNANIMITY:
STRIVING TOWARD GREAT THINGS

Magnanimity (big-heartedness or greatness of soul) is the virtue of contemplative souls who acknowledge the unique dignity and exalted vocation of the human being. It is also the virtue of doers. Magnanimity is directed toward action. Magnanimity is the virtue of contemplation and action. It is the virtue of philosophers and doers. Magnanimous people not only acknowledge their dignity—they affirm it with deeds.

Contemplation	Action
Be mindful of your personal dignity.	Affirm your personal dignity.
Discover your strengths and talents.	Embrace your strengths and talents.
Explore dreams and visions.	Pursue your mission.

Magnanimity is the striving of the spirit toward great things. If you strive for greatness and seek to achieve it, you are magnanimous. Magnanimity is rooted in a firm confidence in the highest possibilities of human nature. Magnanimity is an ideal rooted in trust in the inherent greatness of the human being. It is the supreme form of human hope.

Magnanimity is not pride: if you are magnanimous, you perceive your strength, dignity, and greatness as gifts from God, rather than the result of your own personal activities or merits.

Magnanimity seeks greatness, not recognition. The pusillanimous (the small-hearted) have no sense of personal, inherent dignity: they think they are worth what people believe they are worth. They want professional recognition at any price. They work a lot because they fear they will not be recognized. People with a sense of personal dignity are not dependent on recognition: they have no need for it.

Magnanimity is the first specific virtue of leaders. Leaders are magnanimous in their vision of self, in their dreams and missions; in their confidence and enthusiasm, hope and daring; in their propensity for using means proportionate to their goals; in their capacity to challenge themselves and those around them.

Martin Luther King was magnanimous. He was a philosopher and a doer. He tells us that leadership begins with a dream. In his "I Have a Dream" speech—one of the most famous of the twentieth century—he reveals his dream of freedom and equality in the midst of hatred and oppression. Both the dream and its realization are the substance of magnanimity. Leaders are dreamers who transform their dreams into action. The dream of a pusillanimous heart is a fantasy. The dream of a magnanimous heart becomes a reality: it is directed toward action. Magnanimity is not afraid of mistakes: it is afraid of inaction. In his Letter from Birmingham City Jail, Dr. King wrote:

> For years now I have heard the word "Wait!" It rings in the ear of every Negro with piercing familiarity. This "Wait" has almost always meant "Never." . . . I have almost reached the regrettable conclusion that the Negro's great stumbling block in his stride toward freedom is not the White Citizen's Councilor or the Ku Klux Klanner, but the white moderate, . . . who paternalistically believes he can set the timetable for another man's freedom; who lives by a mythical concept of time and who constantly advises the Negro to wait for a "more convenient season." . . . We have waited for more than 340 years for our constitutional and God-given rights. . . . More and more I feel that the people of ill will have used time much more effectively than have the

people of good will. We will have to repent in this generation not merely for the hateful words and actions of the bad people but for the appalling silence of the good people. . . . We must use time creatively, in the knowledge that the time is always ripe to do right."[8]

Martin Luther King tells us here a very important thing: For magnanimous souls, evil is not something done by others; it is the good that they, personally, failed to do. Magnanimous hearts do not fear mistakes. They fear inaction. Not seizing the opportunity out of laziness or fear—this is what makes a true leader suffer more than anything else.

Europe as we know it might never have come into being but for the magnanimity of a sixth-century Italian monk called *Benedict*. Born in a time and place beset by corruption and repeated barbarian invasions, Benedict saw the challenge facing Europe as essentially spiritual and cultural. He and his followers established a network of monastic communities across Europe, which eventually numbered eighty in Benedict's own lifetime. These communities were repositories of Christian faith and the inherited culture, islands

8. Martin Luther King, Jr., "Letter from Birmingham Jail."

in the torrent of barbarism sweeping across the continent. They were largely responsible for the preservation of Western civilization.

In the East, *Cyril and Methodius*, Greek monks and blood brothers born in ninth-century Thessalonica, displayed a magnanimity that paralleled Benedict's in the West. They conceived a bold vision for bringing the Slavic tribes of Europe into the Christian communion. They created an alphabet adapted to the phonetics of the Slavic languages to allow the Slavs of central and eastern Europe to follow the liturgy in a language they could understand, thereby laying the foundations for Slavic culture. For this they faced torture and abuse. Cyril and Methodius are giants not only of the spirit, but of culture and inculturation: a concern to bring revealed truth to whole nations while respecting their original culture remains a living model for evangelizers of our time. In politics, Cyril and Methodius remind us that the union of peoples can only come about on the basis of respect and love for diversity. Their message was "Yes to unity, no to uniformity!"

▸ **Self-examination:** Identify your enemy. Is it your failure to dream? Or is it your failure to transform your dream into a mission?

HUMILITY:
KNOWING ONESELF AND SERVING OTHERS

Humility is the habit of living in the truth about oneself (self-knowledge). It is also the habit of serving others. We serve people effectively when we help them grow as human beings.

Self-knowledge	Service
Be mindful of your createdness.	Serve others.
Be mindful of your flaws.	Help people grow.
Acknowledge your dignity.	
Be aware of your talents.	

Self-knowledge is *fundamental* humility. It is the result of contemplation. Service is *fraternal* humility. It is the result of action.

Fundamental humility is not pusillanimity (small-mindedness or small-heartedness). Certainly, self-knowledge makes you aware of your limitations and flaws, but it makes you also aware of your dignity and talents (in the same way magnanimity does). If you do not recognize your talents, you are not humble: you are pusillanimous. Magnanimity and humility go hand in hand.

Fraternal humility is the second virtue specific to leaders. Leadership means pulling rather than pushing, teaching rather than ordering around, inspiring rather than berating. Leaders bring out the greatness in others and give them the capacity to realize their human potential. Leadership is less about displays of power than the empowerment of others. Leaders delegate power not because they do not have the time to do everything themselves, but because they know that followers are more likely to grow if they are involved in the decision-making process. Leaders promote their people, rather than themselves. They do not make themselves irreplaceable, but rather plan for their succession. All of this is fraternal humility in practice.

Herb Kelleher, the American businessman, practiced fraternal humility. He succeeded in making the employees of Southwest Airlines feel intellectually, emotionally, and spiritually connected to a vision full of humanity, simplicity, humor, and altruism. Kelleher would say: "The general office is at the bottom of the pyramid, not the top. Our job at the general office is to supply the resources that our frontline fighters need in order to be successful. . . . We have a 'People Department.' That's what it deals with, so don't call it 'Human Resources'—that sounds like something from a Stalin five-year plan."[9]

Kelleher encouraged and applauded out-of-the-box thinking from everyone at the company, from flight attendants to top-level executives. . . . If a Southwest employee submitted an idea, he or she could expect an answer within a week.

Kelleher established a culture of empowerment and collaboration in which people could make decisions and show initiative beyond the scope of their day-to-day responsibilities. "We want all our people to be leaders," he said. "I don't care whether you're checking bags or loading them in the bin or no matter what you're doing. You're setting a standard for other people. You should be inspirational." Kelleher said, "We devote an enormous amount of time to making sure we get people who are other-oriented, who have a servant's heart, who enjoy working as part of the team. . . . And then we try to maintain their interest, their *esprit de corps* by constantly communicating with them and honoring them."[10]

---

9. Julie Aigner-Clark, "I am American Business," video interview, *CNBC, https://www.cnbc.com/id/100000634;* Evan Carmichael, "Business Ideas: 3 Lessons from Herb Kelleher (Southwest Airlines)," EvanCarmichael, *http://www.evancarmichael.com/library/evan -carmichael2/Business-Ideas--3-Lessons-from-Herb-Kelleher-South west-Airlines.html*

10. Aigner-Clark.

Kelleher built a culture that put his employees ahead of customers. "The customer," he said, "is sometimes wrong. We don't carry those sorts of customers. We write to them and say, 'Fly somebody else. Don't abuse our people'."[11]

Kelleher multiplied his leadership in and through others and made it possible for his organization to continue its mission beyond his retirement. Continuity, along with empowerment, is a sign of true humility. Kelleher did not make himself irreplaceable. He created the conditions for others to bring his work to a successful conclusion. He paved the way for succession. This is fraternal humility.

Édouard Michelin, founder of the market-leading Michelin Company, is another example of a businessman who practiced fraternal humility. Six years after he created the company in 1889 in France, Michelin invented and brought to market the first tire for the automobile industry. In the 1930's Marius Mignol, a worker without formal education, was hired to work in the company's print shop. But Édouard Michelin had other plans for him. He told the firm's head of

---

11. Paul Uduk, *Bridges to the Customer's Heart*, (Bloomington, IN: Trafford, 2011), p.141. Kindle edition.

personnel: "Don't judge by appearances. Remember that one must break the stone to find the diamond hidden inside."

Mignol was reassigned to a purely commercial part of the business involving international markets. One day, Michelin noticed a strange-looking slide ruler on Mignol's desk. It was a device Mignol had invented to rapidly convert foreign exchange rates into the local currency. Édouard exclaimed: "This man is a genius!"[12]

Édouard transferred Mignol to the research division at a critical time for the industry. The conventional tire of that time had reached the limits of its usefulness because of its tendency to heat up at high speeds. The conventional tire could not go more than eighty miles an hour without blowing up. To study variations in heat inside the conventional tire, Mignol invented a "fly trap," a tire whose sides were replaced by metallic cables with plenty of space between them.

The resulting "radial tire" (invented in 1941) proved revolutionary. Mignol ended up becoming the tire engineer of the century. Because of

---

12. François Graveline, "Le rayonnement du radial," *Michelin— Son histoire, ses champions, les héros du quotidien*, (Numéro hors série, 2007), pp. 53–54.

its significant advantages, the radial tire spread quickly in Europe and Asia in the 1950s, and in the US in the 1970s. Radial technology is now the standard design for essentially all automotive tires and the Michelin company is the world's largest tire manufacturer.

For Marius Mignol, who invented the radial tire, Édouard Michelin was more than a boss. He was his mentor, teacher, and father. Édouard the boss became the servant of Marius the employee. He helped him discover his talents and put them at the service of the organization, the country, and the whole world. This is fraternal humility.

▶ **Self-examination:** Identify your enemy. Is it your pride ("I am self-sufficient!"), or is it your indifference to the spiritual growth of those you lead ("Things are more important than people!")?

THE CHOLERICS:

THEIR PERSONAL CHALLENGES

CHOLERICS ARE *INTENSE:* they are ACTION-ORIENTED.

Their strengths:

- enthusiastic, energetic
- self-confident and aware of their talents
- eminently pragmatic
- natural entrepreneurs: they start things
- natural managers: they get things done quickly
- comfortable with power, they flourish in competition

Their weaknesses:

- prone to pride, anger

- susceptible to rashness (precipitate decisions and actions)
- slow to admit mistakes
- inclined toward blind activism
- confrontational and domineering
- insensitive; known to disregard coworkers' views and feelings
- likely not to take the time to mold, convince, or teach the people they supervise

PRUDENCE

Deliberation ⊖	Decision ⊕
Cholerics are prone to rashness (to charge ahead without proper reflection).	Cholerics exhibit self-confidence.
Cholerics tend not to seek advice.	

Cholerics have no problem with making decisions; they have problems with making *right* decisions. They must practice self-mastery and moderate their natural impatience. They must also practice humility and overcome their natural reluctance to ask for advice. This will help them deliberate efficiently.

Cholerics must remember Shakespeare's *Othello*: he meets a cruel fate brought on by his failure to deliberate. Ever impulsive, he jumps straight to the conclusion without stopping to think. He shoots first and asks questions later.

And yet, the choleric must not let his deliberations—the time and effort he expends on them—impede his natural ability to decide. Remember: the aim of prudence is not deliberation, but decision. It is a bad thing not to deliberate, but it is much worse not to decide. Not to decide is basically and fundamentally imprudent.

COURAGE

Audacity ●	Endurance ●
Cholerics possess self-confidence.	Cholerics exhibit sustained reactivity.

Courage (boldness and endurance) is not a real challenge for the choleric, provided he knows what the right thing is, and does it. The choleric needs to be sure that his goals and means are just. Courage is a virtue: it implies goodness and is directed toward goodness.

Paul of Tarsus was a choleric who fanatically persecuted Christians. He truly sacrificed himself in this endeavor. This was toughness, rather than courage. After his conversion to Christianity, Paul sacrificed himself for the right cause and employed the right means. This was courage. Paul the persecutor became the greatest Christian leader of all time.

SELF-MASTERY

Subduing evil passions ⊖	Energizing noble passions ⊕
Cholerics are prone to pride and anger.	Cholerics possess strong physiological energy and enthusiasm.

Cholerics can easily energize their *noble* passions, but they must struggle to subdue their *evil* ones, such as pride and anger.

Pride can be overcome by humility: cholerics need to understand that their physiological strength is a gift from God, not the result of their activity. Anger can be overcome by meekness: they must stop viewing every statement of opinion as a declaration of war, they must soften a harsh tongue, and they must never correct anyone while they are still indignant about some failing or shortcoming.

JUSTICE

Communion ⊖	Common good ⊕
Cholerics tend to be confrontational and domineering.	Cholerics strive for the common good through work, family, religion, and social life.
Cholerics tend to be contemptuous of those less forceful and dynamic.	

Because cholerics are action-oriented, they can easily strive for the common good, provided they know what the common good is and are determined to achieve it.

The real challenge for cholerics is interpersonal communion: in their determination to achieve results, they often ignore their followers' feelings. They tend to be confrontational and contemptuous. Cholerics need humility to listen to people, understand them, and respect their dignity.

MAGNANIMITY

Contemplation ⊕	Action ⊕
Cholerics tend to be aware of their talents.	Cholerics are self-confident.
Contemplation ⊖	
Cholerics are prone to blind activism.	

Cholerics are prone to set high goals and achieve them. But they may easily fall into blind activism. They must strengthen the contemplative side of their personality. Magnanimous people are always doers, but never do things just for the sake of doing them; their doing is always an extension of their being, the outgrowth of their contemplation of their own dignity and greatness. Workaholics act in order to escape themselves, and somehow fill the emptiness of their interior lives. The workaholic has little sense of his inherent, personal dignity. Cholerics must avoid workaholism and blind activism at all costs.

HUMILITY

Self-knowledge ✚	Service ➖
Cholerics tend to be aware of their talents.	Cholerics are likely to be confrontational and contemptuous of those less forceful and dynamic. They disregard their followers' feelings in their mania to get the job done.
Self-knowledge ➖	Cholerics do not take the time to mold, convince, or teach the people they oversee.
Cholerics tend not to be aware that their talents are gifts from God.	
Cholerics tend not to admit mistakes.	
Cholerics are prone to pride.	

Cholerics are highly aware of their talents. This kind of knowledge is an important aspect of both magnanimity and humility (self-knowledge).

But fraternal humility (service) is a major challenge for cholerics. They need to take the time to mold, convince, and teach the people they are in charge of. They do not practice inclusion and empowerment easily (they don't like to delegate because they believe that they can do it better and faster themselves and because they enjoy their own productivity). Cholerics tend to be good managers and often attract others through their dynamism and energy. Nevertheless, if they fail to develop fraternal humility, their path to leadership will be blocked.

cholerics

are fundamentally challenged by

humility.

Joan of Arc was a choleric. In warfare, she was a highly efficient commander in the field. Joan was a powerful manager: she drove the English from French soil. But she was also a magnificent leader: she brought out the greatness in her soldiers, changed the hearts of millions of her countrymen, and engendered the spiritual revival of the nation, which had sunk into mediocrity and darkness. Joan was a choleric who practiced humility.

4

THE MELANCHOLICS:

THEIR PERSONAL CHALLENGES

MELANCHOLICS ARE *DEEP:* they are IDEA-ORIENTED.

Their strengths:

- deep, reflective, contemplative
- idealistic and long for perfection
- orderly and diligent
- faithful, patient, and persistent
- grace and aplomb to handle the big crises
- self-motivated: not responsive to reward or punishment

Their weaknesses:

- prone to self-absorption
- fear of actions which risk human imperfection

- pessimistic and magnify difficulties
- averse to risk
- extremely moody
- ineffective team players
- critical or judgmental of others
- overly sensitive and unforgiving

PRUDENCE

Deliberation ⊕	Decision ⊖
Melancholics are deep, reflective, and contemplative.	Melancholics fear action in which human imperfection becomes manifest.
Deliberation ⊖	Melancholics crave certainty.
Melancholics exaggerate difficulties.	
Melancholics tend to be pessimistic.	

In deliberation, melancholics tend to be deep and reflective. But they must overcome their pessimism and tendency to magnify difficulties. They also need boldness to come to a decision. Melancholics love "The Idea," which is perfect, but fear action in which human imperfection becomes manifest.

Melancholics must overcome their fear of the unknown and decide audaciously. Shakespeare's *Hamlet* is a good example of how an obsessive desire for certainty can result in imprudent decision-making. Hamlet craves information to give him greater certainty, but in the end he fails to act. Shakespeare's masterpiece is, indeed, a "tragedy of indecisiveness."

COURAGE

Audacity ⊖	Endurance ⊕
Melancholics see all the difficulties and pitfalls of a new venture.	Melancholics are consistent, faithful, patient and persistent.
Melancholics are overly cautious.	Melancholics handle the big crises with aplomb.
Melancholics worry about the less important.	
Melancholics fear of the future stymies initiative.	

Spiritual depth makes melancholic people enduring. They easily find a meaning in their trials. But melancholics need to be bold: they prefer analysis to action. They tend to be overly cautious and focus on all the potential difficulties of a new venture.

Melancholics must remember always these words of Peter Drucker: "The better a man is the more mistakes will he make—for the more new things he will try. I would never promote a man into a top-level job who has not made mistakes, and big ones at that. Otherwise he is sure to be mediocre."[1]

melancholics
are fundamentally challenged by
audacity.

Martin Luther King was a melancholic: intense melancholia was one of the most striking features of his personality. But Martin overcame his fears and took direct action as a leader of the civil rights movement. A few months after he wrote his Letter from Birmingham Jail, he organized

---

1. Drucker, *The Practice of Management*, p. 128.

and led the March on Washington and delivered his historic "I Have a Dream" speech in which he called for an end to racism. King was a melancholic who practiced audacity.

Maria Callas was a melancholic, but by overcoming her fear of failure she became one of the greatest opera singers of all time. In 1949, maestro Tullio Serafin asked her to replace Margherita Carosio, who had fallen ill, in the role of Elvira in Bellini's *I Puritani*. He gave Callas six days to learn the role. Callas was convinced she was not up to the challenge. First, the role was entirely new to her. Second, a Wagnerian voice cannot substitute overnight for a coloratura soprano. The project sounded crazy. But Serafin reassured her: "I guarantee you can do it." In the briefest amount of time, Callas mastered one of the most complex roles in the repertory, submitting her voice to enormous strain. Her dramatic portrayal of Elvira stunned the musical world and made her, overnight, a star of international renown. She would go on to transform the opera through her talent not merely as a singer but as an actress. Callas was a melancholic who practiced audacity.

SELF-MASTERY

Subduing evil passions ⊖	Energizing noble passions ⊕
Melancholics struggle with anxiety. pessimism. sadness. a critical spirit. oversensitivity.	Melancholics value all that is noble.

Melancholics can easily summon up good passions as they deeply value and are attuned to all that is noble. But they must struggle to control their anxiety (they worry about things that are not important), natural pessimism (they tend to focus on the negative), sadness (they are extremely moody), critical spirit (they easily criticize others and their projects), and oversensitivity (they tend to hold grudges).

Moses, the great prophet of the Jewish people ("God spoke to him face to face"), was a melancholic. He was pessimistic, insecure, fearful, and resistant to taking leadership. Cautious by nature, he weighed all the pros and cons before agreeing to anything. He replied to God with a series of moody attitudes and questions that revealed his inner fear: "Who am I that I should lead these people? Who should I say sent me? What if they don't believe me?" Moses confronted his defects and overcame his natural pessimism: he led the Israelites out of slavery and on to the Promised Land.

JUSTICE

Communion ⊖	Common good ⊕
Melancholics are critical of others and bear grudges.	Melancholics strive for the common good; they are idea-oriented.
Melancholics are bad team players; they do things their own way.	

Melancholics can easily strive for the common good (they are idea-oriented), if they overcome self-absorption and practice audacity. But they are deeply challenged by the virtues of interpersonal communion. They tend to be absorbed with their own thoughts and feelings (melancholics do not "roll over" people, like cholerics—they do not even "see" them). They tend to bear grudges and be critical of others (in other words, treat people unjustly), and be bad team players.

MAGNANIMITY

Contemplation ⊕	Action ⊖
Melancholics are aware of their personal dignity.	Melancholics fear action
Melancholics are aware of their talents.	Melancholics do not like to run risks.
Melancholics are dreamers.	

Magnanimity is the virtue of contemplation and action. Melancholics are prone to be contemplative, to be aware of their personal dignity, and to set their sights on the highest of goals. They tend to be magnanimous in terms of contemplation but are prone to pusillanimity when it comes to acting: they must overcome their pessimism and fear of the future. They must practice boldness.

HUMILITY

Self-knowledge ⊕	Service ⊖
Melancholics are aware of their talents.	Melancholics tend to be self-absorbed.
Melancholics are aware that their talents are gifts from God.	

Melancholics have no problem with self-knowledge: they tend to acknowledge their nothingness without God and their greatness with him. They tend to be aware of their talents, which, unlike cholerics, they gratefully acknowledge are gifts from God. But they may find it hard to serve others effectively: they tend to be self-absorbed. If they struggle to practice the virtues of interpersonal communion (love, empathy, friendship, cheerfulness), they will overcome this self-absorption: they will inspire people and become powerful teachers and educators.

5

THE SANGUINES:

THEIR PERSONAL CHALLENGES

SANGUINES ARE *SPONTANEOUS*: they are PEOPLE-ORIENTED.

Their strengths:

- enjoy people and want to make them happy
- friendly, outgoing, and communicative
- warmhearted, compassionate, and generous
- creative, enterprising, and adventuresome
- attuned to the five senses: a good eye for detail

Weaknesses:

- prone to superficiality and inconstancy
- motivated in large part by fun
- easily distracted by something new
- eager to please and to receive praise

- tempted to forsake what they know is right in order to fit in with the crowd
- attuned to the five senses and easily drawn to tangible pleasures and external attractions

PRUDENCE

Deliberation ⊖	Decision ⊕
Sanguines are prone to superficiality.	Sanguines embrace new undertakings.
Sanguines overlook difficulties.	

It is easy for sanguine people to make a decision: they tend to love adventure. But in the process of deliberation, they tend to overlook difficulties ("Trust me! It'll work out!"). They need to overcome their natural superficiality and look reality in the eye.

COURAGE

Audacity ⊕	Endurance ⊖
Sanguines love adventures.	Sanguines are prone to inconstancy.
	Sanguines are volatile and changeable in their emotions and ideas.
	Sanguines forsake what they know is right in order to fit in with the crowd.
	Sanguines feel uncomfortable when there is a disagreement.
	Sanguines aim to please everyone; they want everyone to love them.

Sanguines may easily practice audacity: they are adventurous. They tend to feel bored if they are not absorbed by something intriguing. But they are prone to inconstancy: they are volatile and changeable in their whims and ideas (fun is often their prime motivator). They need to practice endurance: they must learn to bring their many projects to a proper conclusion.

sanguines

are fundamentally challenged by

endurance.

Sir Thomas More, the English thinker and Lord Chancellor of King Henry VIII, was sanguine by nature. He was always smiling, light-hearted, friendly, and communicative. Someone called him the "laughing philosopher." But More was also deep, constant, and faithful. He even stands as a model of endurance for all ages. He refused to take an oath recognizing Henry as self-proclaimed head of a new English church of his own invention. Although treated cruelly during his fifteen-month incarceration in the Tower of London, and despite the opposition of his king, the bishops of England, most of his friends, and his entire family (including, most painfully, his beloved daughter Margaret), Sir Thomas stood fast in his convictions and suffered martyrdom by decapitation. A "man for all seasons," Thomas More was a sanguine who practiced endurance.

SELF-MASTERY

Subduing evil passions ⊖	Energizing noble passions ⊕
Sanguines find it difficult to control the five external senses (seeing, hearing, feeling, tasting, smelling), and the imagination.	Sanguines are warmhearted and generous.

Sanguine people see everything, the good as well as the bad. They tend to be sensation-seekers. They often love the life of luxury and like to impress others with their expensive clothes and sports cars. Their particular challenge is to control their external senses (unlike the cholerics and the melancholics, who need above all to control their internal senses).

David, the second King of the Jewish people, was sanguine by nature. He had a hard time controlling his external senses. As a result, he committed adultery and murder. But he sincerely repented and eventually became a model of leadership. David is the one God called "a man after my heart" (Acts 13:22, Revised Standard Version).

JUSTICE

Communion ⊕	Common good ⊖
Sanguines are friendly, outgoing, communicative, and compassionate.	Sanguines are unstable in their undertakings and commitments.
Sanguines are good team players; they go out of their way to help others.	

Sanguines are outgoing. It may be easy for them to practice the virtues of communion. But in order to strive for the common good, they need to overcome their instability. They do this by practicing the virtues of endurance and faithfulness.

MAGNANIMITY

Contemplation ⊖	Action ⊕
Sanguines are superficial in their reflections.	Sanguines love adventure.
	Action ⊖
	Sanguines are unstable in their actions.

To practice magnanimity, sanguines need to overcome their natural superficiality and develop the ability to sustain their actions over the long term.

HUMILITY

Self-knowledge ⊖	Service ⊕
Sanguines take into account others and their feelings, though are disinclined to reflect on their own talents and short-comings.	Sanguines are concerned to serve others.
	Service ⊖
	Sanguines are unstable in their service.

Sanguines are prone to serve others, but they also tend to be unstable. If they practice the virtue of endurance, they may become great servants.

6

THE PHLEGMATICS:

THEIR PERSONAL CHALLENGES

PHLEGMATICS ARE *RESTRAINED*: they are PEACE-ORIENTED.

Their strengths:

- scientific in approach to reality
- excellent listeners; they have great empathy for others
- endowed with a strong sense of obligation and cooperation
- known to possess a hidden will of iron; they are constant, loyal, and persevering
- not easily insulted or provoked to anger; calm under pressure

Weaknesses:

- content with the status quo, security, and routine

- indecisive and terrified of making mistakes
- seeking to avoid conflict at all costs
- prone to passivity

PRUDENCE

Deliberation ✚	Decision ➖
Phlegmatics are commonsensical and mentally well-balanced.	Phlegmatics are terrified of making mistakes.
Phlegmatics take a scientific, dispassionate, and realistic approach.	

Phlegmatic people tend to have a great deal of common sense. This is important in deliberation. But they tend to be indecisive. They are terrified of making mistakes. If they practice boldness, they can become powerful decision-makers.

Robert Schuman, the political founder of the European Union, was phlegmatic. He was so phlegmatic that people fell asleep while listening to him. He looked like a provincial notary public, like a man who was born old. He did everything he could to pass unnoticed. Schuman's charisma did not stem from magnetism, but from his profoundly moral vision of Europe and the contribution to humanity this vision entailed. As France's Minister of Foreign Affairs, he said: "Europe must not miss its hour of destiny." He did not let the opportunity pass: in a matter of days he laid the basis for the European Common Market, which later evolved into the European Union. German Chancellor Konrad Adenauer observed: "The powerful and daring initiative of Robert Schuman was an act of extraordinary significance. Thanks to his prudence and values, he laid the foundations for reconciliation between France and Germany and for the construction of a united and strong Europe."[1] The phlegmatic Robert Schuman was prudent because he learned to be bold. Although he was timid by temperament, he made daring decisions and carried them out no matter the consequences. When a decision was made, he was impervious to criticism, attacks, and threats.

---

1. René Lejeune, *Robert Schuman: Père de l'Europe* (Paris: Fayard, 1980), p.150.

COURAGE

Audacity ⊖	Endurance ⊕
Phlegmatics are apathetic and slothful.	Phlegmatics possess a hidden will of iron.
Phlegmatics crave the status quo, security, and routine.	Phlegmatics are patient with difficult people and situations.
Phlegmatics are indecisive and terrified of making mistakes.	Phlegmatics are constant and persevering.

Endurance is not a big challenge for the phlegmatic: he tends to possess a hidden will of iron, to be patient with difficult people and situations, and to persevere. But phlegmatic people need to practice audacity: they tend to love the status quo and are terrified of making mistakes.

Abraham, the great Patriarch of the Jewish people and first prophet of monotheism, was a phlegmatic. He did not argue with his nephew Lot, who chose the best piece of land for his cattle. He did not argue with his wife Sarah when she sent Hagar and his son into the wilderness, although he was greatly distressed. Nor did he argue with God when the Almighty asked for the sacrifice of Abraham's son Isaac. But Abraham was capable of great boldness: he left familiar, comfortable surroundings to establish a home for the Israelites on land designated by God.

SELF-MASTERY

Subduing evil passions ⊕	Energizing noble passions ⊖
Phlegmatics are not easily insulted or provoked to anger.	Phlegmatics want to avoid conflict at all costs.
Phlegmatics stay calm under pressure.	
Phlegmatics exhibit a dispassionate approach to reality.	

Phlegmatics do not find it hard to control their emotions. They are not easily insulted or provoked to anger: they are able to shrug off major insults without skipping a beat. But they need to energize their noble passions: they must overcome their fear of conflict. They must be ready to sacrifice peace and security for higher values.

JUSTICE

Communion ⊕	Common good ⊕
Phlegmatics are sensitive and respectful.	Phlegmatics have a strong sense of obligation and cooperation.
Phlegmatics are excellent listeners.	Common good ⊖
Phlegmatics feel great empathy for others.	Phlegmatics are prone to passivity.

Phlegmatic people are good communicators: they are excellent listeners. At the same time, they are prone to strive for the common good: they seek to contribute to society at large. But they must overcome their natural tendency toward passivity. The common good abhors apathy and lethargy. The common good is something we build.

MAGNANIMITY

Contemplation ⊖	Action ⊖
Phlegmatics go along with the status quo and conform to the expectations and goals of those around them.	Phlegmatics perceive tasks as formidable and obstacles as insurmountable.
Phlegmatics love security and routine.	

Magnanimity is a challenge for phlegmatics because of their tendency to go along with the status quo. They are called to dream and raise the level of their expectations.

phlegmatics

are fundamentally challenged by

magnanimity.

Thomas Aquinas, the most brilliant philosopher and theologian of the Middle-Ages, was phlegmatic. He was careful in thought and speech, logical, methodical, precise, quiet, even-tempered, simple, and dry-witted. But Thomas refused to go along with the intellectual status quo of his time. In the XIII century when the general opinion was that Christian faith is independent of reason, Thomas brought back human reason to theology. Aquinas' restoration of human reason is one of the greatest achievements in the history of Christian thought. Aquinas was a phlegmatic person who practiced magnanimity.

Jérôme Lejeune, the French geneticist, was also a phlegmatic: he was restrained and peace-loving, and he always took a scientific approach. At the same time, he was a dreamer and a doer. He upheld the dignity of human life at a time when tribunals and parliaments were usurping the divine right to determine who shall live and who must die. The phlegmatic Jérôme was magnanimous. He is considered the greatest advocate of the unborn child and the moral leader of the pro-life movement worldwide.

Darwin Smith, CEO of Kimberly-Clark from 1971 to 1991, was phlegmatic. But he set a magnanimous goal for his company: to achieve greatness or perish. He decided to sell all of its factories that had been producing coated paper—the main source of the company's revenue—and use the proceeds to begin producing consumer paper products, deliberately placing the firm in direct competition with market leaders Procter & Gamble and Scott Paper. Wall Street analysts and the business media derided his decision; they were certain it would fail. Smith did not allow himself to be swayed by the conventional wisdom. His magnanimous decision brought about a spectacular turnaround in the firm's fortunes, transforming Kimberly-Clark into the number one paper-based consumer products company in the world.

HUMILITY

Self-knowledge ⊖	Service ⊕
Phlegmatics understate their talents.	Phlegmatics are willing to serve.
	Service ⊖
	Phlegmatics fail to recognize the ways in which they may best serve others.

Phlegmatic people are prone to serve others. But at the same time, they tend to understate their talents. They must learn to serve using the talents they have.

7

DEVELOP THE VIRTUE YOU ARE CHALLENGED BY

CHOLERICS ARE CHALLENGED BY HUMILITY, melancholics by audacity, sanguines by endurance, phlegmatics by magnanimity. You will find below practical advice on how to develop these virtues. This practical advice is directed to all: we are all called to strengthen our virtues, both those that present a real challenge for us, and those that come more easily.

DEVELOPING AUDACITY

- This year, make a few bold decisions in your professional, social, spiritual and family life.
- Carry out your decisions expeditiously.
- Share your ideas, talents, and passions with the whole world.
- Get out of the house. Meet new people. Travel.

- Transform your dreams into a mission, and remember your mission every day.

DEVELOPING ENDURANCE

- Practice "heroic deeds" in the humdrum routine of everyday life.
- Bring the work you are doing now to a proper conclusion, taking care to get the details right, no matter how hard the going may get.
- Learn not to worry about what others may say or think about you.
- Do what you *must* do first, even if it is disagreeable, and then do what you like doing.
- Correct subordinates (charitably) even if you find this hard.
- Stick to your scheduled time of reading/meditation/sports.
- Play with the kids when you get home even if you're dead tired.
- Eat what is put in front of you even if it's not to your liking.

DEVELOPING MAGNANIMITY

- Identify a few magnanimous people whom you know or have heard of, and seek their company. Contemplate them, study them, and try to imitate them.

- Create around yourself a "magnanimous environment." Your environment is the books and the papers you read, the movies you watch, the music you listen to. It is the internet, which can range from extraordinarily good to downright vile. Be selective: filter out that which is base, and fill your heart and mind with that which is noble.

- Make a daily plan of "spiritual and cultural growth" with a set time for contemplation and meditation, reading, sports, and so on.

- Learn to contemplate beauty; admire it and respond to it appropriately.

- "Waste time" with your imagination, nourish it, give it free rein, and push it to its limits.

- Seek greatness in the immediate, tangible reality of your material surroundings: in the fulfillment of your professional, social, and family responsibilities. Use your talents to draw out the best in people. If you are a homemaker, prepare food with professional attention to detail. Your talent, which reflects greatness, will inspire your spouse, children, and friends to similarly give the best of themselves. It is a paradox, but many homemakers have elevated the people they serve spiritually by tending to their stomachs. In investing their work with talent, love, and passion, homemakers can transform food into a metaphor for greatness. Many stories of great cookery are more inspiring as examples of leadership than many anecdotes about the battlefield and the board room.

- Do not compare yourself to anyone. In their dignity, human beings are radically equal, but in their talents, they are radically unequal. Many could do miracles, but because they seek only to please the crowd (or their contemporaries), what they do is reduced to mere triviality.

- Do not let opportunities pass you by. Letting opportunities pass, not seizing them out of fear or laziness—this is what makes a magnanimous soul suffer more than anything else. Evil is not something done by others; it is the good that you, personally, did not do.

- Do not hire yes-men. Seek collaborators who can and will challenge you.

- Remember: as important as it is to struggle against your defects, you should be more concerned to develop and augment your strengths.

- Discover your mission, write it down, and implement it.

- Do not forget: successful accomplishment of your mission must be your foremost decision-making criterion.

- Concentrate your energies on your mission. Do not become distracted by peripheral matters.

- Inspire a sense of mission in those around you.

- If you work in a business corporation or in a nonprofit organization, ask yourself: "To what extent, by fulfilling the mission of my organization, do I fulfill my personal mission?" If you cannot answer this question, you should leave the organization.

DEVELOPING HUMILITY

- Remember: Humility is not a virtue of the weak but of the strong. Leaders do not need to treat people poorly in order to feel important.

- Remember: In order to bring out the greatness in people, we need to love them. Love is the only way to grasp human beings in the innermost core of their personality, to discover their talents and encourage them to actualize their potential.

- Pull rather than push, teach rather than command, inspire rather than berate. Help your friends, children, and colleagues acknowledge their dignity, revel in their personal freedom, embrace responsibility, discover and increase their talents, and put those at the service of the community.

- Delegate power. Leaders delegate power not because they have no time to do everything themselves, but because they want their subordinates to grow (which is what happens when the subordinates are given a say in decision-making).

- Encourage team members to voice their opinions even if they are critical.

- Pave the way for your succession. Do not make yourself irreplaceable. Share information. Create the conditions for others to bring your work to a successful conclusion.

8

DISCOVER YOUR MISSION

HAVING A MISSION AND A SENSE of mission is vital if you wish to grow in magnanimity. You should discover, write down and implement your own unique mission.

A CALL TO ACTION

A mission is not a vocation. A vocation is a call to live, think, feel, and act *in a particular way.* A mission is a call *to do a certain thing.* A vocation is always a call from God. A mission is normally the result of human considerations, although divine missions directly inspired by God must not be excluded (Moses, Joan of Arc, Teresa of Calcutta, etc.).

Our vocation is the framework in which we discover and carry out our mission, which constitutes our specific contribution to humanity. Without a vocation, leadership is *devoid of purpose*; without a mission, it is *devoid of substance*. Many have a clear sense of their vocation, but have trouble discovering their mission. This is because they are insufficiently aware of their talent or insufficiently imaginative. Conversely, many understand that they have a mission, but are not aware that they have a vocation. This is because their religious sense is insufficiently developed.

To discover your mission, ask yourself two questions:

1. Who am I? (What is my story and what is my talent?)
2. What is the cultural or social challenge I am called to respond to with passion and dedication?

Knowledge of self and of the world yield the basic information necessary to discover a mission.

1. Your Story

To answer the question "Who am I?" you need to reflect on your story and contemplate it. Your mission cannot be separated from your story. *Your story, not your whims, defines your mission.* Delve into your past and discern its meaning. You have a story to tell. Contemplate your life and fate, and find the appropriate words to speak about it.

You are a man or a woman with a history and a memory. Your story is not only about you: it is also about the people who live in you, so to speak, because their influence on you has been powerful. You are not a monad closed in on itself and satisfied with its own self-sufficiency. You are not alone, and you are not only "yourself."

Your story is not a limitation, but a strength. It is a light that allows you to interpret reality with depth and originality, and a rock that gives you the energy and the security necessary to make magnanimous decisions. Who are you? Where do you come from? People who can answer these questions with confidence and aplomb are leaders. Their heart is strong. They have a clear direction in life, and they feel the comforting presence of those who live in them.

Write about:

- the people who have been instrumental in your life.
- the books, the movies, and the music that propel you to unexpected emotional and spiritual heights.

- your country—its historical and cultural greatness, and also its failings and weaknesses. Feel
  free to denounce the things you do not like
  about it. Foster in your soul a righteous wrath.
- the ideals you want to fight for.
- the key events in your life until now. Discover their meaning.

Your story must be dramatic, poetic, symbolic, and short. *Dramatic*, to make it attractive
to you and others (you must discover its central
theme or idea). *Poetic*, to capture the greatness of
little things. *Symbolic*, to make it universal and
unforgettable. *Short*, to focus on that which is
important.

According to Vyacheslav Ivanov, Russian
Symbolist poet and philosopher: "There is a mystical meaning in many lives, but not everyone
correctly understands this. It often comes to us
in encrypted form, and we, failing to decipher it,
despair over the meaninglessness of our life. The
success of great lives is often due to the fact that
the person managed to decipher the code that
came down to him, understood and learned how
to proceed correctly."[1]

---

1. Cited in Solzhenitsyn, *The Oak and the Calf*, p. 80.

2. Your Talent

Your mission is related to your story and also to your talent. What, specifically, are you good at? Most people think they know what they are good at. They are often wrong. Listen to others. What do they say about you? Analytical feedback can help you discover your specific gifts.

It is hard to know what we are good at before the age of thirty. Explore many avenues, and ask your friends or colleagues to help you discover your specific talent.

Do not forget that your temperament is also a talent:

- If you are melancholic, you have a gift for bucking the status quo and *generating new ideas.*
- If you are choleric, you have a gift for *starting a big project* on the foundation of these ideas.
- If you are sanguine, you have a gift for *gathering people* around that project.
- If you are phlegmatic, you have a gift *for bringing rationality* to the endeavor, which could bring about long-term success.

3. Your Mission Statement

Your mission statement points to the cultural or social challenge you are called to respond to with passion and dedication.

Your mission statement must be broad enough that you could accomplish it in many different ways, but narrow enough that it speaks to you personally every single day. Here are three mission statements that are pitch perfect:

> "I wanted to be a memory; the memory of a people doomed to tragedy." (Aleksandr Solzhenitsyn)

> "I wanted to become a Mother to the poorest of the world's poor." (St. Teresa of Calcutta)

> "I wanted to uphold scientific truth and the larger moral truth that flows from it." (Jérôme Lejeune)

I discovered my mission late in life at age forty, when I began teaching Virtuous Leadership. *Igniting hearts for greatness and transforming the resultant fire into a powerful habit of the mind and the will—* this is it. I saw greatness in my parents, grandparents, and ancestors. I saw it in my brother and sister, my friends and mentors. At the same time, I saw waves of small-heartedness breaking over the world. I noted with astonishment the rise of new kinds of creatures in our midst like those in Huxley's *Brave New World*: creatures without a past, without a homeland, without family, and without God. I saw the "men without chests" of C. S. Lewis.[2] I found it alarming, and I decided to act. "*Igniting hearts for greatness*" became my mission, my personal answer to this human catastrophe. This personal mission is now a corporate mission: the mission of the Virtuous Leadership Institute.

---

2. "Men Without Chests" is the title of the first chapter of C. S. Lewis' *Abolition of Man*.

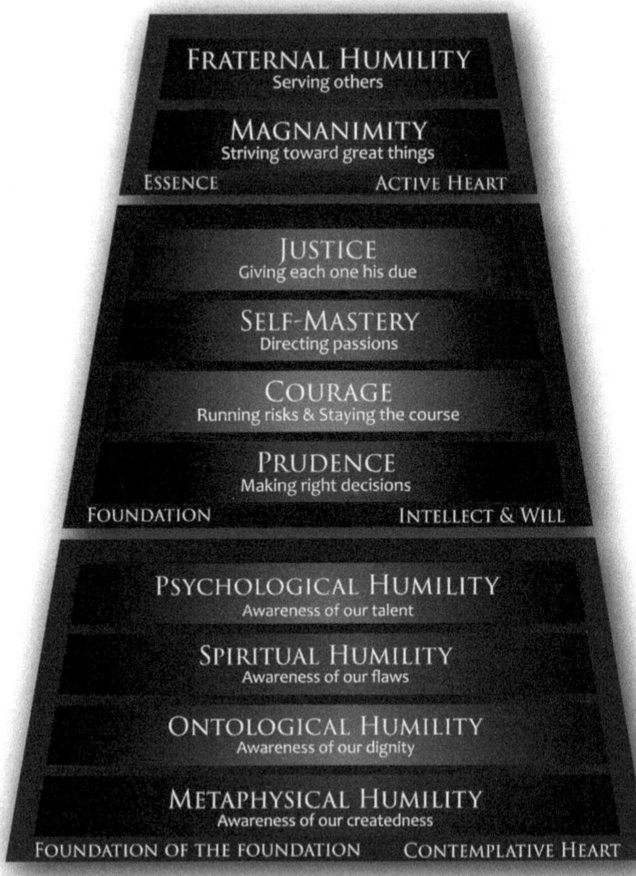
FRATERNAL HUMILITY
Serving others
MAGNANIMITY
Striving toward great things
ESSENCE
ACTIVE HEART
JUSTICE
Giving each one his due
SELF-MASTERY
Directing passions
COURAGE
Running risks & Staying the course
PRUDENCE
Making right decisions
FOUNDATION
INTELLECT & WILL
PSYCHOLOGICAL HUMILITY
Awareness of our talent
SPIRITUAL HUMILITY
Awareness of our flaws
ONTOLOGICAL HUMILITY
Awareness of our dignity
METAPHYSICAL HUMILITY
Awareness of our createdness
FOUNDATION OF THE FOUNDATION
CONTEMPLATIVE HEART

Graphic 2: The Virtuous Leadership Pyramid

9

THE FOUNDATION
AND ESSENCE OF LEADERSHIP

Magnanimity and fraternal humility constitute the *essence* of leadership. These two leadership virtues rest upon the basic virtues of prudence, courage, self-mastery and justice, which constitute the *foundation* of leadership.

1. Magnanimity and fraternal humility constitute the essence of leadership.

- *Magnanimity* is the habit of striving for great things. Leaders are magnanimous in their vision of self, in their dreams and missions; in their confidence and enthusiasm, hope and daring; in their propensity for using means proportionate to their goals; in their capacity to challenge themselves and those around them.

- *Fraternal humility* is the habit of serving. It means pulling rather than pushing, teaching rather than ordering about, inspiring rather than berating. Thus, leadership is less about displays of power than the empowerment of others. To practice humility is to bring out the greatness in others, to give them the capacity to realize their human potential.

2. Prudence, courage, self-mastery, and justice constitute the foundation of leadership.

- *Prudence* is the ability to make right decisions.
- *Courage* is the ability to run risks and stay the course.
- *Self-mastery* is the ability to subordinate one's emotions and passions to the spirit and channel their vital energy into the fulfillment of the mission at hand.
- *Justice* is the ability to give everyone his due and communicate effectively with others.

Prudence, courage, self-mastery, and justice undergird the leadership virtues of magnanimity and fraternal humility. In other words, if we do not practice the four basic virtues, leadership will collapse.

- *No magnanimity without prudence.* Prudence is the guiding light of all the virtues, because it reveals how to behave virtuously in any situation. If you are not prudent, you will not be able to distinguish megalomaniacal behavior from magnanimous behavior. Don Quixote is not magnanimous: he is mad.

- *No fraternal humility without prudence.* Crazy people can hardly be good servants.

- *No magnanimity without courage.* If you lack courage, you will not overcome your fear of making mistakes. Hamlet is a small man because he is a coward.

- *No fraternal humility without courage.* If you lack endurance (the habit of staying the course), you will be unstable and will not serve effectively.

- *No magnanimity without self-mastery.* Intemperance crowds out magnanimity. Obsessed with his power, pleasures, and possessions, the intemperate person conceives of life as an agglomeration of sensations. He shrivels in stature before our very eyes. Oscar Wilde's Dorian Gray is an intemperate rake, and, therefore, a small man.

- *No fraternal humility without self-mastery.* Obsessed with his power, pleasures, and possessions, the intemperate person has no capacity to create space in his heart for other people and for the ideal of serving them.

- *No magnanimity without justice.* If you are not just, your greatness is fake. Vladimir Lenin, Margaret Sanger, and Adolf Hitler (each of them is responsible for the death of millions of innocent people) were not magnanimous: these were people wounded in their childhood in the depth of their souls and manipulated by diabolical powers. Evil can be gigantic, but it cannot be great.

- *No fraternal humility without justice.* Injustice crowds out the very desire to serve.

FRATERNAL HUMILITY
Effective service

SUPREME HUMILITY

PSYCHOLOGICAL HUMILITY
Awareness of our talent
Allows us to appreciate our talents in order
to serve with magnanimity

SPIRITUAL HUMILITY
Awareness of our flaws
Makes us aware of the need to perfect ourselves in order
to serve others effectively

ONTOLOGICAL HUMILITY
Awareness of our dignity
Allows us to see the Face of God in others, so that we
can serve them with love

METAPHYSICAL HUMILITY
Awareness of our createdness
Allows us to see the presence of God in others, in order
to serve them with reverence

FUNDAMENTAL HUMILITY

Graphic 3: The Humility Pyramid

SELF-KNOWLEDGE

IF PRUDENCE, COURAGE, SELF-MASTERY, and justice are the *foundation* of leadership, fundamental humility (self-knowledge) is the foundation of the foundation, so to speak.

Fundamental humility is awareness of our limitations and flaws on the one hand, and awareness of our dignity and talents on the other. We are *fundamentally* humble if we adhere to these truths and live by them.

Fundamental humility has four dimensions:

Metaphysical Humility

- To practice humility is, first of all, to acknowledge one's status as a creature. We are not gods, but created beings. Without God we are nothing; we do not exist. God created us out of nothing and maintains us in being. The truth about the existence of God and the maintenance of all creatures in being is a metaphysical truth. *Metaphysics* deals with the source of being. The humble person keeps his eyes fixed on God, who is the inexhaustible source of his being. Metaphysical humility is the deepest aspect of humility.

- Metaphysical humility encourages us to practice fraternal humility, because it compels us to discover the presence of God in each and every person (by his uninterrupted gift of being, God makes himself present in his creatures).

Ontological Humility

- To practice humility means also to acknowledge one's dignity. Human beings are personal beings, like God. They have a spirit that gives them rationality, freedom, and immortality. This is an *ontological* truth. Ontology deals with being as such. The humble person knows that his dignity is an original, essential, and unalienable gift from God. (Christianity says that human beings become children of God by faith in Christ Jesus. It is impossible to imagine a higher ontological dignity than the dignity of being a child of God. But this truth cannot be reached by human reason).

- Ontological humility encourages us to practice fraternal humility because it compels us to discover in each and every human being a person, i.e. the image of God.

Spiritual Humility

- To practice humility means also to acknowledge our spiritual weaknesses, especially that "something which fights against reason and resists it" (Aristotle). (The Judeo-Christian tradition explains this spiritual disorder—the triple tendency toward pleasure, affluence, and power—as the result of an anthropological disaster: Original Sin. This explanation makes sense only to those who venerate the Bible, although the disorder itself is a fact that cannot be denied: Rousseau's "Noble Savage" is a myth).

- Spiritual humility helps us to practice fraternal humility: only those humble enough to acknowledge and overcome their own shortcomings will be able to serve others effectively.

Psychological Humility

- To practice humility means also to acknowledge our talents. Many people, for *psychological* reasons, never think or speak of their talents (they have the impression it would be a lack of modesty). In fact, one should be able to speak about one's talents with naturalness, without boasting. A truly humble person does not need modesty, because his intentions are pure: he does not seek applause or recognition. He just wants to serve as best he can.

- Psychological humility helps us practice fraternal humility: only those who are aware of their talents can use and develop them in order to serve others with magnanimity.

Fundamental humility (self-knowledge) is the foundation of fraternal humility (service). It is also the foundation of prudence (practical wisdom). The information granted to us by fundamental humility (the information about our personal dignity, our strengths and weaknesses) is indeed necessary if we are to practice the virtue of prudence. Without fundamental humility, we cannot make prudent decisions because we do not even know who we are. Self-knowledge, according to Socrates, is the beginning of wisdom and of any human activity, theoretical and practical.

11

AN ACTIVE HEART

SOMEONE WHO PRACTICES fundamental humility along with the four basic virtues of prudence, courage self-mastery, and justice can be called a *mature human being*.

Mature human beings know the truth about themselves and live by it. They pay attention to objective reality and respect it. They run risks, stay the course, and say "yes" to what elevates them and "no" to what enslaves them. They love people and fulfill their professional, social, and family responsibilities.

Maturity (or integrity) is a necessary step toward leadership. But other steps must be taken. Mature human beings are leaders insofar as they practice also the virtues of magnanimity and fraternal humility. Without maturity there is no leadership, but leadership is more than maturity. Many mature people are far from being leaders.

Without a contemplative heart (fundamental humility), an enlightened intellect (prudence), and a strong will (courage, self-mastery, and justice), there is no leadership. But leadership requires something more: it requires an *active heart*.

An active heart is a heart that transforms contemplation into action for the sake of service. A leader is deep, but at the same time he is full of spiritual energy and initiative. His self-knowledge is neither self-adoration nor self-flagellation: it is directed toward the service of others.

A leader is a mature person, but maturity (or integrity) is not his essential characteristic. Striving for greatness and devotion to service—these are his specific traits.

12

WHY SERVE?

SELF-KNOWLEDGE REQUIRES GENERAL knowledge about the human being—his createdness, sinfulness, and dignity. It also requires a specific knowledge of one's temperament, character, talent, and mission. Our motivation is also something specific to each one of us.

In leadership, a fundamental question is "Why serve?" If to lead is to serve, then leaders cannot fail to ask themselves this question. Altruistic motivation is part and parcel of leadership.

1. False altruism

When we serve, we usually feel good, because we do what our conscience tells us to do. Feeling good is not a goal, but one of the manifold consequences of service.

There are people, nevertheless, who serve in order to feel good. For them, service is a means to an end. Feeling good is their goal. This is false altruism.

We need to check our motives. If we serve the others for our personal satisfaction, this is *feel-goodism*, not leadership.

2. Secular altruism

Human beings are social beings, not mere individuals. Altruism should be a natural tendency, a natural consequence of our sociability. Unfortunately, the spiritual disorder provoked by Original Sin created in man another natural tendency: a tendency toward egoism.

Without faith in a God who rewards people in eternal life for their service to others, altruism is hard to practice. Fyodor Dostoyevsky put it this way: "You cannot replace the absence of God with love for humanity, because people will ask immediately, 'Why do I have to love humanity?'"[1]

For the great majority of people, secular altruism does not work. They cannot be satisfied with

---

1. Fyodor Dostoyevsky, *Mysli, vyskazyvania i aforizmy Dostoevskovo* (Paris: Pyat' Kontinentov, 1975), p. 107.

an answer such as: "There is no God, but you still need to serve other people, because they are people just like you."

3. Religious altruism

Human beings are religious beings. Through spiritual experience and the contemplation of nature, humans discover God in themselves and outside themselves. They understand that the human soul is spiritual and immortal. They acknowledge the person's transcendent dignity, and the person's vocation to eternal and absolute happiness. They see the beauty of persons and decide to serve them.

Natural religion constitutes a sure foundation for altruism.

4. Christian altruism

Christianity is the world's largest religion. It is a revealed religion that does not deny the value of natural religion. Christianity calls people to live lives of service to others.

"The Son of man came not to be served but to serve. . . . Whoever would be great among you must be your servant. . . . As you did it to one of the least of these my brethren, you did to me"

(Mt 20:28,26; 25:40). These are the words of Christ, the founder of Christianity.

Christians serve because they see Christ in each and every person.

The Christian religion constitutes the surest foundation for altruism.

13

THE UPWARD SPIRAL
OF GROWTH

In order to improve, we need to strengthen our heart (through humility and magnanimity), our intellect (through prudence), and our will (through courage, self-mastery and justice).

Reason, will, and the heart blend seamlessly in the human person. We cannot separate them from each other without doing enormous damage to all three. Rationalists elevate the mind above all things, voluntarists the will, and sentimentalists the heart. Each approach corrupts them all.

We cannot practice the virtues of the heart (humility and magnanimity) and the virtues of the will (courage, self-mastery, and justice) without the virtue of the intellect (prudence). Only the prudent man can distinguish audacity from recklessness, endurance from servility, self-mastery from insensitivity, justice from harshness, magnanimity from pride, and humility from pusillanimity.

Virtue is not a midway point between a deficit and an excess of goodness. One cannot be *too* audacious or have *too* much self-mastery. Recklessness is not "too much courage": it is false courage; insensitivity is not "too much self-mastery":

Graphic 4: The Function of Prudence

it is false self-mastery; harshness is not "too much justice": it is false justice; pride is not "too much magnanimity": it is false magnanimity; pusillanimity is not "too much humility": it is false humility.

The prudent man is able to distinguish between truth and falsehood in every situation. The imprudent man is not. (See graphic 4.)

If the virtues of the will and the heart cannot develop in the absence of prudence, likewise prudence cannot develop in the absence of the virtues of the will and the heart. Why? Because the

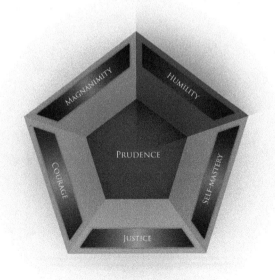

Graphic 5: The Ascending Spiral of Growth

intellect (our prudence) interprets reality through the lens forged by the will and the heart. The proud judge as true whatever flatters their pride; the intemperate, whatever helps them acquire power, money, or pleasure; the pusillanimous, whatever justifies their small-heartedness.

By growing in the virtues of the heart and the will, we improve our ability to deliberate in the light of reason.

All the virtues nurture prudence and in turn are nurtured by it. This is not a closed circle, but an ascending spiral of growth. (See graphic 5.)

14

MAGNANIMITY AND HUMILITY GO HAND IN HAND

MAGNANIMITY AND HUMILITY ARE inseparable. Magnanimity without humility is pride, and humility without magnanimity is pusillanimity.

One needs a pure heart, a strong will, and a bright intellect not to break the intimate link that unites these two virtues.

Magnanimity and humility go hand in hand. An important aspect of humility is to acknowledge our dignity, talents, and greatness. And when we speak of magnanimity, we must never forget to mention that our dignity, talents, and greatness are gifts from God.

Humility acknowledges the strength and greatness of man, seeing them as gifts from God. It constitutes no denial of man's own greatness and strength to attribute them to the goodness of God. Humility offers up to God this greatness and strength, thereby consecrating them.

To acknowledge our talents is an act of humility because it brings us closer to the truth about ourselves. We must have the humility to acknowledge our talents. In so doing, we thank God, who created us. Not to acknowledge our talents is not humility; it is ingratitude.

Modesty must not be an obstacle to humility. Humility is more important than modesty. "Perfect humility dispenses with modesty," writes C. S. Lewis. "If God is satisfied with the work, the work may be satisfied with itself."[1]

In order to understand how magnanimity and humility relate to each other in practice, we need to contemplate the life of virtuous leaders. Take the example of Aleksandr Solzhenitsyn, the Russian writer and Nobel prize winner:

MAGNANIMITY

- *A unique sense of mission.* "I wanted to be memory; the memory of a people doomed to tragedy."[2]

---

1. C. S. Lewis, *The Weight of Glory*, sermon preached in the Church of St. Mary the Virgin, June 8, 1941, Oxford.

2. Interview with Liudmila Saraskina: "Yesterday He Worked until 7 p.m.," *Gazeta.ru*, April 2008, *https://www.gazeta.ru/culture/2008/08/04/a_2800993.shtml.*

- *A powerful human hope.* "I can go on writing that book . . . until the calf breaks its neck butting the oak, or until the oak cracks and comes crashing down. An unlikely happening, but one in which I am very ready to believe."[3]

- *An acute sense of personal dignity.* Solzhenitsyn possessed a high sense of his own dignity at a time when the totalitarian state trampled on dignity to a degree never before seen. This sense of personal dignity allowed him to remain utterly unfazed when he faced brutal calumny from both the Soviet authorities and Western liberals.

- *A greatness that inspires.* "The most talented contemporaries of Solzhenitsyn, having been captivated by him as a writer, did not conceal their shock when they made the acquaintance of Solzhenitsyn the man. It seems the first to discern Solzhenitsyn's magnanimity was the Russian poet Anna Akhmatova. She said about him: 'A bearer of light! [...]. We had forgotten that such people exist [...]. A surprising individual [...]. A great man.'"[4]

---

3. Solzhenitsyn, *The Oak and the Calf*, p. 190.

4. Liudmila Saraskina, *Aleksandr Solzhenitsyn* (Moscow: Molodaia gvardiia, 2008), pp. 896–898.

- *A greatness that elevates.* "Living with him (even if only for two days), you feel small, shackled by prosperity, useless concerns, and interests [...]. The greatness of Solzhenitsyn: he defines the scale, and accompanying him one day, you again begin to be horrified by the triumph of the small-minded of the world, the blindness, the prejudice, and so forth."[5]

- *A greatness that frightens.* "He is the standard of measurement. I know writers who celebrate his merits and his worthiness, but cannot acknowledge him because they are afraid. Next to Solzhenitsyn, their own true worth becomes clear."[6]

- *A greatness that triumphs.* "This was more astounding than anything—one man versus virtually all of the regime's vast machinery of lies, stupidity, brutality, and ability to cover up evidence. This was a conflict waged by a solitary fighter such as comes along once in a millennium. And in every sentence, the

---

5. Alexander Schmemann, *Dnevniki 1973–1983* (Moscow: Ruskii Put, 2013), p. 101. Alexander Schmemann was one of the twentieth century's leading theologians and Dean of St. Vladimir's Theological Seminary in New York from 1962 to 1983.

6. Andrei Tvardovskiy, poet and editor of *Noviy Mir*, as quoted in Saraskina, pp. 896–898.

victor's identity came through unmistakably. But unlike the victories won by the regime, this one had nothing bombastic about it. I call it an Easter victory, one that passes through the medium of death to resurrection. In the *Archipelago* narrative, people rose from the dead, transformed in the dust of the camps, the country rose from the dead, the truth rose from the dead [...]. It was the resurrection of truth in man and the truth about man out of the complete impossibility that this could happen."[7]

HUMILITY

- *Self-knowledge.* "When I was struggling against the Communist regime, I understood that it was not I who was fighting, that I am an insect, that in carrying on such a struggle I was just a tool in the hands of Another."[8]
- *Self-knowledge.* "I had learned in my years of imprisonment to sense that guiding hand,

7. Olga Sedakova, "The Strength That Does Not Abandon Us," *Foma* (December 2008). Olga Sedakova was a 1995 recipient of the European Prize in Poetry.

8. Aleksandr Solzhenitsyn, *Ogoniok* (Moscow: 1998).

to glimpse that bright meaning beyond and above my self and my wishes. I had not always been quick to understand the sudden upsets in my life, and often, out of bodily and spiritual weakness, had seen in them the very opposite of their true meaning and their far-off purpose. Later the true significance of what had happened would inevitably become clear to me and I would become numb with surprise. I have done many things in my life that conflicted with the great aims I had set myself—and something has always set me on the true path again. I have become so used to this, come to rely on it so much, that the only task I need set myself is to interpret as clearly and quickly as I can each major event in my life."[9]

- *Self-knowledge.* "Solzhenitsyn's awareness of his mission is indubitable, but stemming from this certainty is authentic humility."[10]

- *Service.* "My point of departure should always have been that I did not belong to myself alone, that my literary destiny was not just my own, but that of the millions who had

---

9. Solzhenitsyn, *The Oak and the Calf,* p. 111.
10. Schmemann, p.101.

not lived to scrawl or gasp or croak the truth about their lot as jail birds."[11]

- *Service.* "Next to you is a man who accepts the whole burden of service, who gives himself up completely."[12]

- *Service.* "Then came exile, and right at the beginning of my exile, cancer. In autumn 1953 it looked very much as though I had only a few months to live. In December the doctors—comrades in exile—confirmed that I had at most three weeks left.

All that I had memorized in camp ran the risk of extinction together with the head that held it.

This was a dreadful moment in my life: to die on the threshold of freedom, to see all I had written, all that gave meaning to my life thus far, about to perish with me. The peculiarities of the Soviet postal censorship made it impossible for me to cry out for help. Come quickly, take what I have written, save it! You can't very well appeal to strangers anyway. My friends were all in camps themselves. My mother was dead. My wife had married again.

---

11. Solzhenitsyn, *The Oak and the Calf,* p. 111.
12. Schmemann, p.101.

All the same, I sent for her to say goodbye thinking she might take my manuscripts away with her, but she did not come.

In those last few weeks that the doctors had promised me I could not escape from my work in school, but in the evening and the nights, kept awake by pain, I hurriedly copied things out in tiny handwriting, rolled them, several pages at a time into tight cylinders and squeezed these into a champagne bottle. I buried the bottle in my garden—and set off for Tashkent to meet the new year (1954) and to die.

I did not die, however. (With a hopelessly neglected and acutely malignant tumor, this was a divine miracle. I could see no other explanation. Since then, all the life that has been given back to me has not been mine in the full sense: it is built around a purpose.)"[13]

---

13. Solzhenitsyn, *The Oak and the Calf*, p. 80.

15

VIRTUE ETHICS

THERE ARE TWO KINDS OF ETHICS: rules-based ethics and virtue ethics.

In the first system, an action is *correct* if it conforms to the rule, *incorrect* if it does not. In the second system, *good* is that which brings us closer to human excellence, *bad* that which leads us away from it.

Virtue ethics do not deny the validity of rules, but they do insist that rules cannot be the ultimate foundation of ethics. Rules must be at the service of virtue. That is the proper order of things. The goal of life is not the observance of rules and laws: it is self-improvement, personal growth, human excellence. Virtues, not rules, make people great.

Many organizations have a corporate code of ethics. Codes of ethics are a starting point, not a goal. If they do not give rise to virtue, they will be window-dressing and undermine the credibility of the organization.

Virtue gives us many things: spiritual freedom, unity of life, wisdom, creativity, and cultural maturity. Virtue is the only way to achieve self-realization.

SPIRITUAL FREEDOM

Children need rules: they need to know precisely where they stand, what is acceptable behavior and what is not. As soon as they reach the age of reason, however, they must be taught the "why" of rules, so as to grasp their connection with human nature and human perfection. By strengthening their intelligence and their heart, and not only their will, children become virtuous and free. Who rejects evil not because it is forbidden, but because it is evil, is truly free. If free human beings refrain from slandering their competitors, it is less because slander is forbidden by law than because, being virtuous, they would not stoop so low in the first place. It simply would not occur to them. The actions of free persons are determined by their virtues, not by rules. The law acts from outside, virtue from inside.

UNITY OF LIFE

Many people are convinced that there is one ethic for work and another for off-hours. They are vigilant about maintaining a strict code of conduct at work, but regard private life as another matter. Yet they are absolutely certain that they are ethical people because they observe a corporate code of conduct, behave in a generally professional manner, and pay their bills. They are leading a double life. Virtues, by contrast, help you behave virtuously always and everywhere: at work, with your family, among friends, during free time, and even when you are alone. Virtue unifies your personality and daily activities, both public and private, making the living of a double life impossible.

WISDOM

Rules are too narrow in scope to cover the variety of life situations people typically encounter. Virtues are needed more than rules. If you possess the virtue of prudence, you will perceive situations in all their complexity and make decisions in accordance with this perception. You will not be at a loss upon finding yourself in uncharted waters. You will know how to make the right choices.

CREATIVITY

Rules-based ethics tend to produce narrow, unimaginative people little given to reflection on the deeper meaning of things. People obsessed with observing rules do not study problems in depth, investigate concrete circumstances, or take the initiative. They make decisions, but they do not really deliberate. Creativity is not their strong suit. How different it is for those who possess the virtue of prudence! No pre-cooked solutions for them. Virtue is always original, creative, and multi-faceted.

CULTURAL MATURITY

Without the practice of virtues, basic moral standards—such as those conveyed by the Ten Commandments—can easily be tossed aside and replaced by ideology, esoteric spirituality, and vacuous and trendy notions. A person who seeks after virtue will not easily surrender to ideological or commercial slogans. Having interiorized the unchanging principles of human nature, he has achieved a spiritual solidity that renders him impervious to the siren song of a debased mass culture.

SELF-REALIZATION

Virtue makes us grow as *human* beings. People without virtue are not merely immoral: they are the embodiment of the "non-man" as indicated by this Chinese and Japanese ideogram, which represents negation and the lie (interior disintegration) juxtaposed with the ideogram representing man.

───── 16 ─────

VIRTUOUS LEADERSHIP
AND MANAGEMENT

LEADERSHIP IS ABOUT HELPING people grow. Management is about getting things done. If you practice virtuous leadership, you will get things done (more than you can even imagine), because people, not technology or finances, are the aspect of business with the most far-reaching and dynamic impact. People are more important than things.

- Through his virtuous leadership, *François Michelin* (1955–1999) transformed the Michelin Group into the world's leading tire company.

- Through his virtuous leadership, *Darwin Smith* (1971–1991) transformed Kimberly-Clark into the number one paper-based consumer products company in the world.

- Through his virtuous leadership, *Herb Kelleher* (1971–2008) transformed Southwest Airlines into the world's largest low-cost carrier.

The future of such corporations depends on the desire and capacity of their future CEOs to follow in the footsteps of their predecessors.

Not a few businessmen reject the notion that virtuous leadership can be profitable. They say "business is business," which gives them a pretext for immoral decision-making and for treating employees badly, as they feel they have to.

True businessmen know that virtuous leadership does not hinder business, but rather serves it.

17

VIRTUOUS LEADERSHIP AND EDUCATION

CHILDREN LEARN MAGNANIMITY at home when they develop a sense of personal dignity: when they feel they are loved, challenged, and forgiven. They develop fundamental humility when they learn to give thanks to God for everything they receive, and to worship him. They grow in fraternal humility when they learn to serve their parents, grandparents, brothers, and sisters, and practice solidarity with the whole family.

The destruction of the institution of the family leads to the destruction of virtuous leadership. Someone who did not in his childhood experience personal dignity and solidarity with others will hardly understand the meaning of such notions as "greatness" and "service."

Children should be educated in greatness, not only in integrity. They must learn to do that which is great, and not only that which is right. A great thing is always a right thing, but it is more than right: it is great. As soon as children understand the difference between what is right and what is wrong, they should be taught the difference between what is great and what is small. The great thing is not the conquest of an empire, but the building of our personality beyond the borders imposed on us by dominant ideologies or fashionable trends.

18

VIRTUOUS LEADERSHIP AND SUCCESS

WE SEEK VIRTUE FIRST AND FOREMOST in order to achieve human excellence, and secondarily to become effective as human beings. Virtue means first excellence in being (*aretē,* in Greek) and secondarily effectiveness in action (*virtus,* in Latin).

Virtue makes you an effective human being because it gives you a specific spiritual power: the power to make right decisions, to stay the course, to run risks, to energize your passions and direct them to the fulfillment of the mission at hand, to give people their due and communicate effectively, to achieve great things and serve people by bringing out the greatness in them.

Personal effectiveness often contributes to success in professional and family life, but does not guarantee it. Success depends on many factors that you cannot control: luck, health, and the social, economic and political context.

Virtue can help you become rich and famous (Francois Michelin, Herb Kelleher, Darwin Smith), but it may also bring you poverty and social disgrace (Jerome Lejeune, Aleksandr Solzhenitsyn), or even death (Thomas More, Joan of Arc, Martin Luther King).

But virtuous leaders do not seek after success. What they desire instead is existential plenitude—that is to say, fullness of life.

MOVING ON

The Gay Man's Guide
for Coping When a
Relationship Ends

Dann Hazel

Kensington Books
http://www.kensingtonbooks.com

KENSINGTON BOOKS are published by

Kensington Publishing Corp.
850 Third Avenue
New York, NY 10022

ISBN 1-57566-378-3

First Printing: June, 1999
10 9 8 7 6 5 4 3

Printed in the United States of America

Contents

Introduction

It would be too easy—and too haughty—to say this book represents the culmination of fifteen years of real-life research—fifteen years filled with shared joy, sorrow, pain, enjoyment, passion, and finally the sinking realization that despite the meaning and longevity of our lives together, Robert and I simply could not go on in a partnership that we once assumed would last a lifetime. Yet, for both of us, those fifteen years empowered and diminished our lives, defined and discarded components of our identities. It would take fourteen months for either of us to find balance and peace in our lives again.

The realization that Dann and Robert, the couple, would not endure, was devastating—perhaps more devastating than the discovery that one of us had been swept off his feet by another man. Yet, after careful analysis of our former relationship, and interviews with dozens of men suffering the associated symptoms of failed relationships, I determined the existence of infidelities of various brands, makes, and models. We are unfaithful to one another not only when we climb into someone else's bed, but also when we take a committed relationship for granted, or refuse to see the pain in our partner's eyes, or opt for the convenience of silence rather than communication, or choose disregard over understanding. But most debilitating of all is the realization that the distance between us has grown too far. Retracing our steps would constitute a denial of what is best for us, and what's best for the man with whom we shared so much of our lives. We wonder—and yet we know—what went wrong.

It was one way with Robert and me. It is quite another way with you.

Several men who shared their stories expressed their regret that a book like *Moving On* had not been available for them when their long-term partnerships ended. As flattering as I found their confidence in this project, I feared their expectations might be too high. True, *Moving On* charts a course through pain and grief toward recovery and affirmation. It shares the stories of other men whose hearts have been broken, and yet, they survived. It recognizes that losing the most significant relationship in our lives does not signal the end of the world. It demands a confrontation of the reader's values as he takes hold of what's left of his life and rebuilds it. "I was a complete basket case," says Bobby Hanes, 35, a Georgia resident whose partner, David, left him after almost three years. "For a year, dating wasn't even an option, as I mourned having lost David. But I still cherish long-term relationships. When we broke up, I felt I needed someone to replace David. But I've realized that I have to create my own life now. Sure, I'm lonely at times. On certain holidays, I would love to have a partner. But when loneliness strikes, I endure it. I don't try to resist it. Instead, I find some way to treat myself well."

Even now, upon completion, I find myself embarrassed by the sheer presumptuousness of the project. Yet, as I engaged in the process of writing *Moving On,* I experienced changes in attitude, belief, and self-image that made me stronger. Part of my growth resulted from the candor of the men who, sometimes willingly, sometimes reluctantly, opened pages of their lives they thought they had closed permanently. Sometimes, they endured their hearts breaking all over again. Dozens of times I heard the choked disclaimer, "I'm sorry. This is very hard for me to talk about." Yet each time I left an interview, whether that meant walking out of a coffee shop or hanging up the telephone, I was moved in ways that shifted my own consciousness of what had happened to Robert and me. Despite my own loneliness, I realized from these men that I was not alone.

Perhaps our most important realization is just that—we are not alone in our suffering. All of us endure the related shock, disbelief, denial, bargaining, suffering and subsequent recovery—even though they do not manifest themselves in the same ways, nor according to the same time frame. Within each man's story, we discover some degree of resonance, of familiarity, that helps us in the process of our own recovery and growth. "I had my phone number changed so that my ex wouldn't call and upset me," says Michael, 40, of Sherman Oaks, California, who broke up with Joe after seven years. All along, Joe had misunderstood Michael's need for trust and fidelity in their partnership. Finally, Michael couldn't tolerate Joe's disrespect, and ended the relationship. "After we broke up, he would call and cry. He would even call me at work, saying how lonely and depressed he was. 'Can I come to talk to you?' he wanted to know. So we'd set up a time to meet. He'd arrive, but never really say anything. I thought he might want to get back together. But he never said he wanted to try. Back then, I might have been vulnerable enough to say yes to such a proposal, although now, I know it would have been a bad idea. Because now, I have reclaimed my life."

These stories give us hope. These stories inspire us.

Yet the antidote to a broken heart is not hope and inspiration alone. Throughout these pages, I have, hopefully, directed you toward the difficult, often nebulous steps leading you to recovery. After careful analysis of my own grief and recovery, and of the experiences of these daring men, I discovered not only emotional experiences each man can expect along the way, but also specific actions he can take to expedite recovery. I have attempted to clarify what we will inevitably experience, as well as what we *must* experience, as we take responsibility for our own healing. "What was certainly true for me is, I think, true of many men following their breakups," says Kurt Colborn, an engineer in Ohio whose relationship ended after six years. "I found solitude to be very beneficial. I got a lot of work done on the house in the year following our split. I relied heavily on friends. I was certainly very busy in one way or another. One way of coping was working more than usual. Another was to avoid doing things on my own, or that might mean I'd have to be alone with myself. I went out with people a lot. I made sure I talked to friends often. And I'm sure I was acting out sexually—at least, for a while."

Following each chapter, you'll find at least one "clarification exercise." These self-scoring activities are designed to show you where you were emotionally, spiritually, and intellectually when your former relationship soured, where you are now in the process of coping, and how far you have yet to go on your journey toward healing. While all activities were tested on a number of individuals, they do not yield measurements as precise as those standardized tests you took while attending school. However, provided you record your responses honestly, your scores, with a respectable degree of reliability, will help you chart your course toward recovery.

In writing this book, it was never my hope to spare anyone the suffering that accompanies the end of a loving partnership. After all, it would have been an empty hope. Besides, we grow stronger when we face and fight our pain. It *is* my hope that, as you read each chapter, and complete each activity, you find value in your experiences. I hope that, methodically and consciously, you leave your pain behind. I hope that you take control of the inevitable changes in your life, and steer them toward a positive transformation. I hope that you perceive your damaged self-image as a temporary regression, and capitalize on your inherent (but perhaps dormant) strengths. And I hope that, once more, you find love in your life—whatever that means for you—not Tennyson's "cruel madness of love," but a love that celebrates, cherishes, and sustains.

CHAPTER ONE

· · · · · · · · · · · · · · · · · · ·

The "It's Inevitable" Cop-out

Sex and More

Most of us, regardless of the longevity of our partnerships, remember the circumstances under which we first met our partner—the furtive glances at the cute guy sheepishly sipping his cocktail, followed by a longer, less comfortable gaze to make sure his interest was unquestionable. Then, the game of eyeball tennis began. It lasted from five minutes to more than an hour before one of us finally took the initiative to say hello.

"We were celebrating a friend's twenty-first birthday," says Allen Williams, 31, a university professor in Boone, North Carolina. "I had accompanied a group of friends to a local bar. One thing you have to know about me. I'm very out and political in North Carolina; we have yet another politician who is the state-level version of Jesse Helms. I had heard before that a gay man worked for him." As Allen watched the dance floor, he spotted the politician's aide across the room. "I thought he was cute," he continues. "Shortly after we made eye contact, he walked out. Later, I saw him talking to several friends of mine. I thought he was very cute, although a little too conservatively dressed."

"Isn't that the asshole who works for that [conservative] politician?" Allen asked.

"Yes," a friend replied. "His name is Donald."

"I looked at him, and Donald looked at me," Allen continues. "Finally, I approached him."

"I hear our politics are diametrically opposite," Allen told him. "Do you want to dance?"

"That's how we met. We talked for a long time. I promised not to write letters to the editor criticizing his boss's political views if he would have dinner with me later."

In this case, Allen says, opposites certainly did attract. "He's northern, and I'm southern," he explains. "He's conservative and a fundamentalist Christian. I'm an eclectic Buddhist. Part of the attraction was that he was incredibly attentive. He sent me cards and flowers quite often. The cards were nice, but I was a little uncomfortable receiving flowers from a man. I guess that's my own internalized issues at work here. Still, I could see us together. I didn't foresee a problem with my taking him home to meet my parents. Besides, he was nice, and the sex was good."

Another part of the attraction, according to Allen, was that a number of gay men who were attracted to him wouldn't date him "because I was out. Sometimes, I felt like a pariah. And Donald was also something of a pariah because of his politics and his faith. He was also seeking someone who would bring him out of the closet. We were like Rush Limbaugh dating Gloria Steinem. Besides, I always seem to attract Republicans and seminary students."

Like Allen, once we've passed that moment of truth when we realize he can form a coherent sentence, his breath smells fresh, and he doesn't wear Brut, we're ready for Step Two. We engage in superficial, witty conversation, taking great pains to demonstrate our irresistible sense of humor. Our laughter draws us even closer. We talk into the wee morning hours. We cling to each provocative word. Before we know it, thoughts of this guy dominate our every waking moment. Our sleep is restless because his face keeps appearing in our dreams. At work, we find ourselves scribbling his name on important reports. We don't even realize it—until the boss slaps the report on our desk, demanding an explanation.

Maybe we were sexually intimate on the night we met, or maybe we waited a day or two. Doesn't matter. It was a night of some of the hottest sex we'd ever had.

In a week, we're fantasizing about moving in with him.

Of course it wouldn't be a wise decision. We know that. So does he. We're moving too fast. But we feel, totally and illogically, that our lives can't go on without him. The urge to merge has *never* been this strong. We want our socks and underwear in his drawer. We want to shower him with lavish gifts. We want to wow him with our culinary expertise. We want to show him that he hasn't even *heard* "articulate" until we indulge him in dusk-to-dawn conversations with Judy Collins playing softly in the background.

However, not every romance begins with a melody. Even though Bobby Hanes, 35, realized that David was someone special who really loved him, their relationship got off to a rocky start. "I moved into David's pad in Decatur, Georgia, just a few months after we met," Bobby says. "I wouldn't recommend that to anyone. As I tried to fit my things into his space, it took a while to make *his* space into *our* space. But once we survived the adjustment period, we found we really enjoyed living with each other. We were working on that together. Cooking, and entertaining our friends. Things were very, very nice. We were great traveling partners. We loved to get into the car and go exploring places with one another. We took winery tours with each other, and discovered we enjoyed gardening together. We made each other laugh a lot."

In fact, things are so good, we know this partnership *has* to be cosmically ordained. It's written in the stars. Before we even know his favorite color, song, or magazine, we've packed our bags and stuffed them into the Ryder truck. We're on our way to a new adventure with the man we love. Life is no longer uncertain. We may encounter problems along the way, but when we're in love, we can handle anything the nasty future doles out.

Fast-forward a bit. Maybe a few weeks. A few months. Even thirty years. Time is inconsequential, but our feelings aren't. Something just doesn't pass the smell test anymore. At first, it was endearing the way he clipped his toenails while watching *Oprah* in the afternoon. Or squirmed out of the cineplex twenty minutes into a tearjerker to have a cigarette. Now, it's just plain irritating. Besides, it's up to us to empty the ashtray containing a strange mixture of cigarette butts, ashes, toenail clippings, and candy wrappers before our friends arrive for a dinner party.

And then there's that damned Antonio Banderas. It's not enough for our partner to watch *Interview with the Vampire* a hundred times on Pay-Per-View because he thinks Antonio as

Armand is hot. Lately, his attraction borders on the pathological. What happened to our status as the center of this man's universe?

Okay, we can deal with his attraction to Antonio, but we can't deal with his observation that the guy sitting at a nearby table in our favorite restaurant looks a lot like the sexy star. What we suspected would happen has apparently already begun. His eye has started to wander. (Well, so has ours, but we'll never admit it.) We've confronted him about it, but he makes a valid point which invites no argument. We may be "married," but neither of us is blind.

That night, in bed, we're feeling amorous. But the perfunctory good night and the lips that brush lightly across ours are his way of letting us know we can get *no* satisfaction tonight. In minutes, his gentle snoring that we once found as comforting as a gentle rain is driving us nuts. Finally, we fall into a restless, obsessive sleep. We dream of being dumped, with no prospect of finding anyone who really loves us. A new haircut *might* make us look a little more like Antonio, we think. The next morning, when we tell him how hurt we were that he wasn't in the mood, he reminds us that after having been together for so long, it's inevitable that we don't put out as much as we used to.

We're pissed, but we have to admit that he may be right. After all, we've noticed our sexual moves lately stem from our desperation to convince ourselves that we find our partner just as hot as the night we first made love.

"When we first met each other," relates Jeremy Richards, 27, an actor living in Brooklyn, "Clint and I exchanged telephone numbers. We didn't go home together right away, but we wound up talking on the phone that night for four hours. We were strongly attracted to each other; besides, it was always so much fun to hang out with him."

Skip ahead five years. "I think I started getting tired of being in a relationship," Jeremy continues. "My feelings for him weren't as strong as they were before. I fell out of love with him. I loved him very deeply, but I was no longer feeling that attraction. He was always certain that I was the one for him, but my eyes had been roving for a while. I started fantasizing about what life might be like with a person to whom I was attracted."

In all romantic relationships, both gay and straight, sexual intimacy remains the core demonstration that both partners care deeply about each other. It is the affirmation that their relationship contains the element of passion transcending all other relationships. Being in love places partners in the unique position to teach each other the tender and erotic capacities of their bodies. However, it's not a lesson that is once learned, then forgotten. Growth-centered relationships seize opportunities for renewal, and a silent rejection of one's body implies that the whole person has lost value in the eyes of the significant other. Research in human sexuality confirms that physical intimacy is as primal and as essential as a baby's need to be touched by his caretakers. The kissing, sucking, caressing, and holding characterizing all sexual intimacy are extensions of a child's need to be cherished and loved. When we withhold the demonstration of physical affection, we communicate to our partners that we no longer care as much as we once did.

Four years into Kurt Colborn's six-year relationship, he began to experience dissatisfaction. "I wanted a very stable and more monogamous relationship than we had, with a house, dog, and picket fence," Kurt says. "Russell wanted a house in Key West with a houseboy. He wanted a level of newness and excitement that wasn't as necessary for me. It's true that he was less monogamous than I was, but his sexual acting out wasn't the big issue. It was how he behaved when he spent time with me. There are, after all, different levels of intimacy. He was always able to connect with me sexually, but seldom in nongenital ways. I wanted more hugging and embracing than he was able to provide." Kurt, 27, an engineer living in Ashtabula, Ohio, says that Russell offered "a lot of resistance to identifying as my lover. He insisted on maintaining a separateness that I didn't want."

However, touching need not always lead to orgasm. As gay men living in a culture that has historically celebrated a man's ability to score—and to score often—we have encountered few opportunities to learn that eroticism and passion are also elements of tactile communication having no goal other than the pleasure of touch. We have resisted the necessity of reassuring our partners that not being in the mood to score does not constitute rejection. That resistance is not a gay thing as much as it is a male thing. Men have a hard time talking about sex unless in the context of locker room humor—a difficulty that is the direct result of acculturation. To acknowledge our vulnerability to sexual issues might make us appear to be less than men.

In terms of sexual responsiveness and intimacy, gay men face numerous deterrents and challenges, both personal and social. In a society that refuses to validate or acknowledge our committed relationships—hence, the propensity of legislators to pooh-pooh gay marriage and domestic partnerships—we couple with our lovers in a hostile environment. No psychological instrument is capable of accurately measuring our internalization of social hostility, or the frequency with which it perpetuates itself in self-destructive or self-demeaning sexual behaviors. We experience dichotomous love lives alien to our heterosexual counterparts— a tug of war between what we perceive as a necessary and silent self-protection and a desire to affirm the love we feel for our partners. Even in cities with sizable gay "communities"—a word not only misleading in its implication that we are a strongly cohesive cadre, but also damaging as a weapon used against us by the Religious Right—gay men are reluctant to show affection in public, and wary of even an innocuous variety of romantic displays that are perfectly acceptable for straight couples. As a result, we sometimes act out internalized feelings of self-loathing through promiscuous sexual activity that is threatening to our partnerships, and psychologically damaging to ourselves. Ultimately, casual sex becomes the Dance of the Social Pariah.

"You develop an intuition about this kind of thing," says Tony Lake, 53, a teacher in Lubbock, Texas, who was partnered with Jonathan for eighteen years. "There were times when he would come home, and not be interested in sex, or anything else having to do with me. I thought he was tired. Then, one Sunday afternoon, he started crying."

"I've been very unfaithful to you," Jonathan sobbed. "I know we pledged monogamy, but I've betrayed our commitment."

Tony's reaction was one of anger and sadness, but he remained outwardly calm. "Jonathan, obviously our relationship has broken down somehow," he said. "We need to start repairing everything."

Wholeheartedly, Jonathan agreed.

Or so Tony thought. "We intended to have continual open

communication. We would converge even closer, physically and spiritually. We would make certain temptation wouldn't come between us again."

But Jonathan couldn't make it work. "His promiscuity started happening all over again. But he kept it quiet, all right." Tony sighs. "I always wonder if the way I perceived things, and the way I so willingly forgave him, and turned the confrontation into something of a positive experience, if my stance was not perceived as subliminal permission."

There was no end to Jonathan's infidelity. "He goes out and sleeps around. Here I am, devastated after eighteen years of what I thought was a monogamous relationship," Tony says. "But what are you going to do? You're powerless to stop it. So you go back into denial."

Interviews with fifty gay men who have experienced the dissolution of their love relationships reveal that many of us attempt partnerships with the "understanding" that sexual fidelity is a social construct best reserved for straight couples (who, by the way, experience an exorbitant divorce rate frequently precipitated by—sexual infidelity). However, even when both partners agree to the terms of so-called "open relationships," sleeping around often leads to jealousy and betrayal. It erodes the core commitment characterizing the relationship from its inception. Frequently, we cannot predict that, even in anonymous or casual sexual encounters, unanticipated emotional involvement has the potential to erode even the most solid relationships. At best, emotional adhesion to what began as a casual fling leads to conflicts that are often irreparable, even in couples counseling. The classic contention that "there are promises made in any bed" proves valid. An encounter intended only for sexual pleasure cannot guarantee that the participants will not discover a more transcendent connection. Occasionally, open relationships work, but they seem to be the exception, rather than the rule.

Another deterrent to the longevity of our partnerships is the absence of opportunity for public celebration of our commitments. Although we can take our "vows" in commitment ceremonies—usually in a local Metropolitan Community Church, although several mainline churches have begun to recognize our committed relationships—those ceremonies don't possess the same clout or legitimization as heterosexual weddings. Those men who *do* "tie the knot" take a big risk. Homophobes could find out about the walk down the aisle, and possibly sabotage their social or employment standing. Take, for example, Gerry Crane, a former high school teacher in Michigan. When local fundamentalists discovered that he had taken a vow of commitment to his partner, Randy, they initiated a movement to oust him from his teaching position. Although he won a financial settlement from the school district, he lost his job—and his life. The stress related to his fight with the school board—and the lack of acknowledgement or support from his own parents—ultimately killed him when he had a heart attack.

Yet some of us are lucky. We enjoy a few close friends, both straight and gay, who know we're in love, respect our love relationship, and regard us as a couple. The unlucky among us cannot tell anyone of our commitment—even our families—leaving us to lead lives in what some gay couples disparagingly regard as the "marriage closet."

The public distinction between gay men who are close friends and those who are romantic partners is the sexual component of the relationship. In fact, we cannot be fully gay until we are part of a relationship. Being in love, and living a committed life of openness in love, makes us gay. Our involvement in a relationship erases the element of doubt. People may have suspected our homosexuality. They may openly wonder whether we are, in fact, gay. But loving commitment to a partner shreds all doubt, and forces our friends, families, and colleagues to acknowledge us in the fullness of our identity. If we aren't brave enough to acknowledge our loving commitments proudly and publicly, and to demand society's respect of our love, then what does our reluctance imply about our ability to take commitment seriously?

What does our willingness to stay in the closet say about our own regard of our partnerships?

"Unfortunately, because we haven't had the socialization to be healthy as gay men, there haven't been models of homosexual relationships," says James E. McKeon, 41, a professional artist and jewelry designer in Miami, Florida. "That doesn't mean we have to model our relationships after heterosexuals. Based on honesty, two men can make a decision about the parameters of their relationship. I think it's great that two men want to see other people *if* they agree on it. But most of us don't like the idea that our partners are screwing around. We are afraid of possible emotional attachments. It's not so much sex, as the danger of attachments. Personally, I want to have deep levels of intimacy with one person. You lose that potential when you start diffusing intimacy with multiple partners."

When Putting Out Means Pretending

We crawl into bed with our partner, then snuggle up close and kiss him goodnight. We reach to turn off the bedside lamp. Hungrily, he pulls us into his arms, and kisses us passionately. His hands are all over us. We respond, but our heart isn't in it. In fact, neither is any other crucial component of our anatomy. Still, out of a sense of duty, we go through the paces, moaning "Oh, baby!" on cue, pretending to be hotter than we've ever been.

He sees through our charade. We never doubted that he would. He knows us better than anyone else, and we can't fake passion. He asks: "Is anything wrong, honey?" We say too quickly: "No. Nothing at all." Then, we add: "Why do you ask?" The patronizing question is a dead giveaway. Hurt and disappointed, he rolls over and slides as far away from us as he can without falling off the bed. Shrugging, we turn out the light. When we drape an arm around him, we feel his muscles tense. We turn the light on once again, sit up, and demand to know why he's being so cold. He turns the question back on us. Before we know it, we're having an argument just minutes after we "made love." Soon, he's sleeping on the sofa. We think that perhaps it's time to consider going our separate ways.

Or maybe it's time to start communicating.

"I suppose I should have recognized several signs from quite early on," says Chuck Parsons, 55, a stage actor and director living in Canada. "At the five-year mark, I had it confirmed that he had slept with a couple of friends of mine. This hurt a lot because he had professed total fidelity and made a big requirement that we have an exclusive relationship. That commitment took considerable effort on my part. By that I mean there were lots of opportunities for me to have slept with other people, or to have carried on a clandestine relationship without his knowing. But I had been completely faithful." However, after his partner's infidelity, Chuck stopped the charade. "But anything I did—and I put definite limits on those activities—was merely sex: nothing that actually threatened the relationship itself. I am not proud of those things. I was very judgmental about myself, in fact. Partially, I rationalized my actions by thinking that while I had been working hard at an exclusive relationship, he had been indulging himself. He continued to deny it. I'd have been hurt if he had admitted it, but I think I could have taken it. Maybe we could have talked, and worked something out. But he would not talk about 'us' issues, except to reaffirm that I had to be exclusively his."

Discussions about sexual responsiveness often lead to positive opportunities for honesty—an occurrence not possible in Chuck's relationship because he and his partner did not communicate well. However, candid communication often renews passion. Lack of sexual interest indicates that we have grown apart in some way—that we need to re-open channels of communication in our relationship. Love needs frequent affirmation (saying "yes" to our commitment) and confirmation (assuring our partner that our "yes" is an honest response). Sex affirms; talk confirms. It's a truth to which partners in successful relationships frequently allude.

When sexual attraction for our partner subsides, we might spend a few moments of quiet introspection to determine the reasons why. Perhaps he has said that our mother is an overbearing woman who always insists on dominating the conversation during holiday feasts. Maybe we even recognize that what he's saying is true. But we don't like to be reminded of this flaw in our mother's personality. Instead of allowing resentment to grow, we should express to him our feelings about his comments. We should frame our response in terms of how his comments made us feel. We should take great care to use assertive statements— "I feel annoyed when I hear negative comments about dear old Mom." These "I-statements" compel him to identify and empathize with our feelings, without our devaluing his. Together, perhaps we can think of ways to help Mother become more charming over the holidays.

Or perhaps we feel irrational jealousy over his attraction for Antonio Banderas. "I know it's unreasonable," we proffer, "but I really feel angry, hurt, and jealous when you observe how sexy he is. It goads me when you say he can put his boots under your bed anytime. I feel as though our relationship isn't really that important to you—that you might be receptive to an encounter with some other hot guy."

More than likely, our partner will reassure us that he was just being glib, that his comments were made in jest, and that his entire world revolves around no one but us. Or if there *are* problems in our relationship, he may use this opportunity to vent. Either way, honesty, no matter how uncomfortable, is essential. Hopefully, we *want* to know of problems in our relationship; we *have* to know of them, to determine if there is a chance for resolution.

Let's say he admits to feeling trapped. He thinks both of us need to examine ways to make our relationship a more vital one. Ruts are hell on relationships. If we consider our partner a major contributor to our stasis, we sure aren't going to find him all that sexy. After communicating the problem clearly, we might examine ways to revitalize our romance. We should give our suggestions time to work before opting to move on to step two, or throwing in the towel. Better to make love two hours earlier than we normally do rather than adding stress to the relationship because our partner is too tired to tango by the time we get horny.

If stasis is only a temporary problem, and our steps to remedy the routine of our lives are successful, then our romance will be back on the right track. We'll also see our partner in a different light. The prospect of sex with him will excite us almost as much as it did when our relationship was just beginning. After all, then, both of us have made life changes so that we aren't the same people we were yesterday. We'll feel as though we're falling in love all over again—well, almost. "It's been my experience that all successful couples grow something together, some kind of outward thing," says Allen Williams. "When things get rocky in their relationship, this thing brings them back together. I know many long-term couples. Their support groups encourage them to stay together, to work their problems out. One long-term couple said they had been together for fifteen years. Two common elements for that kind of longevity are that successful couples grow something together, and they respect their partners. Even if long-term partners have an open relationship, they have the same understanding. 'I expect that you occasionally cheat,' they think, 'but you will come home.' Or they expect that both partners will be monogamous. It's the idea of a common expectation that makes a relationship work.''

But what if nothing changes, even when we've made one another aware of the need for change? Then, we have a problem. Some men report that upon determining their relationship had reached a standstill, they tried to use sex as a remedy. Unfortunately, sex in frozen relationships only serves as a placebo. If both of us are unwilling to confront, honestly and openly, our concerns about the issues that have stunted our growth, then our relationship will die a slow, agonizing death.

Eight common warning signs related to our sexual responsiveness often hide the fact that our relationships are in trouble. While recognition of these signals is easy, the determination of whether our relationship problems are temporary ones with permanent solutions, or warnings that to continue in the relationship would be spiritual suicide, is more difficult.

God, how you've let yourself go. The small patch of baldness we thought was so cute when we first met our partner has grown so large now that the reflection of florescent lighting in that patch impairs our vision. Or that cute ass we affectionately dubbed ''Bubble Butt'' now looks like a good replacement for that tattered sofa cushion.

If our partner no longer takes pride in his appearance, we have every right to complain. The manifestations are easy to see. He eats like a pig, and has the waistline to prove it. He scoffs at our suggestion that only twenty percent of his daily caloric intake should be composed of fat, and swears that his weight problem is genetic. Or recently, he stopped an exercise regimen he once considered a religious ritual; what we remember as muscle has turned to sagging flab. Or he no longer shops for stylish clothes. Instead, he wears relics whose fashion period we can't even remember—and he doesn't care. Issues of physical appearance are addressable issues; we owe it to our relationship to activate channels of communication before our once-gorgeous partner looks like Austin Powers. Perhaps our couch potato hasn't even realized that what he's doing—or *not* doing, as the case may be— is driving us up the wall, and he just needed to hear our concerns.

But what if certain characteristics of his appearance bug us out until we realize that they haven't really changed all that much since we first met? Then, we can safely bet that *he* hasn't changed; *we* have. Emotionally, we're separating from him. The truth is hard to admit to ourselves, so we look for tangible characteristics to criticize. By finding flaws in his appearance and personality, we've shifted the blame for *our* emotional detachment. Projected blame is serious business, a portent of even bigger trouble ahead. We must analyze what has happened between us, then confront it directly. If issues can't be resolved, then our relationship might be on the brink of disaster. Regardless of the pain involved in candidly analyzing our relationship, the diminution of sexual interest can't be dismissed as a mere inevitability.

Who needs a shower, anyway? Remember those courtship days when we spent half an hour in the shower, and another thirty minutes in front of the mirror before he picked us up for a date? Now, we've determined all that primping is more trouble than it's worth. So, when we climb into bed, the decision is clear. Either we hold our breath during sex to avoid the pungent aroma of armpits and bad breath, or we feign fatigue and a headache.

Let's face it. Unless we're into grime, nothing is a bigger turnoff than a man who doesn't respect our relationship enough to practice good hygiene before hopping into the sack. Early in our relationship, neither of us would dream of going out together without a shower and a shave. A sign that we're no longer cherished, and our relationship is taken for granted, is that layer of dirt separating us from our lover boy. Cleanliness is not irrelevant to desire after he's become as familiar as our favorite pillow. If our partner doesn't care how he smells when we're in the sack, he probably doesn't care a hell of a lot about how we *feel* in the sack. Give him a bar of antibacterial soap and a sponge, then light the candles and the incense while he showers.

You never hold me anymore. At work, during a conversation in the break room, Allen overheard a straight man berating his wife for something she'd said after making love the previous night.

"Hold me, darling," she had said, after intercourse. "Please hold me." The man, however, repeated her words mockingly, as though hugs were strictly a "female thing"—something a man does to humor his female. The other men in the break room laughed uproariously.

The patriarchal nature of society characterizes men as performance-oriented, even in terms of sexual responsiveness. We don't need physical intimacy beyond getting our rocks off. If touching doesn't culminate with ejaculation, then we have failed in the bedroom. "A lesbian couple I know said that if you both can agree on the room temperature for comfortable hugging," says Allen, "then that cements the relationship. It's true of gay relationships, too. We want hugs as much as women do."

However, a common complaint among gay men in recovery after a breakup was that a physical closeness transcending orgasm was missing from their relationships. Even when sex was fantastic, they felt cherished only in bed. Romantic affirmations of their value to their partners, "pet names," hugs and caresses were missing in their interactions with their partners. A kind of emptiness ensues when we fall into the more comfortable roles of friend, advisor, and sex partner. To be a lover requires significantly more imagination. When we're in love, our minds and bodies crave more substantive, more spiritually affirming interactions. If our relationships stop providing imaginative, romantic fulfillment, we run the risk of falling out of love. We might come to regard our partners as best friends with no claim on our love lives. Such evolution occurs when we do not work on growing our relationship. We lie to ourselves when we regard the loss of intimacy and desire as inevitable. In essence, we deny the nature of touch—physical, emotional, and spiritual—as a dynamic witness to our commitment.

Why is it so dark in here? Lawrence left work a little early, stopped by the liquor store to purchase James's favorite wine, and raced home. He placed the wine on ice, then pulled from the crock pot the roast that had been simmering since early morning. He glanced at the clock. James would be home in less than an hour.

As James pulled into the driveway, Lawrence played his favorite music on the stereo, dimmed the lights, and stood at the door, with a glass of wine in his hand. The moment James entered, he looked annoyed. "Why is it so dark in here?" he demanded. Immediately, he turned the lights up and the stereo off. "It's been a long day," he said, half-apologetically when he noticed the pained expression on Lawrence's face.

Both of them would remember James's thirty-fifth birthday, all right. But not with the same degree of fondness.

Early in our commitments, we frequently plan to turn our time together into special events. These activities—whether they are nights on the town, weekends at beach or mountain resorts, or quiet evenings at home—remind our lovers of the importance they have achieved in our lives. All too often, as we feel "sure" (a dangerous word) that our relationships will "work" (an equally dangerous word), the routine of our lives overrides the potential for spontaneity. We overlook the frequent opportunities for those boosts of novelty that could energize our romance. While not wholly untrue that after the honeymoon is over, monotony sets in, our imagination empowers us to plan ways to beat that monotony, and to show our partners how much they are cherished.

When our partner rejects our efforts, and doesn't seem to care about the quality or diversity of our lives, trouble lies ahead. Or if we feel reluctant to do anything special for "that man," then it's time for a reassessment of our relationship. When we mix the right ingredients into our partnerships, should we ever feel our efforts at sustaining the relationship aren't worth the energy?

He's just a friend. All of us have experienced the sensation that there is more to a situation than meets the eye. At no time is that sensation stronger than when our partner nervously introduces a nice, attractive man as "my new friend." Later, when we question him about the "new friend," in tones of jealousy and suspicion, and wonder why he hasn't mentioned this guy before, he tries to reassure us. "Look. You're just being paranoid. He's just a friend."

And perhaps he is. But we must not discount our ability to sense a potential threat to our relationship. Whether sex is involved in this friendship or not, we gauge the degree of intimacy, if any, this new friendship drains from our partnership. Occasionally, even if our partner isn't sexually involved, the friendship can be erotically charged. Although our partner's friendships should never be universally suspect, a new friend who monopolizes our lover's time, about whom he speaks in affectionate, reverential tones, and about whom he entitles us to limited, filtered information, might be a threat. It's a difficult call, and one that has to be made with great caution.

"I received a phone call from this guy whose voice I didn't recognize," says Michael, 32, a senior financial analyst in Sherman Oaks, California. "He wanted to speak with Evan. He said he had gotten Evan's name from a sex hotline. When Evan came home, I confronted him about the call. He denied everything. Said it must be a joke someone was playing on him. Indeed, it was the only call he received from this individual, so he could have been telling the truth."

At work, Evan also received several bouquets of flowers from his doctor's male receptionist. "I started not trusting him as much," Michael continues. "I started investigating when he would go out of town. I found porno videos in a drawer that I didn't know anything about, as well as the phone numbers of several different guys. He left his car at home once when he was away on a business trip, and his glove compartment was filled with condoms. I never confronted him with most of my discoveries, but he said he had gotten the condoms from Gay Pride. Then, at a Christmas party, I discovered our bedroom door was closed while the rest of our apartment was filled with people. I couldn't understand why the bedroom door was closed, nor could I understand why he just had one man in there alone with him. He said he was showing off a quilt his grandmother made. Then, he went to Ohio, and left his car again. I found a parking ticket. When I looked up the address, the ticket had been written in front of a sex shop. That was pretty much it for me." Later, Evan ran away with the same "friend" admiring Evan's inherited quilt.

So what's wrong with doing it seven days a week? Or . . . Not up to the Marathon Event. Frequent hot sex is every man's fondest dream. One benefit of being in a committed relationship is not only the availability of sex, but also that sexual intimacy is more exciting with someone with whom we're in love and with whom, together, we can comfortably explore ways to be sexually creative. Although we know the conclusion from experience, studies have shown that sexual activity during the first few months of a relationship occurs with much greater frequency than after we've been partnered for a while. Perhaps that's Nature's way of ensuring that our lives are not totally given over to carnal pleasure—or to put it crudely, that we're not always fucking our eyeballs out. After all, we need time for the pursuit of other important goals in our lives. So, to conclude that our relationship is in danger because its sexual intensity has diminished indicates that it was based on very little substance from the beginning.

However, sex is an important component of any partnership; when either we, or our partner, loses interest, we should be concerned. Chronic brush-offs—either his or ours—with no logical justification mean that the separation process has been activated. We handle rejection of sexual intimacy by feeling hurt, angry, and confused. We find the topic difficult to address and, despite our concerns, are inclined to dismiss lack of sexual interest as a temporary condition. But without communication, weeks without sex can grow into months, or even years. One man reported having sex with his partner only once in three years—and then only when his lover woke him in the middle of the night for a quickie. Later, during the process of their breaking up, he discovered that the single amorous advance resulted from his ex-partner's erotic dream of an underwear model he had recently seen in an *International Male* catalog. It is not farfetched to conclude that lack of sexual activity with our partner exacerbates the lack of connection we're already experiencing. If we're not regularly making love with our partner, then we're probably also missing out on those long, loving conversations that often follow. Sexual intimacy results in the kind of vulnerability that opens us to other modes of connecting to the most significant person in our lives.

"We didn't have sex the last seven years of our relationship," says John Eastwood, 48, a telephone operator in Washington, Kentucky. "I would be in the mood, and Dane would roll over and go to sleep. Anytime there was any sex throughout our relationship, I was always the one who made the first move. Sex went from ten to zilch."

For Jim, 46, an editor living in Champaign, Illinois, there was no sex for the last two years of his seventeen-year relationship. "Sex was okay in the beginning, but Jay would then try to perform sexually when he was drunk. It would get painful to do anything with him. He was so clumsy and awkward. Finally, I moved into another bedroom. He would try to sneak into my bed and spend the night with me. We'd get into a big fight, and I would sleep on the couch. He was extremely possessive. Literally, he wanted to wrap around me. He reeked of alcohol all the time. I just blew up one night and told him I was moving into the other room. He got really nasty about it. Eventually, I put a lock on my bedroom door; he would pound on it for a while, and then pass out."

A word of caution is in order. Before concluding that an apparent lack of sexual interest portends the end of our partnership, we need to determine whether other issues are at work. If a personal crisis has recently occurred, or a medical condition has been diagnosed, we are less than likely to feel all that sexy. Still, it's important to communicate clearly that our seeming lack of interest is attributable to circumstances beyond our control, not to any problem or conflict in our relationship. Then, we are positioned to express our love in other ways, like supportive words of encouragement, communication of the value of our partner in our lives, and frequent, physical displays of affection.

Three's not a crowd. It's a family. Lance and his partner, Rob, are having drinks at the local watering hole one Friday night, when Lance leans across the table and says, in a quiet, intense voice: "You see that guy over there? I talked to him when I was ordering our drinks, and he's interested in a *ménage à trois*."

"I'm sure he can find a couple of guys in here who'd be willing to take him up on that offer," Rob replies.

Lance chuckles, but looks annoyed. "He's interested in a threesome with *us*."

"Yeah, but *I'm* not interested," Rob says in a terse voice.

The rest of the evening is spent in virtual silence. Rob asks several times if anything is wrong; always, Lance denies it, but Rob notices he doesn't make eye contact with him all evening. At home, Lance admits his interest in "adding a little variety to our relationship. Besides, who says we're capable of falling in love with only one person?"

Despite encouragement from some pundits in the gay media to reject traditional heterosexual mores and establish ways of relating that are unique and comfortable to us, many men report that the involvement of a third partner in a relationship poses more problems than the initial excitement is worth. They wonder, first of all, why their partners wanted to embrace a third man into their sex lives, causing them to question their own value in the partnership. Second, they recognize the possibility that either or both of them run a significant risk of attachment to the third man. They fear the emotional far more than the physical investment, because they understand that we are not completely in control of choosing the recipient of our love.

We *should* be alarmed when the parameters of our relationship have eroded to the degree that we are willing to allow another individual to compromise our commitment. As one man put it: "Threesomes are ways to search for what we perceive to be a better relationship without relinquishing the security of the old one." While a number of gay men place some credence in the idea that the "nature of the male animal" makes monogamy difficult, they also admit that few of us have reached the point in emotional development to deal with sexual encounters outside the core relationship.

So, when we invite a third playmate to the party, we're playing with fire.

Brian, 26, a teacher in Austin, Texas, discovered that computers also provide an effective way of destroying relationships. "I guess what happened is sort of ironic, considering Ben and I met through a personal ad on Prodigy," he says. "When we finally hooked up, and would go out to bars together, he would question me every time he suspected I was looking at another guy."

"Do you want to fuck him?" Ben would ask when he "caught" Brian admiring another guy.

"I don't think there's anything wrong with looking," Brian explains. "I know where my heart is." But one spring, Ben informed Brian that when he had alleged that he had been "out" with his friends, he had actually arranged, through Prodigy, a rendezvous with Andrew. "They went out together, and Andrew performed oral sex on him. That really pissed me off. For the first seven or eight months of our relationship, he couldn't climax when I was fellating him. He even boasted to me that Andrew could bring him to climax. The implication was that Andrew was more sexually adequate than I."

For a while, Ben and Brian separated, but soon talked through their problems and got together again "full force." "Still, because of the distrust factor, things weren't the same."

James McKeon found out through a friend that his partner was seeing someone else. "I saw Ethan with a very young guy in Crumpets Café," his friend told him.

"So I asked Ethan about it," James says. "He said it was nothing, that the guy was just an old friend of his. But I finally discovered that he had been having an affair with him for six months. Later on, I discovered the young man was employed at the same gym where Ethan and I worked out several times a week."

Once James and Ethan separated, the young man apologized to James. "I had no idea you were in the picture," he said.

"An interesting twist to the story is that once Ethan and I split up for good, the young guy and I started communicating. I asked him to dinner. We hit it off, and ended up having an affair for a few months, even to the point of living together. When Ethan found out, he wanted to get back together again. Somehow, my having the affair with the twenty-one-year-old influenced Ethan to ask me to come back to him." He paused. "Yeah, we got back together for a couple of years, but they were rocky. We should've stayed apart, but neither of us wanted to be alone."

That old football injury is acting up again. Suddenly, we wake up, but it's not the sun glaring in our face. It's the angry countenance of our partner. He demands to know why, in the middle of the night, we left a perfectly comfortable bed and his sparkling company to sleep on this ratty old sofa.

The first time our partner confronts us, we can get away with a reference to the knee injury we sustained while playing college football. After all, middle age is staring us in the face; it's not uncommon to experience nagging little aches and pains. However, when that nagging little pain happens to be our partner, it's time to reach deep, and determine what it is about him that compels us to build walls of separation. To accept anxiety and conflict as part of the evolution of our relationship is self-destructive. If we don't monitor that evolution closely, we may find our partnership on the endangered list.

Okay. Maybe we *do* have a physical problem that makes a lousy mattress unbearable. Or perhaps we worry that our discomfort causes us to toss and turn, hindering our partner's sleep. But if we retreat from the nuptial bed with little or no explanation, we have opened opportunity's window for our partner to question our motivation and our relationship.

In the absence of sexual intimacy, and our unwillingness to sleep with our partner, we have, consciously or not, altered the dynamics of our partnership. What we have created, if we are still communicating openly and honestly with one another, is a close friendship. Not that there's anything wrong with friendship, as long as we've both agreed to it. But if the terms of our relationship are ours alone, and we lead our partner to believe separation is temporary, we are guilty of yet another lie certain to cause significant emotional scarring over the long haul.

We must, for the sake of our relationship and our integrity, understand the physical separation for what it is: either the symbolic withdrawal of our emotional and spiritual involvement, or our way of not dealing with real circumstances about which both of us are entitled to know.

Reflections

Not that the common denominator of all gay relationships is sex, but the way we handle sexual intimacy is a reflection of other issues that damage, or sustain, our relationships. Once we grow comfortable with our partnerships, sex can, without insight and self-knowledge, become a way to mete out rewards and punishments, aggression, gratitude, and a host of other primal emotions. When sex becomes less than a spontaneous expression of love and passion for a partner to whom we are committed, the sexual experience itself diminishes us as individuals, and scoffs at our relationships. The Romantic poets of English literature regarded sexual expressions of intimacy as pathways to a higher spirituality. Orgasm was regarded as the sublime experience of total unity with one special individual and, through him, a feeling of unity with the universe. To undergird sexual expression with values other than love and passion erects barriers that will eventually corrode the innocence and joy we felt when we first met our partners. When we no longer employ the imagination in sustaining our partnerships, we fall out of love and into an existence that does not begin to touch the magic of our lives.

"It isn't perfect, but we made it clear to each other what we want from our partnership," says Brian of his relationship that began seven months ago. "I'm at a point in establishing a relationship that if a partner can't give me what I need, then it's goodbye. But we wanted commitment, monogamy, and all of the old-fashioned things. On April 6, we exchanged commitment rings at Dupont Circle in Washington, D.C. Of course, we have to deal with stressors in our relationship. But we never go to bed without saying, 'I love you.' This morning, he had to report to work at six o'clock. Before he left, he gave me a hug and a kiss, and said, 'I love you.' These little things we do for each other make our relationship so special. On our monthly anniversary, he's gotten me cards, flowers, and various coupons that he generates on the computer for things like free foot rubs, bubble baths, and free trips to my favorite restaurant. Personal gifts like that—the kind that reflect the nature of our intimacy—mean more to me than even the flowers."

But what happens when the magic disappears? What happens

when the desire and motivation to treat one another as someone special have disappeared?

How do we know when it's time to be concerned?

Your Romance Satisfaction Quotient (RSQ)

You're worried. Things just aren't the same in the bedroom— or in any other room, for that matter. The romance that once typified your relationship has slipped away, and you want to know: Is it time to think seriously about breaking up?

Here's an activity to help you decide how satisfied you are with the romance in your current relationship. Or if you've already broken up, this clarification activity will affirm how much of the romance had been drained from your partnership by the time you made the break. In the table below, place the rating (1-5) that most closely corresponds to your feeling about each statement. (For right now, ignore the letters in the first column of the table.)

5—I feel very strongly that this statement is true.
4—I feel this statement is somewhat true.
3—I feel neither positively nor negatively about this statement.
2—I feel this statement isn't very true of my relationship.
1—I feel this statement is farthest from the truth about my relationship.

1. My heart races whenever my partner is in the same room.
2. Occasionally, I fantasize having a sexual encounter with a man other than my partner.
3. I don't look at other men as much as I did before my partner and I got together.
4. I cringe when I realize my partner wants to have sex with me.
5. I'm more interested in my partner's sexual satisfaction than in my own.
6. I can't wait for my partner to get home from work.

7. My partner and I have invited a third man into our relationship to increase our sexual excitement.
8. I am easily aroused sexually by my partner.
9. I have had at least one affair that I tried to hide from my partner.
10. My partner inspires my creative energy, such as writing poetry, painting, music, and the like.
11. We love to be creative during sexual intimacy.
12. I wonder whether I would stay with my partner if we weren't obligated to each other financially.
13. We never have disagreements over how we express our sexual intimacy with each other.
14. I've noticed that it takes my partner a long time to get sexually aroused when we're in bed together.
15. We are just as sexually attracted to one another now as we were when we first met.
16. My partner and I never run out of conversation topics when we're together.
17. I prefer masturbating to making love with my partner.
18. We never have disagreements over the frequency of sex.
19. I know that my partner has had at least one affair.
20. I enjoy buying my partner things with little thought of the expense.
21. My partner has no personal habits that drive me crazy.
22. Antonio Banderas can put his boots under my bed anytime.
23. My partner stays in my thoughts most of the time.
24. The thought of my partner having sex with someone else turns me on.
25. Our attitudes about sexual fidelity are in line.

A.	1.	6.	11.	16.	21.
B.	2.	7.	12.	17.	22.
C.	3.	8.	13.	18.	23.
D.	4.	9.	14.	19.	24.
E.	5.	10.	15.	20.	25.

Calculating Your RSQ: For each row (A through E), calculate the sum of the five ratings, then indicate that sum in the corresponding box. (For example, add Responses 1, 6, 11, 16, and 21.) After completing all five rows, add the sums of Rows A, C, and E. Place that response below.

Response 1 (A, C, E): _____

Now, add the sums of Rows B and D. Place that response below.

Response 2 (B and D): _____

Next, subtract your smaller response from your larger response to get your RSQ. Place that number here.

Your RSQ: _____

What the RSQ Means

When Response 1 is larger than Response 2 . . .

. . . and your RSQ is less than 35, you're experiencing some problems with romance in your partnership.
. . . and your RSQ is more than 35, and you're having a problem with your current partner, it has very little to do with romance.

When Response 2 is larger than Response 1 . . .

. . . and your RSQ is larger than 15, you're having a serious problem with the romantic component of your partnership.
. . . and your RSQ is less than 15, there's room for improvement, but things may not be hopeless yet.

CHAPTER TWO
. . . .
Warning Signs

Substantial Penalties for Early Withdrawal

A self-indulgence. The slow, agonizing dissolution of the couple our friends and colleagues knew as "Robert and Dann."

We were both doing it, this "separation thing." This drifting away from each other yet not knowing how to call each other back. It was the coldest, loneliest feeling. First, we experienced sadness that the chasm between us widened and deepened with each passing day. Then came anger that neither of us could build a bridge sturdy enough to sustain our partnership until help arrived. After that, resignation that the end was near. No need to fret anymore. All we had to look forward to was a period of waiting until the final collision came and we would sink like the *Titanic*.

Sometimes I felt—as I'm sure he did as well—empty, silent spaces all around me when he entered the room. What happened to us? I wondered. Was it too late to recapture the joy, the excitement—the connection—we had lost?

How could we possibly know where to begin?

We didn't know the answers, which slithered farther from our grasp the more desperately we needed them, to any of those questions. When spending time together, we either endured one another's silent company, or engaged in yet another confrontation. Eventually, we began to examine the steps necessary to dissolve the relationship.

Our withdrawal from one another grew increasingly onerous and irrevocable. Psychotherapy, intended to help us rekindle our romance, became an exploration of ways to separate and still maintain a friendship—an objective substantially difficult because of the psychological distance between us.

"I realized I didn't matter anymore," says Robert. "It didn't matter whether I was there for Dann or not. I even felt that he wouldn't miss me if I disappeared. There were other things, as well. My mother was dying throughout our relationship problems. I was hurting a lot, and it didn't matter to him that I was hurting. I was in mourning for so many things. Leaving was my trying to shake Dann up enough to make him choose me all over again. But he wasn't emotionally ready to make a decision about anything. He was a wreck when I needed him to be strong."

The tendency of unhappy couples to withdraw from their partnerships is characterized by distinct signals alerting us to the inevitability of separation. To disregard those signals prolongs our unhappiness as we reach a point where splitting up is our only option. Prolonging an unsatisfactory partnership is unfair to ourselves, our partners and our own potential for love.

"A couple of months before we broke up, I noticed a distance in our relationship," says Duncan Teague, a research coordinator in Atlanta. "Like he was always thinking about something. Then, I felt a real dread of ending the relationship. It was never anything David said. Just something I sensed."

"Well, I have a slightly different perspective," David, a research physician at the Centers for Disease Control, says. "Some of the things that attracted me to Duncan were also the difficulties in the relationship. He's very committed to gay activism, and is extroverted and gregarious. He really likes to be involved socially. At times, I need more solitude. I prefer small groups to large ones, yet Duncan gets his energy from social encounters. I was the one who first felt like this relationship really wasn't going to work. It was really hard because I never stopped loving Duncan."

According to Duncan, a difficult struggle is knowing that "you want to be with a particular person, but not knowing whether you'll be happy with him. We both grappled with the issue of whether the quality of our lives would be what we wanted with this person we love very, very much. When we broke up, there was no malice in our relationship—besides the fact that he never bought me diamonds."

David laughs. "Like Duncan, I'm very glad of our relationship. I'm also glad we still have a friendship. I don't know that our break-up strengthened either one of us. I still have sadness over what happened. I don't think breaking up was ennobling or strengthening. But we go through it. It hurts, but we go through it."

How do we know it's time to call it quits? In all honesty, certainty about such matters is elusive. But once we reach an intolerable depth of unhappiness and dissatisfaction, we are compelled to take action. For example, the avoidance of spending time with our partner because his presence drains us indicates that we have, at least subconsciously, entertained the idea of singlehood. However, we don't wish to make the leap right away to the assumption that our partnership is over. For our sanity, and in fairness to our relationship, we strive to understand the source of our unhappiness. Additionally, the determination of whether our problems are chronic and incurable, or temporary and situational, is essential.

"I knew Rick was in love with someone else, and didn't want to be," says James Courson, 37, a nurse in a large Minneapolis hospital. "That's the worst kind of infidelity. What made it worse was the fact that the other guy—Scott—was a friend of mine before Rick and I hooked up. Rick asked me to give him time. He promised he would work through his feelings—that *I* was the man he wanted to spend his life with. How could I not believe him? Our partnership had already lasted ten years."

Ultimately, Rick and James ended their partnership because James could no longer deal with his feelings of rejection. "It seemed the harder he struggled, the more deeply he fell for Scott. After eight months of feeling the walls closing in around me—of feeling horribly lonely—I did what I thought was best. I broke up with him."

What's happened to us when we plan quiet, romantic evenings with our partner, and the romance is noticeably lacking? Is it possible that we have nothing left to talk about? When we try to force conversation, we often reach impasses which lead to silence or arguments. He feels shallow to us. He drains our energy. Maybe it's nothing he's done, specifically, but the spark that once kept us up all night in rapt conversation has been extinguished.

How could we have screwed up this badly? Whatever made us think that we would *ever* want to spend our lives with this guy? Could we have been this naïve? Could passion have made us so blind?

Probably not. Our partnership was good when it started. We ought to give ourselves credit for that. But people grow. They change. Their paths sometimes diverge so dramatically that they cannot be rediverted toward common ground. Humans are both tenacious and malleable. We must reject the temptation to beat ourselves up because we regard ourselves as failures in sustaining our partnership. If we don't communicate as effortlessly as we once did, we don't rashly conclude that we have failed. While building our relationship, we also erected barriers—personal observations, insights, and attitudes about which we never told our partner, because we worried about how he'd react. Now, they have become our little secrets and our shames, no matter how innocuous they really are. Maybe now, we want to talk about them, but fear encumbers us. He'll want to know why we never entrusted him before. As a result of our fear to continue the intimacy we began, we accept unpopular shifts at work to avoid spending time with him. Or we establish a network of friends we don't share. We establish a life quite separate from our partner so that, when the time comes—and we are certain that it will—we can cut the ties cleanly and painlessly. That goal becomes our own illusion. We think growing the distance between ourselves and our partner will be enabling. Perhaps in that space we can find our happiness again. We love our partner. But how can we live with him, if we want any of the love to last? So, our decision is made. Withdrawal is necessary to end this relationship that no longer makes us grow.

"Everything turned to shit," says Jeff, 34, a vice-president of administration and finance in Lexington, Kentucky. "We were no longer equal partners. I became someone I wasn't before. Cory drained me dry emotionally, psychologically, and in the end, financially. He just took. Cory is a collector. He was like that with people. The relationship deteriorated the more manipulative he became. He even had me convinced that no one else would ever want me. Often, he even forbade me to have anything to do with many of my friends."

If we are still in love with our partner, yet recognize the signs indicating the relationship is no longer synchronized, we should examine his behavior toward us, and the way our interactions make us feel. When he hurts us and doesn't care, he diminishes the sanctity of our relationship, and cheapens who we are to each other. We suffer a sense of loss, of wandering and disequilibrium. Does he sleep most of the day when he has a day off instead of spending time with us? Does television monopolize his every waking moment? Is his exclusive topic of conversation the cubic zirconium stone he saw on the Home Shopping Network, or the new wrinkle in Rexella's face on the *Jack van Impe Show*? Perhaps we finally decide to tell him how neglected we feel. He dismisses our concerns with a curt admonition that we worry too much. Yet, even our faithful dog, Rover, gets preoccupied and depressed when he's not taken out for exercise now and then. Our relationships should also have a little fresh air and some stimulation from time to time. Atrophy is comfortable. It's predictable. But it's not healthy. People who allow their lives to erode risk losing everything—including their spirit. Eventually, they snap—or they're put out to pasture.

"When Lance and I broke up, that triggered my battle with manic depression," says Gene Gilfus, 44, an aging services program coordinator in Albany, New York. "They put me on anticonvulsants. Now, I'm doing lithium therapy. I also suffer from agoraphobia and mood disorders."

Gene compares his circumstances to the death of a loved one. "I felt a terrible loss like I never had in my life. It was very, very rough on me. I had lost my major friend, companion, and lover. I felt very much deceived and betrayed, but I was never filled with hate. Anger, yes. I always loved him, and I love him now. God damn it! I wouldn't be having these problems if he were around."

It's easy to be thrown off-guard by all the trappings of a life into which we've grown comfortable and secure. Although we generally know what's best for us, we're often willing to relinquish the passion in our lives for the convenience of the nest egg we've built.

Don't rock the boat, baby, or you'll fall out. If you're not careful, you'll drown.

But drowning is exactly what happens, whether we rock or not. Our relationship has been reduced to a Pandora's box of secrets. Not the sordid kind, like the sexual fantasy we had this morning, or the new Gay Billy doll we must have—and not just because he's anatomically correct, although we'll see more of the doll's anatomy than our partner's. The secrets we're keeping are the secrets of our dissatisfaction with our partnership. Why do we hide our feelings, our concerns? Because something scares the hell out of us about not being a pair again. Maybe we're frightened of looking inside, or discovering, on our own, who we are all over again. Maybe we're afraid of dwindling away to nothing if we're not part of a set. We know that, if we tell him that we don't want to be his partner anymore—or he tells us the same secret—life becomes saturated with pain. When we withdraw from our partner without explaining to him why we must, we are desperately trying to avoid pain, even if it means doing what we've never been willing to do before—keeping secrets.

This particular secret—*that we want out*—is the biggest one of all.

And the one we keep the longest.

The Growth of Resentment

Topping the list of reasons that resentment creeps into our relationships is our inability to communicate effectively. While tempted to regard this lack of communication as a personal failure, we can't always assume that is the case. As much as we want to open channels of communication with our partner, the truth is, we don't always know exactly *what* we wish to express. Often, the best we can do is to recognize that something is wrong. When relationships are on the fritz, we wrestle with all kinds of issues and feelings, many of which are intricately interwoven or whose explanations linger just out of reach. Therefore, explanations might sound cryptic, at best. To consider a communication failure at fault in a relationship's dissolution might be a simplistic rationalization that says little about why we've fallen out of love. Instead, it merely touches the surface of layers of issues contributing to our breakup.

"I didn't realize there was anything seriously wrong until Jason came home in the wee hours of the morning," Les Wright, 44, an author and scholar living in Boston, says. "He told me he had spent the night with someone else. Our agreement was that we could be sexual with other people, but not get emotionally involved. It was clear he wasn't just having sex."

Les was surprised he had not detected a problem "because I tend to be a sensitive person. But I was head over heels in love with him, and completely blind to what was going on. I just wasn't picking up that he wasn't one hundred percent honest with me. I guess I should have suspected, because he was very good at playing the role of perfect spouse. To this day, I have not been able to see where the reality and the role-playing diverged."

Furthermore, we may be dealing with issues that, while affecting the tone of our partnership, are not directly related to it. Perhaps we are grieving the recent loss of our parents, or confronting a perplexing middle-age crisis. Maybe we've uncovered a deep resentment of straight people because of social repression and discrimination, or heard through the office grapevine that several colleagues will have to be "terminated." Combined with problems directly associated with our relationship—like the loss of sexual attraction or our partner's cultivation of interests different from ours—the challenge of identifying other personal issues poses a serious dilemma when we're striving for clear, compassionate communication with our partner. If we're unable to define concisely those issues bothering us, then we're likely to inflict even more damage on our relationship with muddled, cryptic, or even cruel messages. Perhaps, under the guise of "communication," we say to our partner: "I think it's time we both admit it. If we found someone 'better,' we'd jump at the chance to start a new relationship." The subtext of such a statement might be that we have been feeling neglected and uncherished lately, and we'd like to work toward reestablishing those special qualities that characterized our relationship in the past. By injecting uncertainty into conversations about our partner-

ship, we communicate that we want to check out of the partnership, rather than work out real, vital issues.

Sometimes, for several days in a row, Keith Schrag's partner
wouldn't even speak to him. "Occasionally, he would be upset
because I mentioned something about his behavior I didn't like,"
Keith says. "Often, his silences would have to do with something
that needed to be done around the house, but Dirk wasn't in
the mood. Or his smoking. He resented the fact that I didn't
allow smoking in the house." Finally, Keith, who is nineteen
years older than his partner and considers himself a "peacemaker
and a giver-in," lifted the no-smoking house rule, as long as Dirk
turned on the exhaust fan.

"But it really didn't matter what I said or did," Keith adds.
"Dirk was trusting me less and less, and shared less with me.
Sex became very infrequent. Maybe his resentment was building
because while we agreed not to have a monogamous relationship,
he would have preferred monogamy as a condition."

Another impediment to communication is the bitchy way,
weakly camouflaged as humor, we are capable of hurting each
other. Because we use humor to soften the blow—or so we
think—we are often surprised when our veiled criticisms come
back to bite us on the ass. Because of our partnership's vulnerable
nature, we discover secrets, desires, dreams, and even sources of
shame unshared by our partners with other friends. They're no
big deal to us because they are close to the core of the man we
love. So what if our partner was molested by an older cousin?
We accept that trauma as part of our partner's being. So what if
he has a heart-shaped birthmark—which we consider sexy—on
his right ass-cheek? So what if we argued vehemently because
the Godiva chocolates we gave him for Valentine's Day weren't
packaged in the holiday box he wanted? Even so, our knowledge
of each other should never become part of the public domain.
Once the boundaries between private and public are no longer
clear, our relationship is running out of steam. We're admitting
that either we don't know our partner as well as we once did, or
that we don't care about him as much.

However, it would be capricious to conclude that our partnership is over because we have done a few shitty things to each
other. Sometimes, when we fall into a rut, the daily routine of

our lives saps our energy. As a result, we bitch a lot to jar our partner into an awareness that our relationship needs work. It's our way of reminding him that we won't be taken for granted. Or so we think. Instead, cattiness often wages a battle of wits. When we, or our partners, disregard indicators that our relationship as it's presently configured really sucks, and willfully continue the verbal jousting, we should seriously consider where we're headed as a couple. Have we erected barriers of hostility against real intimacy to ensure that our wish for separation comes true? If so, the end is indeed near, along with scarring, bitterness, and resentment that linger long after we've gone our separate ways.

John Eastwood knows from experience the frustration partners suffer when they build barriers. "Often, I'd fester instead of confronting him—though once I told him he needed his head examined," John says. "Because we didn't communicate, I was oblivious to the fact that things had begun to deteriorate until he wanted to take a week's sabbatical to think about things."

Once Christopher left, John got only two hours of sleep per night. "I was a basket case," he explains. "I would lie down to go to sleep, and still be wide awake."

On the Friday that ended Christopher's "sabbatical," John picked him up from work, but gave him the silent treatment until Sunday.

"Aren't you going to say anything?" John finally asked.

"I've been waiting for *you* to say something," Christopher replied.

For weeks, Christopher found other excuses not to come home.

"I thought it was time to start doing things to make him wake up and take notice," John said.

However, his plan backfired. When, to get a reaction from Christopher, John allowed a friend to move into the spare bedroom, Christopher saw an easy escape. "That's fine," he said. "I'll just leave."

And leave he did. "He had all of forty-eight hours before a twenty-year-old redhead moved in with him," John said.

Understanding other pitfalls to communication is essential in determining how seriously the engine of our relationship is malfunctioning. Sometimes, relinquishing certain behaviors rekindles our romance; at other times, terminating the relationship is the only way to reenergize our lives. As responsible partners, we do everything we can to make our partnership work. What's difficult is determining when we've exhausted all our resources toward resolution. Prolonging the agony of a dead-end relationship forebodes a greater difficulty in sustaining a friendship with our ex-partner—an important consideration for most men, who prefer friendship to enmity. Feelings of hostility and resentment impair our ability to start our romantic lives anew. How can our lives move forward when we spend each day defiling the corpse of the old relationship?

Gay men who have faced the challenges of long-term relationships agree that lack of communication is the fastest way to destroy a partnership. The most injurious mode of poor communication is passive-aggressiveness, by far the easiest way to avoid dealing with emotions. Instead of experiencing "negative" emotions, then working through them, we act them out. All of us behave passive-aggressively at times. If we're angry with our partner, for example, we choose not to tell him. Hell, we don't even talk to him. Instead, we slam household objects around, or kick the dog. And it's not anger alone that compels us to behave like a drama queen. We might be sad because he doesn't pay enough attention to us, or hurt because he didn't remember our anniversary.

A wealth of behaviors falls into the passive-aggressive category. Instead of dealing with an uncomfortable domestic confrontation, one of us drives his car around the countryside for hours. *Anything*, to avoid facing this disruption of our equilibrium. Or if he asks us what's wrong, we say, "Nothing," but continue to sulk and pout. Or for revenge, we refuse to fulfill what is traditionally considered our "duty," just to inconvenience the asshole.

As Michael Burdick's suspicion of his partner's lip service to fidelity mounted, he also stumbled on another ugly surprise. "Neither one of us did drugs—or so I thought," he explains. "As I was looking through a bathroom drawer, I discovered that Joe had poppers."

Michael decided he could no longer trust Joe, but instead of talking things out, he dealt with his realization in a passive-aggressive manner. "I went out and got drunk, then went to a gay movie theatre," he says. "I scored with somebody else."

At first, Michael evaded an admission of the truth. "Joe had been invited to a New Year's Eve party with his bowling buddies. They were always trying to get him to do things without me. When I reminded him that we had been invited to another party as a couple, he said he had committed himself to attending this party. It's true, he asked me to go with him, but not feeling comfortable around his friends, I declined."

Michael came home the next morning at five-thirty, and slept in the spare room. "Joe awoke me around eleven," he says.

"Why didn't you sleep with me?" he asked, then added that he didn't know Michael's favorite club stayed open so late. "I heard you come in. It was past five o'clock."

"After playing twenty questions, I finally admitted that I wasn't at the club," Michael said. "I told him the truth. I'd had sex with someone else that morning." He sighed, still upset at the vengeful games he and his partner had been playing. "That blew our relationship right there."

Is passive-aggressive behavior a signal that it's time to end our relationship? Absolutely not. In fact, this particular mode of communication is fairly easy to fix, with the assistance of a good behaviorist—or strong determination. But if passive-aggressive behavior is one among a number of symptoms which characterize interactions with our partner, we had better take a close look at the dynamics of our relationship.

Another warning sign that our relationship has run aground is continuous, biting sarcasm. Some of our best zingers are products of a sarcastic wit, but our lover should not be a sparring partner against whom we're competing for the best line. No other style of interaction can degrade another human being like sarcasm. Sarcasm belittles us, angers us, depresses us, and puts us on the defensive. Sarcasm has led to more arguments than the cute young thing who just started going to the bar. No one can forget how belittled he feels during a sarcastic battle of the wits. Nor should he.

One couple, together for three years, made all their friends very uncomfortable because sarcasm had become the *only* way they could relate to each other. Obviously, Graham was intellectually superior to Wayne. At first, their friends wondered what they ever saw in each other. Later, one friend commented that Graham needed a whipping boy to feed his withering self-esteem. Whenever Wayne's conversation revealed his immaturity or naïveté, Graham was quick to deliver a sarcastic retort. Their friends laughed uncomfortably, not certain whether both Graham and Wayne were willing participants in this game. Clearly, Wayne was the loser in this sinister competition. Before long, their friends figured out that, while Graham enjoyed showcasing his caustic sense of humor, Wayne suffered irreparable hurt. Soon, their friends avoided them like the plague.

Ultimately, Graham grew increasingly contemptuous of Wayne. One day, after a particularly hostile battle of wits, Graham disappeared while Wayne was working, and never returned. Wayne never heard from him again.

"Living without him was very difficult at first," Wayne admits. "After a while, I realized that I had become very accustomed to his always cutting me down. There was never any love, really, in that relationship—not for me. It's taken me a very long time to get beyond the resentment I felt for Graham. To be honest with you, I don't care if I never see or hear from him again—not after what he did to me. He robbed me of my dignity and self-respect." Wayne grows tearful. After a moment, he clears his throat, and continues. "Look. I know I'm not the smartest guy in the world. I'd rather be in the kitchen, cooking for my lover, rather than arguing politics with him. Graham didn't respect what he thought was my shallowness. At first, maybe he did. Or it was flattering to him, having someone wait on him hand and foot. After a while, I guess I just got boring."

Sarcasm can veil any number of relationship subtexts. On the most superficial level, it can mask extreme distaste for our partner. Unfortunately, some of us launch a relationship based on initial infatuation, only to realize later that romance cannot be sustained solely by physical attraction. We discover, after pledging an eternity of undying love, that we really can't stand our partner.

"I met Marc at a Metropolitan Community Church social," says Chris, 26, a graphic artist in Phoenix. "He's blond, blue-eyed, very handsome—the kind of guy you might see in a fashion spread in a glossy magazine. Instantly, I fell in love—or more accurately, I was infatuated.''

Marc and Chris struck up a conversation, and found they liked each other. "Although Marc was only twenty-three, he was a very polished conversationalist," Chris explains. "I adored his sense of humor, and he seemed well educated, although he made his living as a waiter in one of Phoenix's nicest restaurants."

In less than two months, the two young men moved in together. "For the next year, we couldn't get enough of each other sexually," Chris continues. "Ours was a passionate, exciting relationship. What red-flagged my involvement, though, was the recognition that intellectually, he was 'used up.' His sparkling, original insights had a ceiling to them—like he had memorized a script that would make him intellectually interesting for only so long. As unkind of me as it was, I got very sarcastic with him. I looked for opportunities—and there were many—to ridicule him. Maybe I was trying to push him to grow. More likely, I was trying to push him away. Ultimately, we reached the point where we couldn't stand to be in the same room together, much less making love."

Sarcasm can also serve to maintain power over our partner. For example, we might be two highly competitive men who can't wait to establish a partnership. However, we're hardly an even match. One of us discovers that he can control our relationship by issuing damaging taunts and barbs. Subsequently, the victim withdraws until he barely even speaks anymore.

Often, sarcasm is a defense mechanism against an injury inflicted by our partner. "I've always admitted that I'm the jealous type," says Joe. "When I discovered that Andy had been downloading porno pictures from the Internet, I considered the act itself as a negative reflection of my desirability. In my mind, Andy had cheated on me. So, to punish him, I honed in on his weaknesses. I made sarcastic cracks about him every chance I got. I even made fun of him about the downloading thing, calling him sleazy, a computer nerd, a cybersex fiend—anything to put him down. But the bottom line was that I felt inadequate. Obviously, he preferred looking at those models than at me."

Regardless of why we interact with sarcasm, it's a communication style best avoided, except when we want to trash politicians, entertainers, and other public figures in fun. We've learned from hit-and-run comedy sitcoms that sarcasm is acceptable. In fact, some of us even attempt to pattern our lives on the television characters we like. Sitcom actors, however, are paid to endure the abuse. Our partners aren't.

An acclaimed educator once said that good teachers *have* to be manipulative, if they want to be effective in the classroom. Essentially, he referred to communication skills which make students *want* to do what's best for them in a learning environment. A teacher manipulates his students with the promise of a reward, such as a good grade or a free period, if they do what he expects of them. In fact, our national education system is based on a paradigm of benevolent manipulation.

However, willful manipulation has no role in a loving relationship. Good lovers recognize that each man is a free agent, and that he is involved with his partner because of decisions freely made. The moment we begin maneuvering situations to coerce our partners into meeting our needs, we till the field for resentment to grow. Manipulative tactics include promises of sex, a seductive gaze, the promise of money or status, the use of the lover's cherished possession, a gift, a vacation, or a host of other "perks" in exchange for a service, a behavior our partner desires, or a favor. While those rewards may be ample payment for a while, we will eventually feel victimized by manipulative tactics. Subsequently, we will rebel against these infringements on our free will and benevolence. However, when we resist a communication strategy that has characterized our relationship for a long time, our partner may perceive our attempt to change as a personal rejection, or as an indicator of trouble.

Manipulation clears the way for the growth of resentment. And little distinction exists between large and small manipulations. When "Would you like some coffee?" means "Would you make some coffee for me?", manipulation occurs. When our partner offers us his expensive sports car to drive on a vacation we've long deserved, yet he can't get away from his job, and we discover his generosity was a deflection of our attention from his invitation to a neighbor for fun and games, we have been manipulated. Once we discover an ulterior motive behind some gesture or action we interpreted as generous or considerate that led to our performance of a service on our partner's behalf, we have been taken for a ride.

"It was the way I was brought up," explains Tommy, 28, a mechanic in Houston, Texas, who admits he has been unsuccessful in sustaining relationships for more than three years at a stretch. "The whole idea of being nice to somebody in exchange for them being nice to me controls the way I relate to people. Sometimes, I actually hate my family for teaching me this lesson. I can't seem to hold a steady job because I always feel that the harder I work, the less I'm appreciated. Finally, I say 'fuck it,' and quit."

Which describes his approach to romance. "With my Leonardo DiCaprio features, I don't have a hard time finding a man," he admits. "It's just impossible to keep him. After a while, I start feeling I'm giving more than I'm getting. I know that's not true, but how can I stop feeling that way? I might spend an entire day shampooing carpets, but I'm not thinking of making the house look nice. I'm thinking that maybe Sam—or whoever my lover is at the time—will buy me some nice clothes—or something else I want—because I worked so hard. Simple gratitude isn't enough, because I feel shortchanged with a simple thank-you."

How did Tommy, who attended Texas A&M "for about a year," come by these insights? "Quite honestly, I'm tired of behaving this way," he says. "So, yeah, I've been seeing somebody—a shrink, I mean. He's helping me a lot. Never thought I'd pay to get counseling, but I'm afraid of growing old all alone."

A severe derivative of manipulation is exploitation. Those of us who have been victims know how psychologically damaging exploitation can be. In the beginning, we don't even realize that our partner is exploiting us. Our awareness grows subtly and progressively. Finally, the nagging perplexity strikes that our lover is using us to shirk responsibility that he rightfully owns. Still, we fear confrontation because, if we *are* misinterpreting, we stand a good chance of hurting him, thereby damaging our relationship. The murkiness of exploitation makes it extremely difficult to detect. Many individuals with selfish personalities possess little awareness of their motivations. Involvement with these men is often workable because, once aware of their behaviors, they are often eager to change. However, we should be extremely wary of those men who, when confronted about their behavior, grow defensive in their denial. They know exactly what they're doing, and don't care if they take us for every penny we have.

Take, for example, this fairly common scenario. An older gay man meets a gorgeous hunk who, during conversation, is cryptic about how he makes a living. During a subsequent date, he alludes to having several irons in the fire, but he doesn't specify which irons. Some deal, as yet unidentified, is bound to happen soon. Meanwhile, the first guy falls in love with him. They set up housekeeping together. Soon, the anticipation of that business deal looks more and more like freeloading. Not only is the older man concerned, but he is also convinced that he is perceived less as a lover, and more as a meal ticket. And he's probably right.

Even if he doesn't want money or a "free ride," the exploiter *is* after something his partner possesses that he values tremendously. Perhaps he's zeroed in on higher social status, a nice house, an exciting city of residence, or a desirable circle of friends. Or maybe he's chronically unlucky in sustaining a relationship. With his current partner, he finds even the *idea* of falling in love again very appealing. The exploitation is manifested in the *image* he has of his partner; in essence, he has no inkling of his partner's identity. From his narrow perspective, all he needs to know is that he feels safe in this new relationship. He is no longer alone. A lover's presence in his life gives validity to his existence, even a sense of reality. He has never taken the time to make friends with himself. He only knows he's lonely, and is convinced he cannot survive alone. Without a partner, he ceases to exist.

One of exploitation's saddest examples occurs when a gay man falls in love with a previously heterosexually identified man. Because of repression experienced in their youth, or because of parental or professional expectations, a significant percentage of gay members of the Baby Boom generation decided to play it straight. Their straight marriage might have lasted if these men had not decided they could no longer lie to themselves or to others about their homosexual orientation. So, shortly after a "passing" homosexual comes out, he meets another gay man usually less closeted, likes him, and wants to continue seeing him. Ultimately, the "ex-straight" guy indicates that he is willing to leave his wife to be with the gay man. What he promises sometimes never happens. The gay man feels used, no more than a convenient piece of ass for a man who wants to have his cake and eat it, too.

Or maybe he *does* leave his wife, then moves in with Mr. Right. Soon, however, he starts seeing other men—not that anyone should take it "personally," he says. It's just because he's new to the gay scene, and "there are so many beautiful men out there." Perhaps awakening this man sexually is satisfaction enough—if the gay man has a strong altruistic streak—because that's just what he did. Probably without even realizing it, Mr. Having-It-Both-Ways used the gay man as a step toward his new self-understanding. The "ex-straight's" exploitation of the man who knows who he is as a gateway to the "gay community" is not premeditated. In fact, he probably committed himself to the partnership with all good intentions. Still, we would be wise to make such a commitment fully aware of the possibilities—and not all of them are positive.

"That's the most difficult question—to strike the balance between his living with his wife, and seeing me frequently," says Richard Epstein, 55, an actor and director living in Los Angeles. "Let's be perfectly candid about it. I was under the impression that he was in the process of getting a divorce. I was under the impression that he was already separated. We were in the relationship at least three or four months when I realized that he was neither."

Even later, he discovered Ron's aspirations toward a political career in their community. "I could understand it from his point of view," Richard continues. "In his political situation, he might need to appear straight. He basically assured me that everything was all right, that his wife knew about us, and that she was okay with it. How she made that accommodation, I don't know."

Because the men had fallen deeply in love, Richard, in spite of his misgivings, could not pull away. "He would say he was leaving his wife, and would get an apartment, yet he never did. He kept saying, 'Next week, it will happen,' but it never did. Instead, I made a lot of adjustments to my schedules, and to the number of my theatrical commitments, so as not to cut into our potential time together."

However, even Richard's concessions did not guarantee they would get together, or that they would be able to enjoy time alone. "We traveled a lot, and his wife would usually go along," he continues. "Then, when I needed him most, he would disappear, later telling me that he was spending time with his wife as her reward for accepting our 'arrangement.' Once I had to handle the aftermath of a family crisis totally alone. Although I had told him how shaken I was, he took his wife off to Europe the next day. I should have recognized what was happening. Soon, they totally changed their lifestyle by adopting children. He was making a sweeping choice of family life over what he had with me."

Hostility can easily be counted as another mode of toxic communication. In some relationships, communication has become so dramatically impaired that one wonders why these guys got together in the first place. Few friends have been masochistic enough to stick by them because their company is not only unpleasant, it bites! These guys don't even know how to fake civil behavior. When bad luck puts them in the same room together, the air is electrified by the disgust they feel for each other.

Severely hostile couples have no courage. Their partnership cries out for help, or for termination. They don't have the courage to take action. If their relationship possessed any redeeming qualities in the past, it has certainly lost them now. Perhaps the two men can't read the writing on the wall because they have grown too comfortable with their mutual hostility. Yet, the truth remains. They are fearful little ferrets, hiding their fear behind what might easily pass as hatred.

Meanness corrodes a man's spirit, the way salty, humid air damages a car's finish. We can easily spot a person who has been victimized by constant hostility. He either seems ready to pounce, a nervous wreck, paranoid, suspicious of what anyone says; or he is like a puppy who pathetically craves affection, pandering to anyone who gives it to him. Chronic hostility easily shapes a noxious training program, the results of which are either the production of docile men, or domineering, argumentative ones. But one thing is undeniable. It's mistreatment, pure and simple.

Unfortunately, some men grow so accustomed to hostility, they don't recognize their victim status. Or because healthy gay couples are often inaccessible to us, we might consider such interaction part of the normal progression of gay relationships.

"I got so tired of all the bickering," says Brian, a teacher in Austin, Texas. "Ben bitched at me for little things. He was never pleased with what I did. He never arrived for dinner on time. I got tired of being taken for granted. I realize relationships are work, but if you fight each time you get together, there are some things wrong."

Brian says that things got so bad, Ben even suspected he was having a heterosexual affair. "He was jealous of Denise, a friend I'd known for eight years, and who is like a sister to me. I couldn't even talk to her without his jumping down my throat."

Soon, Brian broached the inevitable subject of breaking up. "Ben went ballistic. At the time, I wasn't out to my parents. He threatened not only to tell them we were lovers, but also to present the information as though I had seduced him, then coerced him into a relationship. He even threatened to tell his own mother that I'm gay. She works for the same school district that I do, and he knew I could lose my job if I stepped too far out of the closet."

When they finally broke up, Brian attempted an embrace. The hostility had become so ensconced that Ben placed his arms loosely against Brian's hips. He did not squeeze, looked away, and said nothing.

Lately, the body of writing dealing with domestic violence in gay and lesbian households has increased. Slowly, our community—as well as service organizations which have historically ignored us—is recognizing that domestic violence occurs more frequently than we imagined. To understand that an abusive partner has problems with which he must grapple is certainly insightful, but no rationalization to remain in such a relationship—particularly if our partner is unwilling to seek treatment. What conclusions may be drawn about us when we stoically endure physical abuse, often feeling we deserve the treatment he doles out?

An occasional fight, even when it becomes physical, does not necessarily qualify as domestic violence. The key is the pattern and frequency. When the black eye heals, or the muscle soreness dissipates, the nose mends, or the sneaker tread marks fade away, and he continues to use physical violence as his principle mode of communication, then our household suffers a problem that many gay men are reticent to admit. No matter how adamantly we assert our liberation from patriarchal attitudes and stifling gender roles, we find the admission that another male has been using us as a punching bag difficult indeed. Such candor violates the genetically encoded message that we, as men, should be able to hold our own against another male. That hang-up, coupled with the dread that others will regard us as "wimps" or "sissies," seals our lips and keeps us silent. Because of stigma, many of us felt weak and inferior as children. We hardly want those feelings to recur. Better to endure physical pain than to suffer the humiliation that accompanies the exposure of our "inadequacies."

Unfortunately, our partner's violent characteristics do not often reveal themselves during the courtship and honeymoon phases of our relationship. Usually, we're already part of a "stable" relationship before we notice that, lately, Dr. Jekyll has been turning into Mr. Hyde with growing frequency. Emotional and verbal abuse often precipitates physical abuse. Before the hitting and the kicking begin, we, as victims, may be subjected to degrading comments and ridicule, both public and private. Our partner's intent is to reduce our sense of self-worth to zilch. When we have reached bottom, he "punishes" us for our worthlessness via physical attacks. If we are not as constitutionally strong as he, then serious physical injury may result.

After the destruction of our self-esteem, we are desperate to hold on to the relationship. We no longer feel worthy enough to attract the interest of any other man. In our codependency, we want the violence to stop, but we're willing to endure the abuse as long as we can hang on to the relationship. Some gay men report feeling suicidal after long-term abuse. They feel completely out of control of their lives—a feeling that is warranted. After all, they have relinquished control to the abusive partner. Sometimes, it takes a near-tragedy to empower us.

Jeff, 38, a vice-president of administration and finance in Lexington, Kentucky, was such a victim of domestic violence. Although his partner, Cory, was dating Jeff's best friend, he wasn't willing to let Jeff go. When Jeff decided enough was enough, Cory's violent streak surfaced. "Screw this, it's my life now," was Jeff's sentiment. "My best friend hangs around Cory, so fine. I love him, but I don't understand what's going on with him."

Jeff began a tentative, nonsexual relationship with another man. "One night, after driving him home, I return to my house to discover the lights off and the chain lock on," Jeff recounts. "It's snowing outside. After twenty minutes of my knocking and shouting, Cory answers the door."

"I thought you were already in your room," Cory said.

"Like hell you did," Jeff replied angrily. "You locked me out intentionally."

At first, Cory laughed. Suddenly, his mood soured. "You were having sex with that asshole friend of yours, weren't you?"

"It's none of your fucking business," Jeff replied. "You have no more to say about my life or what I do with it."

Suddenly, Cory punched Jeff in the mouth, and threw him against the closet door. "Blood is pouring down the front of my shirt. He had hit me only one other time, so I'm scared. Besides, he looks crazed."

Next, Cory realizes what he's done. He's frightened by Jeff's threats to call the police. "Give me your shirt," Cory says. "Let's get the blood off everything."

"No, I said I'm calling the fucking police."

Finally, Cory convinces Jeff not to call. "The next day, I can't speak," he says. "My mouth is swollen. I have a huge gash in my lip line. I am drained more than I've ever been before."

The abuser who expresses post-violence remorse exacerbates the codependent relationship. If we truly love him, his tears are difficult to resist. We are often inclined to renew our commitment, thinking, falsely, that circumstances will improve. We can't accept the fact that our partner is locked into a pattern of behavior over which he has no control. Without intense therapy—an option with a mediocre success rate—the only way to reclaim our lives is to dissolve the relationship entirely.

Cory's violence against Jeff continued until they ended their relationship permanently. "Cory beat me up three more times," Jeff relates. "I was too embarrassed to tell anyone. I would never strike back because I was convinced that would only make things worse. I had a sneaker tread down the side of my face the night I was scheduled to appear in *A Chorus Line*. Cory beat me up that night, then threw me down the stairs.''

Jeff began to sleep with his bedroom door locked. ''Cory would actually pick the lock and come in and punch me in the face,'' Jeff continues. ''Several times, I had to get up and get out of my own house.''

The abuse finally ended during a cast party. Drunk, Cory cornered Jeff in the kitchen.

''Why can't we be like we were before?'' Cory asks.

Jeff pointed a finger in Cory's face and told him off. ''A man I was seeing had just broken off with me because Cory kept intruding into my life, and I was pissed,'' Jeff explains. ''If it wasn't for a redneck friend of mine, I'm not sure what would have happened.''

''Are you okay?'' Bubba asks.

''No, I'm not okay,'' Jeff snaps.

Bubba grabbed him and physically lifted Jeff out of the corner. Amazed, Cory watched, but didn't budge.

Bubba turned to Cory. ''Look, asshole. Don't you ever get within three feet of Jeff again, or I will break your neck,'' he warned.

Cory never bothered Jeff again.

Less serious than domestic violence is a partner's disregard of our personal boundaries. Frequently, his unwillingness to allow us privacy and individuality results from his inability to trust us. A distrustful or paranoid partner is often still grappling with unresolved issues of abandonment from his childhood. More than likely, we did not enter a relationship to be anyone's therapist, or his mother. If, after several affirmations of our trustworthiness, he continues to feel that we are out to get him, then a close examination of the relationship's potential is in order.

Several men reported incidents where their distrusting partners searched through personal effects while they worked in the office. When confronted, their partners expressed a fear that the investment in their relationship was one-sided. Their search for evidence was intended to support or invalidate their suspicion. Others read personal journals, only to let a bit of personal information slip at inopportune times. Another man frequently called his partner's secretary to check his time of departure. If his partner's trip home took longer than usual, he would face an interrogation to verify he "was not up to something." Yet another man, so convinced was he that his partner was seeing another guy, stalked his partner. The most extreme example involves a man who kept close track of odometer readings in his partner's car. Each day, he questioned his partner about his daily activities, tracked the accurate mileage count based on the information he obtained during an "interrogation," then compared his calculations to the odometer reading. Once, he asked his partner if he had taken the car out since coming home from work. The answer was no. Not satisfied, he placed his hand against the car's hood to see if the engine was warm, since he was certain of having seen the car in a popular cruise area. Only when he determined the engine was sufficiently cold did he relinquish his certainty that his partner had been searching for anonymous sexual encounters.

Internalized homophobia is a partial explanation for distrust. If we accept that gay men are promiscuous, fickle, immoral, incapable of love, or any of the socially proscribed stereotypes, then it is little wonder we find it difficult to trust another gay man. We may also feel uncertain about the quality of our commitment; in that case, our distrust is a projection of our own doubts. The leap that is difficult to take, once we establish our partnerships, is that gay men are individuals, not collectives of some giant homosexual assembly line. Manufacturers don't use standardized parts. Each product is unique. And unique individuals defy generalizations and compartmentalization. We learn to trust only by trusting, by letting go of our fears and insecurities, not by believing everything we hear. What's true of our neighbor's partner is not true of ours.

"When the promiscuity started happening all over again," says Tony Lake, "I realized that Jonathan had perceived my earlier forgiveness as subliminal permission. Once, when he returned from a trip to the East Coast, he wanted to use a condom. We never used one before."

"With AIDS going around," he said, "we should be safe. You just don't know in this day and age."

Tony suspected that Jonathan's caution was only the tip of

the iceberg, and started watching for little things. "Meanwhile, we started writing a musical together," Tony explains. "I did historical research. The musical was very successful, and was even performed overseas."

On a tour in Seville, Spain, Tony noticed many odd occurrences. "Jonathan always wanted to go into town alone. His reasoning was that foreigners are better received if they are alone. Later, a Flamenco dancer started calling for Jonathan. And when I wanted to have sex, he exploded."

"Just because you think a lot of guys are hitting on me, you get horny and want to have sex," Jonathan shouted.

"God damn it, I want to have sex because I love you," Tony retorted.

The next day, Tony begged to know what was going on. "Be honest with me," he said. "That's all I ask."

But Jonathan kept denying all accusations of infidelity.

When they returned to Texas, Jonathan wanted to sell their house. "We need to move to a city more open to the arts," Jonathan said. "I will never make anything of myself in Austin because it is so limited."

The next day, Tony returned home to find a real estate sign in the front yard. "What's going on here?" he demanded. "I never agreed to sell the house."

"Too bad," Jonathan replied. "I've already signed the contract."

Several days later, Tony heard Jonathan's voice as he stepped out of the shower. "He's on the phone, and mentioning my name a lot. I stop to listen. He's telling about all kinds of personal details that involve us."

When Jonathan hung up, Tony demanded to know who was on the other end. "It was no one," Jonathan answered.

"There are too many things going on," Tony said. "I've been lied to, fooled, and cheated. We *are* going to talk this time."

"Fine," Jonathan said.

He confessed everything—the affair with the Flamenco dancer, his promiscuity, his lack of interest in salvaging the relationship. "And I'm faced with reorganizing my life in a gay world that has changed tremendously," said Tony who, for so long, trusted Jonathan.

When we don't trust, we no longer regard our partner with the same respect we afford an equal. Therefore, we permit ourselves to disregard *his* personal boundaries while we may respect a stranger's. Each time we open his journal, or call his secretary, or cross-examine him to determine his daily activities, we're adding yet another brick in the construction of a prison, not a relationship. Prisoners spend most waking moments lamenting the freedom they have surrendered, while plotting their escape.

No one likes to consider money as an important part of a relationship, but we flirt with disaster when we don't. Discussions of money are disdained because we equate financial issues to the practical, the coarse, and the mundane. A romantic relationship is none of these things. However, our survival depends on how well we manage our financial resources. It would be a serious judgmental error to discount the fiscal elements of our relationship as irrelevant. If our relationships are to survive, we must be willing to address our values and attitudes toward money.

First of all, we must be very clear with one another about our attitudes toward our dollars. Together, we should explore our feelings about earning, managing, and spending them. How possessive are we of our personal resources? To what degree can we, as partners, pool our financial resources toward the goal of establishing and maintaining a household? Who will be responsible for what expenditures? Will we divide all expenses in half? Will we assign payment of certain bills to our partner, while we assume responsibility for the others?

During the course of a long-term relationship, we may determine a need for a career change. Always, such a decision creates stress. Risk factors, the initial excitement over a new job, an increase or decrease in income, and the degree of our partner's involvement in making a career decision influence the administration of household finances. If we do not enjoy our partner's full support, we may feel our judgment is in question, or our partner is determined to increase his control over us. Naturally, if the move to a new position requires less or equal investment of time, or a substantially increased salary, we have little to worry about—most of the time. But if the new career demands more travel than before, or a temporary (or permanent) decrease in salary, then the strain on our relationship deepens.

"We were both spending a lot of time at work," says 35-year-old Bobby Hanes, a manager of a retail establishment in Decatur, Georgia. "Both of us had extremely stressful jobs. Mine required me to work weekends, as did his. While Donovan's company was going through a major reorganization, I had the boss from hell."

Bobby admits they weren't spending enough time together, just doing ordinary things, "or even having meals together. Both of us were very focused on keeping things moving in our job situation." As a result of drifting apart socially and emotionally, Donovan eventually met someone new at work, fell in love with him, and dumped Bobby. "I would've preferred to have the separation go a little slower," he says of the abrupt ending of their three-year commitment. "At this point, I was still in love with him. It was sort of like being thrown out of the house."

Inevitably, our households will encounter occasional financial setbacks. Perhaps one of us is unemployed for a while, and has to rely on the working partner to make ends meet. We should keep the lines of communication open, and periodically appraise the financial soundness of our household. If, during a period of unemployment, he develops an affinity for this new role as full-time house husband, we'd better make sure both of us agree to these terms. Though we don't like to admit it, our partnerships occasionally dissolve because one of us feels financially exploited. If we communicate *honestly* about financial matters—for example, we don't say his income doesn't matter when we know damn well it does—we can avoid the pitfalls that often result from a partner's need for a break from the rat race.

Another explosive financial issue involves a discrepancy between partners' incomes—or income potentials. Clarity and honesty are extremely important when discussing fair allocation of resources. If we are well-heeled bluebloods, or have exorbitant incomes, we can honestly say to our partner, who works for little more than minimum wage: "What you make, honey, doesn't matter to me—just as long as we're together." Still, couples who experience income disparity have found that their relationships are healthier when neither partner feels as though he's being "kept." Many couples formulate a percentage scale. The lower wage-earner contributes to the household the amount he can comfortably afford. His contribution may never be an issue for the wealthier partner, but his own self-worth may diminish if he isn't a contributing member of the household.

"I could see—or was it projection?—that my meager income was a sore spot for him, even though he kept expressing confidence that I would eventually find a career that 'suited' me," says Gary Jacobi, 28, now the proprietor of a print shop in Soda Springs, Idaho. "I don't think his concern had so much to do with money as it did with my own self-image. He was afraid of losing me if I couldn't find an anchor. To him, that meant having a career. I have to admit, too, that I wondered why Sandy wanted me around, a good-for-nothing freeloader."

After almost three years together, Gary called it quits. "I hurt him tremendously, and myself as well," he admitted. "In retrospect, it all boiled down to my conviction that Sandy *was* going to break up with me, sooner or later. My pride and arrogance insisted that I do it before he did. Besides, I knew the split would hurt even more if we kept putting it off."

Gary and Sandy remain friends today, although both admit a certain caution when in each other's company. In fact, Sandy contributed financially to Gary's new business.

"Will we get back together?" Gary shrugs. "I doubt it. We don't want to risk hating each other's guts. But at least we finally understand the degree of misunderstanding we had of each other's attitudes toward money during the years we were partners."

Many in the gay community have chosen careers in the arts. If we are serious about our "calling," we must be sure that our partner understands the frustration, the uncertainty, the volatility of the profession toward which we aspire. If he doesn't see much value in culture—or worse yet, has no faith in our talent—then he might not possess the tenacity to stick with us as we struggle to get our foot in the door. Our dream of success may turn out to be, for him, a recurring nightmare. Besides, he may remind us, many a freeloader has fancied himself an artist.

The bottom line should be clear: Regarding financial matters, we need to define our values with our partners. Say, for example, we feel spending is the sole purpose of money. Stingy people bore and annoy us. However, our partner holds a dramatically different attitude. He spends only those dollars that are absolutely necessary—while only occasionally throwing away a few on fun—

and saves the rest. He grows horrified when we order an expensive gift from the Hammacher Schlemmer catalog. We are appalled that he's *still* wearing that atrocious pair of shoes. Once we internalize the idea that there is no "right" and "wrong" way to regard money, we're able to respect, rather than disdain, one another's approach to fiscal management. As in most aspects of our partnership, it's all about compromise, but without sacrificing our own individual standards.

By now, we have examined most components of our partnership whose dysfunctions frequently cause a good thing to collapse. Still, doubts about our relationship linger. We think the end is near, but we're still just not sure.

An examination of five additional critical issues should help us make up our minds.

Growing Apart

Let's face it. As gay couples, we probably didn't waste very much time discovering whether we were sexually compatible. It's not that we regard dating as a waste of time. We just don't allow the values of June and Ward Cleaver to get in the way. But then, who does? (This point bears repetition. We are all individuals. Sexual opportunism isn't always true of us. But most men represented in this book waited, at most, no more than several days before hopping into the sack.)

As our knowledge of one another deepened, we discovered numerous similarities—personally, socially, spiritually, and politically. We grew our relationship on acres of common ground. We were soulmates.

Conversation flowed easily. Soon, we could even finish each other's sentences—not a good practice, but it was nice to know we could, given the right circumstances. We found humor in similar circumstances and situations. Our lifestyles were compatible. Our identities as gay men were lifted from the same page. If some moron made reference to our sexual *preference*, rather than orientation, both of us would enjoin him to take a flying leap. And while we might not enjoy *exactly* the same foods, compromises in the kitchen were relatively easy to make. Our palates grew accustomed to both *kosher* and Southern-fried. We enjoyed a harmony of interaction never established with any of our friends. What other evidence could there be that our partnership was cosmically ordained?

But people being what they are, things changed. *We* changed, and so did he. No matter how hard we tried, we couldn't reestablish that feeling of connectedness, the strong sentiment that no matter what challenges we had to face, we would, together, find the courage and the cunning to overcome them. As much as we wanted to talk in the easy way of the past, not caring about sense or syntax, we grew alarmed upon discovering a poignant, yet mutual, discomfort—a discomfort leading frequently to pregnant silences or volatile misunderstandings. What once we both thought outrageously humorous, he now thinks stupid or sophomoric. He thought our membership in the Metropolitan Community Church was just a cop-out. After all, he said sarcastically, it's just a gay-themed traditional church making no inroads into modern theology. He told us we might as well be a Baptist. Worse yet, he became a Republican. Once, we both thought right-wing politics incompatible with a gay identity. The Democrats always had our vote. Yet his affiliation with the Republican Party provided the much-needed impetus for him to come, swinging, out of the closet. He had a purist's view of Republican politics. We have to admit, the politicos in DC drag who scream lies from their Congressional pews have given him bravery we admire. But we are not ready. We are not ready.

We considered our relationship a gift from an unknowable God, from Luck, or from our talent for finding a desirable man. Maybe our confidence was part of the problem. Nice gifts we like to display, keep them dusted off for guests to admire, but it's always the newer stuff that gets the most attention. We took it for granted, this thing we had. We took each other for granted. We never hated each other, not for longer than those few moments when we were getting on each other's nerves. But those moments scarcely seemed to count. Now, we're not sure what we have. Nice things, a roof over our head, an adorable dog, and some really good friends—a few of whom we've seen through their untimely deaths. We have nice wheels. We have comfort. Maybe it's the comfort that's driving us crazy. We're too predictable. Too reticent and too quiet. We suspect there's so much going through one another's heads, but we don't know how to share anymore. We've lost that early talent of reaching out, of grabbing hold and pulling one another back into the fold. It has something to do with losing track of who we are to each other. Of losing each other.

"It was *too* much of a storybook romance," Brin says of his two-year involvement with his ex-partner. "I was not communicative enough, I think. He was an emotionally dominating kind of person, without necessarily meaning to be. The way he looked at the world and mine didn't exactly match. Still, I freaked when we broke up, and fell apart. In retrospect, I could see warning signs, like a general misunderstanding of what was necessary for me to make him happy. He needed to know me. He *needed* me to tell him there were some things I didn't like. I lived by the 'nothing-can-go-wrong' mentality. I treated the relationship working as fact—no effort, no concern, really."

So what we have left is a tally of all the losses, and a vague recollection of the gains. They don't seem to matter much anymore. Together, we feel so separated, so alone. Funny how that is. How we can feel so lonely when we spend so much time together? What is it that we have lost? We've tried to keep track, but lately, all we do is feel sorry for ourselves, feel like failures, because we know where this loneliness leads. With him, there is no music anymore, and no chance for harmony. Here is what it all boils down to: It's about cutting our losses, cold kisses, and a constant analysis of how we have created such distance. Somehow, we think that reclaiming our lives depends on relinquishing this one.

Both of us feel this way. Truth by consensus, he's always said. We planted early—perhaps too early—on common ground, yet our relationship yields little that we can harvest. It's an awful feeling. A lost feeling. We are lost boys who don't know what's real anymore. Give it up, give it up, the voices keep telling us. Maybe they are the voices of delusion, but they seem awfully smart. We know we have lives ahead of us, mysteries yet undiscovered. Yet, what we are to each other holds us back. To find ourselves again, we have to lose each other.

Ironic, isn't it, this idea of gain being contingent on the concept of loss? Which is stronger—to stay in a place that makes us unhappy? Or to look like cowards and flee?

Intellectual Connections

One reason we pledged our love to each other was an intellectual connection we seldom noticed with other men. We never thought we were the smartest guys on earth. But we discovered that, regardless of conversation's focus, even if we didn't agree, our brains were an even match. We could follow the critical points, his reasoning, without demanding an explanation. We were never too dense to understand each other. When we needed a break between all the hot sex, we could always find topics of conversation to intrigue us.

We never made the mistake that some of our friends made. Some guys are such suckers for a pretty face, but the mouth belonging to that face can seldom construct a coherent sentence. When *we* conversed, we experienced an intellectual stimulation rivaling what we felt in bed. Not so long ago, we couldn't imagine another couple who could be such a perfect match, body, mind, and soul.

Lately, during our infrequent talks, we no longer connect intellectually. The ideas that made the man we knew not so long ago don't even begin to describe the one sitting next to us now. His thoughts belong to another place, another time—maybe to another planet. The intellectual meter that measured us a match years ago wouldn't even register now. We can't respect his ideas anymore. We can't even relate to them. And it's not just a matter of disagreement. It's deeper than that. His ideas repel us. How can we love the man on the other end of this intellectual tug-of-war that relating has become?

Time passes. It's not happening, this mind match we used to have. He's smart; that's not the problem. But he's not smart in the way we'd like. He's not talking the talk—not the way he used to.

And then, what about us? We've grown intellectually as well. We get, from him, the kind of gaze he gets from us—that "look" that says, "I don't know you anymore. Who are you, this man sitting in my lover's favorite chair?"

Suddenly, we know the reason we seldom talk anymore. We're more strangers now than the night of our first kiss. Then, the effort was worth making.

Values Discrepancies

As important as the compatibility of intelligence are issues of personal values. Do we, as partners, adhere to values that, if not the same, are at least compatible? Ideals make the man—not his mind, his physical attributes, his profession, or the social roles he plays. A man is defined by what he believes in, those truths that characterize his life. If we can't interface with our partner's values, whether or not we believe in them for ourselves, then fantastic sex and his vast intelligence don't matter. Neither does the fact that everyone at our favorite social haunts considers him a hoot. In the privacy of our homes, where compatibility *really* counts, we're not going to click.

Although the religious right would like to convince us that moral values are guided by an unalterable set of "thou-shalt-nots," the truth is that real morals are a panoply of affirmations surviving years of challenges and tests. They stick around to guide our lives. Standards of feelings, attitudes, and behaviors keep us in harmony with ourselves. If we value honesty, for example, then a partner's lying will be a source of revulsion. Our own lies will cause us to feel guilt.

"We broke up five times and then got back together," says Allen Williams. "Our relationship was very volatile, to say the least. Opposites may attract, but they don't stay together. When one person picks up the paper and says, 'How awful!' and the other thinks the events of the story are great, you're going to have problems. I concluded that you can love someone, but if you don't respect him, a relationship is not going to work. Also, we didn't communicate very well. He didn't respect some of the things I did, and vice versa. He respected my community work— helping gay kids and stuff. But my religious views?"

No way. The men's positions on religious values were polarized throughout their two-year relationship. "Everyone has his own way. I challenged him about doing the local Christian Coalition newsletter and being gay. I asked him to see the connections between what he was doing and what that organization does to us."

Another potentially contentious issue is that of religious values. Many gay couples who subscribe to different faiths are able to maintain a healthy, vital relationship. However, they realize the necessity of maintaining a respect for and understanding of the religious beliefs of their partners. Relationship problems arise when our perceptions of the nature of the universe and our places in it differ so dramatically that our patronization of our partner's beliefs erodes our respect for him. For example, we feel that his belief in an afterlife constitutes a way for his church to control the behaviors of its members. In other words, if people are afraid of going to Hell after they die, they will be on their best behavior in this mortal life. On the other hand, we believe that when we die in this life, there is no other. After the infatuation has diminished, we begin to perceive his beliefs as pandering to primitive religious values. Or if we adhere to strong religious beliefs, we might attempt to change the way our partner believes. To bring to a partnership a missionary's zeal for conversion invites disaster.

All of us possess patriotic values influencing our perception of ourselves as gay American citizens. Do we choke up when we see the Stars and Stripes pass during a parade? Or do we feel an urgency to rip the flag from the color guard's hands and set fire to it, protesting the injustices we've had to endure as gay citizens? Are we the kind of individual who, in exercising our rights and responsibilities, works within, around, or against the system? If we could choose our country of residence, would we choose the United States, or gay-friendlier Holland? Are we the kind of person who never neglects to vote in an election, or do we feel our vote isn't going to matter? Regardless of our patriotic sentiments, how would our partner answer these questions? If we're on opposite political poles, can we handle those differences? Or do we use every opportunity to lambaste his political beliefs, making him feel as though he's Gore Vidal cohabiting with a ponderous William Buckley? As with religion, sometimes an agreement to disagree is most prudent.

While moral values encourage social harmony, and religious values cosmic harmony, personal values guide us in our routine, day-to-day lives. Categorically, personal values hold the potential to be the biggest sore spot in our relationships. We have numerous personal values guiding our daily lives, with an equal number of opportunities for conflicts. If we like to bathe daily, while our partner prefers only biweekly baths, thus causing the sheets and pillowcases to require more frequent cleanings, we have a potential personal value conflict. Or we like to be in bed by midnight, but our partner *has* to see *Star Trek*, which doesn't play until twelve-thirty. How do we compromise in a situation like this? Does it matter that we go to sleep alone? Does a perfunctory goodnight kiss substitute for holding him as we fall asleep?

Another area of potential conflict is the discrepancy in energy level. Do we prefer an evening at home in front of the fireplace, while he prefers flitting around the city like a social gadfly? It doesn't matter that he wants us to accompany him on all his social calls. What matters to us are our colleagues' comments about our puffy eyes when we drag our asses into work the next morning.

"Although Sandy was only five years older than me," Gary explains, "he seldom had the energy to stay up or out as long as I could. At first, when our relationship was brand-new and highly sexual, that wasn't a big problem. But as we needed to branch out as a couple and as individuals, I often grew irritated when he either urged me to stay home, or rushed me to leave a social gathering. I came to regard him as a sloth, though I knew he really wasn't. His peak energy schedule had to do with his circadian rhythms, not inherent laziness. But while we were together, I was less inclined to be understanding. I thought my lover should operate on the same schedule as I. Selfishly, I regarded my peak times as ideal times to have fun—and totally disregarded what was comfortable for him."

What about the compatibility of our tastes? Does he prefer floral patterns, while we like bold, geometric ones? Does he adore watching all-night marathons of old sitcoms, while we abhor the concept of television? Our cultural and entertainment tastes are subject to all manner of differences, and some compliance will always be necessary to accommodate individual tastes. The question is: How much compliance and compromise can we take?

As society debates our place "at the table," we may also find wide discrepancies in our self-images as gay men. Does he feel his sexual orientation is nobody's business, while we seek every opportunity to out ourselves? Eventually, his cringing every time we come out to our baker, grocer, clothier or stylist will lead to confrontation. He will want us to keep our mouths shut about our orientation when we're in public together. We will see his wish as an unreasonable plea to stay closeted.

Perhaps he needs the presence of the "tribe" every Saturday night, when he expects to visit the local gay watering hole. We feel perfectly content to see our gay friends in calmer social settings, like dinner parties or support groups. Maybe we feel threatened by the bar scene, thinking that the highly sexualized atmosphere makes it easy for our lover to stray. He thinks our attitude is ridiculous. Sure, someone might *try* to pick him up, but we should trust him to just say no. Besides, he says, the shoe could easily be on the other foot.

"In Lexington, once a couple is committed, outside forces try to break up their relationship," says Jeff. "Other gay men do everything they can to sabotage it. It's just the most ironic behavior I've ever seen. And yet, these same men bemoan the fact that they don't have a lover."

A personal value loaded with various subjective viewpoints is the work ethic. While we are devoted to our jobs, and willingly work overtime when necessary, he sees employment as an inconvenience to gain the means to have fun. To us, his attitude appears cavalier. As a result of his attitude toward work, he changes jobs frequently. To us, the dedicated professionals, his caprice causes tremendous anxiety.

Last, but certainly not least, discrepancies occur in our attitudes toward sexual values. Our attitudes about our sexuality may be the most difficult to negotiate. Some of us may feel rejected if we're not putting out every night, while others are perfectly satisfied with once or twice a week. But far more difficult an issue is the conflict between an "open" and a "closed" relationship. We can usually reach an agreement about the frequency of sexual intimacy with our partners, but often irreconcilable is the conflict resulting from differing attitudes toward monogamy. Once we open a committed relationship to a variety of sexual encounters, it is often for the convenience of one partner. The other partner usually feels not liberated, but hurt. However, some men enter a partnership with the clear understanding that monogamy will not be a condition of their commitment. Under those circumstances, the partners have no expectations of monogamy, and casual sex doesn't threaten the core relationship. However, very few partnerships begin within these parameters.

Allen says that it is during a crisis point when couples start talking about opening up their relationships. "And it may very well portend the end of the relationship," he asserts. "Men *say* they can handle it. But our mothers don't casually say our fathers are out fucking the secretary while they're doing the milkman. In the heterosexual world, affairs aren't taken so lightly."

On several occasions, Allen has received e-mail messages from men in both rural and urban areas who say they are attracted to men, but they're not into the gay scene. "I just want to meet a nice guy," they say, "but I don't want anybody to know."

Allen tells them that "you could have all the sex you want, and no one has to know you're gay. But the minute you have a relationship, you're going to be pulled out more and more. Sex is *not* what makes you gay. It's the relationship. That puts a huge amount of pressure on a couple."

When Allen came out, he tried to locate books about how gay people lead their lives. "But they simply aren't available," he says. "While growing up—well, your childhood sets how you live your life. Myths are powerful. They invoke solitary figures, or pixies and fairies fucking everything. These archetypes you can recognize on some level as gay. The hard thing for gay couples is knowing the reality and having a standard to set your dreams by."

Lack of Common Goals

Once we sealed our commitment to each other, we made plans and set goals. Our daily journey to our jobs seemed less burdensome because now, we weren't bringing home the bacon just for ourselves. We *wanted* to work hard because each paycheck brought us closer to the dreams we shared. Together we decided to build a home in the hills or on the oceanfront. We decided to open a joint savings account or to invest wisely toward growing a business for ourselves. We purchased a state-of-the-art entertainment system we just couldn't live without, and picked some exotic vacation destinations. This goal planning energized our relationship, elevated our feelings of security, and deepened our affection for each another.

As time passed, we achieved some of our goals, revised others, and established new ones. Although we no longer expected quite as much excitement in the bedroom, our mutual dedication to our dreams constituted a deeper excitement. In fact, the heightened intimacy of goal setting and dream chasing was frequently manifested by seeing our partner with new eyes. As we made plans and set goals, his boy-like enthusiasm made him sexier. No man could look better than one whose eyes brightened as he ranted on about winding porches, spacious kitchens, and Caribbean cruises.

God, we'd marry him all over again!

One day, we realize we've achieved only a fraction of our goals. Our dreams seem as ephemeral as a scarlet sunset. We are struck by the horrible feeling that someone has pissed in our corn flakes. Now, when we discuss our goals, the gleam in his eyes has dulled. Frankly, we also wonder what we really want. Life has grown tedious. We feel a little silly, spending hours in conversation about dreams that seem a far cry from reality. Wouldn't we be better off with a good night's sleep?

Time, as they say, marches on. The feelings don't change. The dreams are nice, but with this man? We don't *think* so.

It's not that we hate him. We can't possibly feel animosity that extreme. We shared with this man some of the best times of our lives. We once felt a completeness with him where now there is none.

We still want to transform our dreams into reality. But lately, we've felt as though to continue these plans, to talk this talk, would be tantamount to lengthening a prison sentence.

Yeah, maybe we'd like to fall in love again someday. Perhaps what we *really* want, deep inside, is to start over. But right now, all of our thoughts are on endings.

Breaking Apart

By far the most difficult part of dissolving a relationship that's not fulfilling us anymore is the inevitable heart-to-heart conversation. Together, we must determine that we have no other option. It doesn't matter who arrives at the decision first. Breaking up isn't going to be easy. One or both of us will resist. Then, when we finally face the broken dreams, the aching heart, the nagging sense of failure, the real work begins.

When Robert and I decided to separate, we had already spent long hours revisiting the good times and the bad over the fifteen-year history of our partnership. Both of us were popping antide-pressants. I was seeing a shrink once every two weeks. Sometimes, Robert and I had great conversations during which we would decide that all this talk about breaking up was nonsense. We just needed some time to regroup, to think, to reaffirm. Any hurt for which we were responsible was not intentional. Only those things that normally happen in the daily lives of partners hap-pened in ours. How much easier it would have been if we had intentionally set out to hurt one another. But the passion had simply disappeared. So had our energy and motivation. Our lives had taken different turns, and in effect, we had established dramatically different focuses. I wasn't sure what he believed anymore. I wasn't sure who he was. I'm certain the same was true of him. When we pledged that no matter what happened, we would remain the best of friends, I felt enormous relief. I didn't want to lose *him*. I just wanted to lose the emptiness I felt. Once the decision was made, I felt a freedom I hadn't felt in years. That sense of freedom, however, did not eradicate the insupera-ble guilt I felt at having "failed" in maintaining our relationship.

"But the decision created a host of feelings," Robert adds. "I was very scared. I experienced a sense of mourning, and a feeling that while I really didn't want to leave, I had no choice in the matter. A lot of it was a control issue. I had no control over a lot of things, and in this situation, I could take back some degree of control of my life.''

In looking back, one of the most insurmountable head trips of any long-term relationship that has soured is a sense that we have failed each other. Yet how can we be failures when we no longer have the capacity to answer the needs of our relationship? The only option we have, besides the misery that pretending brings, is to terminate the partnership. Hopefully, the breakup doesn't end our friendship. But lying almost always will. ''You have to *want* to maintain the friendship,'' Robert says. ''And the ex-partners still have to respect each other.''

Perhaps the most constructive way to regard our empowerment to end the partnership is to celebrate our courage. Inevitably, we feel pain when admitting to ourselves that our relationship no longer cuts the mustard. We feel a sense of loss akin to that which we feel when a loved one dies. We endure stages of misery and grief before we even begin the recovery process. But endings are also beginnings, a time of impending opportunity and challenge. That's what we must hold on to.

''I'm just coming out of my grieving process,'' explains Tony. ''A couple of months ago, I relinquished the guilt, the self-doubt, feelings of rejection—all that is part of it. I simply admitted to myself that I did the very best I could. My best wasn't good enough. In life, not everything is going to stay good permanently. I make no apologies to anyone for the things I did. I forgave myself. I have nothing to feel guilty about. I moved on. And now, Jonathan and I are the very best of friends.''

A psychologist suggested an unorthodox ceremony to end a relationship. Instead of wandering off to parts unknown with our tails between our legs, he suggested inviting our mutual friends to a party honoring our divorce. Not only does such a celebration acknowledge the love we've experienced through the years, but it also affirms that we have not closed the door on our lives. We look toward the future with hope. We are certain it will bring good things.

If we end our partnerships on such a positive note, we can say our goodbyes with minimum psychological damage, and diminish the time we need for healing.

Determining Your Intimacy Quotient (IQ)

The frequency and the intensity of putting out aren't the sole indicators of the level of intimacy you enjoy with your partner. In fact, if you've come this far, you're wondering whether there's anything you can do to save your relationship. Using the evaluative guides below as responses to each statement, place the numbers which correspond to the most honest response in the chart below. Then, you'll discover just how far apart you and your partner have grown.

3—This happens a hell of a lot.
2—This happens occasionally, but not often.
1—This happens very infrequently.
0—This never happens.

1. I feel annoyed or resentful when my partner even tries to talk to me.
2. My partner seems impatient when I try to interact with him—as though he doesn't have enough time to be bothered.
3. My partner and I snap at each other.
4. My partner relates to me in a very sarcastic way.
5. I say very hurtful things to my partner.
6. My partner does very hurtful things to me.
7. The time we spend together is spent in silence, or in our own spaces.
8. When I think of my partner, I have very critical thoughts of him.
9. The words "I love you" get stuck in my throat.
10. We don't hug and kiss.
11. To be honest, I find that I'm more intimate with my colleagues and coworkers than I am with my partner.
12. This relationship feels more like a business affiliation than anything else.
13. I do not respect my partner's beliefs, standards, and attitudes.
14. My partner criticizes my values.
15. To be honest, I don't really care about my partner's feelings.

16. I take on professional, personal, and volunteer activities to avoid spending time at home with my partner.
17. We can't agree on how to spend the time we have together.
18. I suffer an overall sensation of feeling trapped.
19. We don't do anything together as a couple.
20. I feel dissatisfied with this relationship.
21. I feel all gay couples fall out of love after they have been together for a while.
22. My partner is easily provoked into actually hitting me.
23. During interactions, we talk in very aggressive tones.
24. During conversations, we talk of only superficial subjects.
25. I feel as though I'm nothing more than a money dispenser for my partner. (Or I feel I am a financial drain on my partner.)

1.	6.	11.	16.	21.
2.	7.	12.	17.	22.
3.	8.	13.	18.	23.
4.	9.	14.	19.	24.
5.	10.	15.	20.	25.

Now, add the numbers in each column, and place the sum in the empty block beneath the column.

Now, add those five numbers in the bottom row, and place the answer here:

What the Responses Mean

A score of 45 or below means that you and your partner possess great capacity for intimacy. You are involved in a relationship that has more positive characteristics of intimacy than negative ones. A little fine-tuning can go a long way for you.

A score between 45 and 60 means that your IQ is moderately deficient. While your relationship may be salvageable, you and your partner will have to work hard to recapture the level of intimacy you find fulfilling.

A score above 60 is considerably deficient. Consider utilizing the services of a qualified couples counselor, and proceed to Chapter 3 now.

CHAPTER THREE

● ● ● ● ● ● ● ● ● ● ● ● ● ● ● ● ● ● ●

Breaking Up Without Cracking Up

Winners and Losers

A common experience that occurs when ending a relationship is our tendency to regard ourselves as either winners or losers. However, the analogy of the boxing ring is not appropriate for relationships. Certainly it's hard if our partner comes to us with the bad news—hard to swallow, and hard to resist feeling that we're the victims of an unevenly matched contest. But we were partners, not opponents, and there are few reasons why we should become opponents now.

What can we expect to feel once the disorienting decision is made? First of all, accurate forecasts of our emotional responses to breaking up are next to impossible. However, veterans *can* provide clues to some emotions we might expect. Each individual may experience all of them, just a few, only one, or even none at all. We must accept that we'll be hurting for a while. So we try to survive the experiences, while maintaining awareness that our lives will get better. As long as we are willing to take the reins again, the pain eventually subsides.

One prevalent experience? Rage. No need to fight it. We must try to let ourselves go and feel the rage completely. Rage directed inward is certainly more damaging than a few broken dishes, or even damaged furniture. One man completely ripped his toilet from the floor, having not only to replace the fixture but also to spend hours cleaning the bathroom and shampooing the carpet in the adjacent bedroom. However, he felt a sense of catharsis, even though releasing his rage in a destructive way.

Although it scared the hell out of his ex-partner, it did *him* a world of good.

What if we don't particularly want to incur major household expenses when letting it all out? We can find various modes of expression. Rage produces energy; that energy, in turn, can be utilized in productive ways, such as exercise, neglected lawn care, or housework. Perhaps a trip to an isolated place where our screams won't terrify the neighbors' kids works for us. Or journaling provides a wonderful opportunity to express our feelings. We can vent all kinds of vile desires and methods of revenge in our journal entries without hurting our ex-partner and running the risk of a prison sentence. Good friends, even counselors, may also be willing to hear us out. In fact, verbal expressions of rage provide opportunities for us to clarify the source, the sensations, and the issues that push us over the edge. "I experienced a lot of rage," admits Bill Van Patten. "I was really angry. I have always dealt with anger by internalizing it. I am not the type of person who takes it out on other people. Finally, though, I had a revelation that sometimes, you have to ask people if it's okay to share your problems. I asked a colleague if it was okay to unload. I sat for three hours talking to him after dinner. It was the most cathartic experience I ever had."

Releasing rage, through whatever means, constitutes only part of the process of letting go. To fully recover, we must also be willing to put our rage to good use. As we've already established, expressions of rage purge negative emotions; they bring us nearer emotional equilibrium and self-comfort. However, productive expressions of rage help us to access our pain, our negative feelings toward our ex-partner, and our disillusion with our former relationship. When we verbalize our rage, a process of clarification begins that cleanses the residue of our "failed" partnership, leaving a pristine space for new self-knowledge and growth. Upon analyzing our personal shortcomings, the shortcomings of our partner and of our relationship, we are more prepared for our positions as better friends, better lovers, and indeed, better human beings.

As the field of psychology relinquishes its grasp on traditional theory, counselors increasingly experiment with alternative treatment modalities. One such method is rage therapy. Often conducted in a group setting, where participants are "strongly encouraged"—some participants say "provoked"—to confront hidden hostilities, rage therapy is not for everyone. But participants often report feelings of peace and strength upon completion of the sessions. During the therapy, patients relate and reexperience repressed conflicts and emotion-laden incidents from their past, such as subconscious hostility toward their ex-partner. Once these feelings surface, they are easier to deal with. Successful completion of the therapy often leads to an elimination of the repressed emotions. But even if we don't hire a therapist, uncovering repressed pains leads us toward an experience of catharsis. Eventually, we can move on with our lives.

Occasionally in relationships where one partner is not ready to confront the inevitability of breaking up, we may resort to vengeful, vindictive behaviors. These behaviors are our way of getting even with the man who has hurt us. In a way, vindictiveness and aggression are natural ways of dealing with pain. Research scientists have observed such behaviors among members of all vertebrate species finding themselves in direct competition with one another over food, dwelling places, and mates. So, when we realize that another man is shamelessly determined to steal our partner away, we prepare ourselves for the attack. Knowing as we do the weaknesses of our ex-partner, we are likely to wage the attack against him, rather than confronting the "enemy." Against our ex-partner, we have a better opportunity to win. Many of us suffering and surviving the loss of a partnership have battled with almost irresistible inclinations to inflict physical injury on the jerk who dumped us. (Or if we dumped him, he may also experience similar feelings toward us.) We may entertain deliciously murderous thoughts, wish for deadly accidents to befall him, or visualize what we would do to him if only he had left a forwarding address. Fortunately, the materialization of revenge seldom occurs. Vicariously, we retaliate hurt-for-hurt, rather than attacking our ex-partner, primarily because of our instinct for self-preservation. We wouldn't mind messing up *his* face, but we hold back because he just might put a dent in ours. "For a year, I was on automatic pilot, emotionally," says Bobby Hanes. "It was a very hard year. I had lots of evil dreams which involved my ex-lover—dreams in which he gets badly hurt. But I'm getting to the point where I can remember the good times without animosity. A friend once told me that I might need as much time to get over this relationship as the length of time it lasted.''

So, rather than risk physical injury, or being cuffed and hauled away for a night in jail with Tiny, our greaser of a cellmate, we tap into our imagination to express vengeful feelings in socially acceptable ways. One reason we crave revenge is the genetic encoding that mandates payment for the damage we've sustained. Getting even, we are convinced, will make us feel better. But we must consider the bigger picture. After rolling up our sleeves, pushing the Maserati off the bluff, then clapping the dust from our hands, we are likely to feel great for a while. But sooner or later, the self-satisfaction will disappear. We will suffer guilt, low self-esteem, or shame for what we have done—even if, during the reading of the will, we discover he *didn't* leave the Maserati to us. Though difficult, maintaining control over aggression is essential. Healing *will* occur. We don't want remorse tainting our sense of well-being and peace—feelings that we will, eventually, experience.

Those of us who have suffered over a loved one's death understand the feelings of anger at life for its unfairness. Essentially, the aftermath of breaking up with someone who shared our bodies and our lives is the same. Often, we vent our anger on those closest to us. In our minds, they are the lucky ones, the survivors who cannot possibly understand the pain we have endured, or the insuperable loss we have suffered. We take a logical, understandable journey into self-pity. We experience grief we aren't sure we can survive. We may hate our lives, our friends, even our God; as a result, we may say or do things ordinarily uncharacteristic of us. Without self-awareness, we may even develop attitudes which forever jeopardize our future experience of happiness, passion, or satisfaction. Consequently, it's best to find space to experience vengeful sentiments without acting them out. One fundamental question remains. Do we want to end our relationship with our partner, or transform it? Vindictive behaviors will hamper the healing process and block any chance for forgiveness.

Another consideration during the process of breaking up is the motivation for our actions. Our ex-partner may perceive some of the business-taking that we do as vindictive. But what about the reality of our motivation? Perhaps what we do is necessary to the satisfying resumption of our lives. After clarifying within our own hearts the reasons for our actions, we might need to explain our motivations to our ex-partner. If, to pay our rent, we have to sell a precious antique that we purchased together, we have acted not out of revenge, but self-preservation. To honor the former relationship, we might discuss our decision with our ex-partner to reassure him that the transaction was necessary. Often, break-ups create havoc in our lives. Decisions have to be made quickly. Most of us understand that we have just as much capacity for screwing up while we're breaking up as we did while we were together. "I was having a tough time making ends meet," says Drew. "So I pawned the expensive ring Mitchell had given me. Later, I wished I had called my creditors to explain what was going on. Maybe they would have worked with me. All I know is that I sure do miss that ring."

Without self-knowledge, we can easily act spuriously and carelessly. Just as communication was important during our relationship, it is just as important when we're breaking up. Negotiation, not retaliation, is the best course of action—an often unpalatable option when we've been hurt. It's easy to say we don't care how the jerk feels about what we're doing, but such obstinance leads only to more resentment and bitterness. By the same token, if we think our ex-partner is behaving in a vindictive way, perhaps we should take the time to explore his thoughts and feelings. That's not to imply that we passively accept his actions, but opening channels of communication may close wounds created by perceived malice. Some of us discover that our ex-partner reaches out to our good friends after we've broken up. Logically, we first assume that he intends to gather forces against us. Then, we grow jealous because we think he is attempting to alienate us from our dearest friends. Just as likely, however, he is strengthening his friendships to assuage pain and loneliness. After all, he probably has done little rejoicing after we broke up. The bottom line? The *desire* for vindication and revenge is probably inevitable. But we must take great care not to act out those emotions. Otherwise, we cheapen the value of our former partnership, sour the present experience of our lives, cause our friends to question our character and integrity, and erode our future capacity for loving.

How, then, do we manage vengeful feelings? When we recognize their occurrence, we simply don't allow ourselves to act on those feelings. We make a conscious effort to reverse them. Instead, we enjoy an hour of solitude, invite a friend for coffee, or if possible, explore our feelings with our ex-partner. Coping is more difficult than revenge, but it reaffirms our humanity and compels others to regard us as a desirable friend. Besides, a vindictive act against our ex-partner invites him back into our lives. He is forced to respond to our demonstration that we haven't disengaged ourselves from the partnership. Vindictiveness is never a path toward freedom, but the most effective way of growing inward. It is a way to relinquish our identities to dreams of a past our ex-partner no longer wishes to share with us.

A frequent consequence of falling out of love—and one we don't always take seriously enough—is depression. After Robert and I ended our partnership, I immersed myself in the details of survival—rearranging finances, cultivating friendships both old and new, and making other lifestyle changes. I was unaware of the depressive feelings creeping into my heart and soul. I vacillated between feelings of anger toward Robert for leaving me, and anger at myself for not being a better partner. Although I felt no chronic sadness, there were times when I sulked or even cried because of what I'd lost. In retrospect, I realize my moods shifted from mania to depression—not so dramatically that my doctor could diagnose a bipolar disorder, like manic depression. But sometimes, I felt an immense optimism which surfaced through hyperactivity and cheerfulness. However, those feelings of liberation were followed by matching sensations of suffering and loss.

As gay men dealing with a relationship crisis, we should not be ashamed to acknowledge feelings of depression. When depression interferes with our lives, we should seek professional counseling. When money is a problem, as it often is following a breakup, we can easily locate psychiatrists and psychologists at state- and community-supported mental health clinics. It is always a good idea to question our counselors to make sure they have no hang-ups about treating homosexuals. If they do, we should request a different shrink. Of course, if we can afford a private practitioner, the choices are infinitely more numerous than with government-supported agencies. No rule stipulates that we're stuck with the first shrink with whom we make an appointment. It's hard enough, dealing with our breakup. Who the hell wants to add homophobia to the problem?

How can we distinguish the blues from depression? Earlier, I mentioned unawareness of depressive symptoms until my life settled down and Robert moved away. Although I was dating someone steadily, a sensation of sadness, despair, even disorientation hit me like a ton of bricks the moment Robert drove away. While pleased with the new man in my life, I found a relationship of three months compared to one of fifteen years did not possess the same qualities or comfort. Occasionally, I found myself pretending to be happy while spending time with Josh when, in reality, I was still grieving over the loss of Robert. Furthermore, I wondered whether I had given myself sufficient time to cultivate the qualities I needed to make another relationship work. Or, would I make the same "mistakes" all over again? I also experienced guilt because I mourned Robert's loss when I should have been enjoying my relationship with Josh. Consciously, I concealed my remorse about the failure of a partnership I thought would end only when mortality demanded that one of us pay up. All the while, the bills piled up, a couple of creditors were calling my office, and my cash flow slowed to a trickle. Not only did I feel helpless to resolve these financial problems, but I was not very hopeful my circumstances would ever improve.

Other manifestations of depression had begun, as well. Everything that once provided pleasure in my life could no longer sustain my interest—except sex. I finally realized that as much as I enjoyed physical intimacy with Josh, sex had become a way to avoid confronting myself. Biking, which I once enjoyed, became a chore I finally relinquished. An avid reader who sometimes digested several books a week, I found I could scarcely start even one. And I had begun to behave self-destructively. I talked with Josh all night, every night, on the telephone, although work started early in the morning for me. My appetite became erratic; one day, I might binge, devouring everything not under lock and key. On other days, I might nibble on a Pop Tart now and then. Fortunately, after sharing these symptoms, my counselor referred me to a psychiatrist who prescribed an antidepressant.

Each of us owes it to himself to be aware of feelings that might indicate a diagnosis of depression. Disturbances in sleep and eating, loss of initiative or motivation in several aspects of our lives, and self-punishing behaviors are common warning signs. Withdrawal from friends and family, inactivity, frequent sleeping, and slowed thinking could also indicate a serious case of clinical depression. We may find concentration impossible; our minds wander when we're reading, repairing the car, or filing an important report at work. We may also eschew decision making, discovering that we would much prefer someone else to take responsibility in both social and professional situations. More severely, some of us even relinquish decisions about our personal lives to friendly meddlers who are more than happy to control us. When we're depressed, we not only notice a severe decline in our energy level—we scarcely feel like doing *anything* other than watching television and renting movies—our thinking process slows down as well.

But what should be most worrisome? Suicidal ideation—generating mental images of our own self-inflicted death. The moment we entertain the question of whether our lives are worth living, professional intervention is essential. We must always hold onto one inarguable tenet: No man is worth the sacrifice of our lives. "When we broke up, I was struck by one electrifying realization. This relationship was what all that love poetry is about," says Les Wright, a professor in Fitchburg, Massachusetts, and author of *The Bear Book.* "The joy I had in this relationship was incredible, but the despair was just the exact opposite. At some point, something snapped. I alternated between states of uncontrollable crying and just being driven. I would go out walking for hours and hours. I stopped sleeping and lost fifty pounds in three months. I became suicidal. I subjected myself to therapy through the support network for alcoholics. After three months, there was still no end to this crying."

Though painful and debilitating, depression *can* provide an impetus for change. On the most fundamental level, depression alerts us that we're not dealing well with some component of our lives. Subsequently, when we refuse to fold, we are enabled to analyze our repressed emotions and desires, our insecurities and fears, and our inadequacies. Les, for example, realized that he was also grieving for other issues—like friends who had died from AIDS, and childhood incest which he had never properly confronted. Self-examination, even if medication is prescribed, is the only way depression can be beaten. Furthermore, depression also serves as a cleansing system, a necessary step in the grieving process when our partnerships end. Personally, my willingness to confront my depression allowed me to filter both the joys and sadnesses of my years with Robert. That journey included pain, resentment, anger, and occasional hatred, but it opened up a healing space where we could work on friendship. Depression has to be one of the worst experiences associated with breaking up, but once we survive, we can safely assume that we have finished the worst part of the journey. We hold fast to the unalterable fact that depression is an important part of healing. Properly confronted, it can help us reclaim our lives. And no matter what anyone says, prescribed antidepressants are not ways to avoid dealing with the symptoms of depression. If our doctors recommend them, pills level the playing field so that we can reclaim the energy and the insight to fight our way back to the enjoyment of our lives.

Breaking up also provides the opportunity to face other issues impeding our growth as human beings. Caring, loving, touching, and nurturing, characteristics of all romantic partnerships, are experiences strongly rooted in our childhood. When we lose those components in a long-term relationship, alarms are sounded, causing us to experience similar anxieties and fears that hark back to our childhood. If we have depended on our relationship to provide security, or even a sense of identity, we are likely to discover repressed feelings of dependency and worthlessness. "Now, I'm more aware of that tendency to throw myself into somebody else's life, and leave my other life," says Russ Souchak. "After breaking up, I'm more aware of my tendency to lose myself in someone else. I know it's not a good thing to happen."

Or if we spent much of our childhood feeling rejected or uncherished, a breakup might incite a recurrence of those feelings. If our parents weren't affectionate or physically demonstrative, perhaps our romance provided a means for having those needs met. Upon breaking up, we may also crave affection, attention, or human touch—all of which sometimes provide common rationalizations for promiscuity. The list goes on, but any developmental issues that are revisited because of breaking up, when dealt with honestly and with willingness to change, will prepare us to enter into other relationships with a far better capacity for success.

While depression, properly faced, places us on the precipice of positive change, we should not be content to remain there. Depression is an energy drain, a negative space where we risk growing too comfortable. Ultimately, we lose sight of the value and purpose of our lives, which can all too easily lead to self-destructive thoughts and behaviors. Before such deterioration occurs, we might seriously consider a battle plan to combat depression. Many of us enlist the services of a counselor who, while unable to force change upon us, can objectively listen to our issues. But even if we aren't comfortable on the doctor's couch, we have other options for dealing with depression. Challenging exercise produces endorphins in our bodies which generate feelings of well-being, with the added benefit of whipping neglected muscles into shape. Maybe we'll never be an Adonis, but a fine-tuned body communicates our concern about ourselves. We might also indulge again in those activities which once gave us pleasure. After relationships end, it's easy to be convinced that we are doomed to feeling like shit. During a relationship, we frequently neglect activities and pastimes we once loved because our partner wasn't crazy about them. But he's not interfering now. If we stopped going to the mosh pit every Saturday because what's-his-name thought it silly, then it's time to put on that tattered T-shirt and ratty old jeans and have some fun. We feel good about ourselves when we indulge in activities that remind us who we were during a happier time of our lives.

"After we broke up," says Michael, "I did a lot of praying. I'm Catholic, you see. I pray regularly anyway, but this time, it really helped a lot. In June, after we split up, I got my navel pierced. I made that decision after losing a lot of weight. It was also an expression of freedom. Right after that, I got my nipples pierced. I just know he would never have allowed me to do this kind of thing.''

Research has indicated that the foods we consume also influence our moods. While as many "feel-good" diets are available as there are dieticians, a common thread runs through all of them: Keep the saturated fats low, get plenty of exercise, and eat until your body has had enough, not until it's full. When we regard food as a drug to be taken in moderation, and only when the body needs it (about once every five hours), we set the stage for a physiological equilibrium rather than a roller coaster "mood ride" that results when we toy with blood sugar levels. Good eating alone is no cure for depression, of course, but coupled with other strategies, it can be a tremendous step toward emotional well-being.

Other constructive responses to depression can also speed healing. Instead of listening to the sad songs of love lost on the stereo system, we might consider soothing, healing music, or something upbeat and exciting—music that forces us off our butts and into our dancing shoes. Not to refute the ultimately cathartic effects of those sad songs, or to trash Cher's album *It's a Man's World,* we don't want to purge our CD collection of everything except the music that makes us cry. We might also rekindle friendships that have fallen by the wayside. Sometimes, reconnecting to old friends is a humbling step to take, particularly if, once we fell in love, we didn't stay in touch. Most friends understand the pressures of relationships, and will welcome us back. In fact, they will probably be honored that we came to them when we were hurting.

A more dramatic response to depression? Changing our image entirely. Perhaps we've already begun a new diet and exercise plan. What's to stop us from going a few steps farther? Are we tired of those streaks of gray? We can always revitalize our hair color with bottled chemicals. In fact, why not change the color entirely? While we're at it, perhaps we could go shorter (or longer) with the hairstyle. And *really*—isn't it time to replace those tired old clothes with a brand-new wardrobe?

After their relationships ended, some men opted to take an even bolder step—changing careers. "After we broke up, I had nothing in my life," says Greg. "It's not that I wanted to commit suicide. It's just that not living would be so preferable to what I was living then. One day, my therapist asked, out of the blue, why didn't I go to medical school, since I had mentioned to him that I was interested in one day becoming a physician. And that's exactly what I did." Sometimes, for the sake of financial security, or to avoid becoming a financial burden on our partner, we remain in professions that no longer fulfill us. Considering that work is such a large part of our lives, finding happier employment improves our self-image and alleviates the drain on our energy. Certainly, many of us are perfectly content with our careers, so a dramatic change would not be a viable option. But if we have experienced long-range dissatisfaction with our work, what better opportunity could there be for us to explore other options? Perhaps we could even go into business for ourselves. What better way is there to put our strengths and our talents on the line?

The most effective prescription for licking depression is change. Of course, the most unnerving change of all has been forced upon us. It was never totally within our control, even if *we* called it quits, this breaking ties with the man with whom we thought we'd spend the rest of our lives. It is empowering to take life by the reins and effect change, rather than being negatively affected by it. Why sit at home alone all the time, staring at the same walls hour after hour? Instead, let's implement a game plan. Even if we don't go out every night, we can talk on the phone to friends, who usually discourage us from taking ourselves so seriously. We can rearrange the furniture so that the new arrangement bears little semblance to the configuration when our ex lived with us. We can paint the walls a different color, alter the décor, reshuffle the kitsch. We can rediscover the library or the bookstore, and choose self-help books about healing, growth, and getting in touch with ourselves. We can keep a journal which chronicles our emotional progress. We *can* become better human beings; as a result, we have more to offer both friends and lovers. In turn, we become gracious recipients of their support, kindness, and affection. We become better listeners and more insightful confidants. We establish a healthier connection with humanity. With such a noble accomplishment, our loneliness subsides.

Another leviathan to face after breaking up is fear—fear of

the unknowable future, fear that we might not have done the right thing, fear for our own survival. Fear is a basic instinct shared by all species, but we are the best equipped to cope. After breaking up, however, we wonder how that could possibly be true. We have fallen to our most vulnerable level. Fear keeps us on our toes, makes us cautious of shifts in the direction of our lives. We may even grow defensive when we think our complacency is in danger. Sometimes, we don't even know what we're afraid of. The fear is generalized, embedded so deep that it defies penetration. But penetrate it we must, if we hope to re-ignite our lives.

What are we afraid of? The most basic fear we experience is that we won't be loved this much again. Let's face it. Our world has been shattered; what we perceived as the best thing that ever happened to us has gone down the tubes. Regardless of what happened, we share the blame, in our hearts, for the relationship's failure. Essentially, we are plagued by doubts that we possess any surviving human qualities worthy of another man's love. We even fear that we won't be able to surmount this shattering loss, that we are doomed to an unhappiness whose end is not yet in sight. "After sixteen and a half years, we broke up," says John Eastwood angrily. "I'm dealing with another breakup right now, after six months. This hasn't been a very good summer. My best friend died of AIDS. The next month, another friend died. My ex laid the bomb on me the following weekend. How was I to deal with that? I'm *still* dealing with it." John lowers his voice. "I lived for one year as a single person, and I don't like it."

We also fear for our future. As a spouse, we experienced security in our relationship—a harbor to which we could return after our daily exploits. "If we're not tied to anything, we can never be free," Pippin sings in the Bob Fosse musical of the same name. Pippin's sentiment captures the essence of the feeling we once had. We could tackle challenges and take risks because even if we failed, we could always return to home base and to the man who loved us. Once our relationship ended, we felt trapped, imprisoned by an aimlessness at a point in our lives where we might have found new freedom.

Fear undermines the faith we have in our own actions and decisions. Constantly, we wonder if we have made a mistake, yet we have little basis for evaluation, no one who loves us enough to offer honest advice, no great book with all the answers. We are, as they say, on our own. We must shit, or get off the pot. Root, hog, or die. Fear blocks movement, yet we have little recourse. We don't know what mechanism moves fear. We don't know how fear works, or why it causes us to malfunction. One bit of advice is offered by a Knoxville, Tennessee, psychologist who has treated both gay men and lesbians caught in the aftermath of a broken relationship. "It's a hard truth to accept," she says. "Hard to internalize. But we all must realize there are no mistakes. What happens is supposed to happen. And that should be a liberating thought." If we accept her observation, we can overcome the inclination to hold on to that which has ended. Our future is our own; we are fit to face the battles ahead.

What else do we fear? We fear we won't be able to make it without him, that in some metaphysical way our strengths are intertwined with his. Without him, we are only half a man, capable of accomplishing only half of what we have set out to do. Can we make it financially? Can we establish our own sustaining friendships as a single individual? Will our employers notice how severely our confidence has been shaken? Will other members of our social circle blame us for what has happened, and fail to see that our ex-partner had any significant role to play in our separation? Will our families see the end of our relationship as evidence that gay men lack the necessary traits to make a relationship work?

Facing these questions is necessary to defeat the beast of fear. When we answer the questions honestly, we maim the sphinx guarding the city's gates. Too often, we yield to the temptation to avoid the hard questions, to run away, with the beast in pursuit. But when we own our fears—when we are willing to face them— wonderful things begin to happen. Problems once perceived as insurmountable have solutions. We absolve ourselves of the blame for what happened between us and our ex-partners. We free creative centers of our minds to deal with life's challenges, and we find we have what it takes to survive. We confront the illusion of fear, and we go on.

Finally, bravery emerges. "Where am I now? I enjoy having the freedom to share physical relations with another man I might find attractive," says Jeremy Richards, "but I'm not looking for another husband. This is the happiest I have ever been. [My ex] also seems more motivated and healthier than I've ever seen him. Friends we have in common have said they can see us both shining brighter than ever. My light has always been shining, and he acted as a reflector. Now my light has gotten more intense, and he has found his own."

The Practical Matters

"Money, money, money, it's so funny," Abba sings, "in a rich man's world."

Yet, when gay partners break up, money matters are far from funny. In the past, we've been a team, a kind of security net for one another. Even if we never pooled our resources, the expenses were cheaper when two of us shared them. Now, almost everything seems twice as expensive—the utilities, the mortgage, even entertainment. We can hardly expect that, because only one of us consumes electricity, the monthly bill will decrease by half. We know it doesn't work that way. While the bills are lower, they aren't *that* much lower. The mortgage doesn't change, and now that we're single again, we may require even more entertainment outlets. So, as distasteful as financial matters are, they are not an insignificant part of any relationship—and certainly not when that relationship ends.

Before making lifestyle changes that reflect our new circumstances, we have to examine how our finances interrelated with those of our ex-partner. If we rented an apartment or condo, the solution to living accommodations is quite simple. We assess whether we can afford the total rent, or we move into a more affordable space. However, decisions become touchier when a mortgage is involved—particularly when the loan was issued in both names. Do we attempt to sell the house? Or do we try to find renters? And if one of us decides to stay in the house, are we on amiable enough terms to discuss the management of mortgage payments? Is it fair for us to pay one hundred percent of the monthly payment, while the ex reaps the benefits of a positive credit reference and fifty percent of the tax deduction?

Or should we attempt to change the terms of the mortgage so that only one partner's name appears on it? Beware of the ex-partner who offers to pay his monthly half, even after he moves out. No matter how well intentioned, he will inevitably encounter a financially bad month (which will turn into three). Our recourse? Not a damn thing. The courts don't recognize our partnerships, so his default is ours, too. No questions asked. While he's living it up in his new boyfriend's townhouse, we risk losing our home. Once, we joked that the house was so small, we might as well live in a box on a street corner. Now *that* joke isn't even remotely funny.

Many couples open joint checking and savings accounts, while others decry such maneuvers as unnecessary. But those who *have* pooled their resources may have a difficult time dividing funds equitably—unless they have kept precise records over the years. Time has a way of revising memory so that, often, we exaggerate our contributions or shortchange his. The area of joint accounting is a potentially explosive issue, opening possibilities for major arguments—so much, in fact, that some men advise a fifty-fifty split just for the sake of maintaining peace. Yet such a division hardly seems fair when we have been depositing thirty percent of our income into savings while he has only forked over ten. If we have been consistent in depositing a specific percentage, splitting funds according to those percentages is the best way to avoid hard feelings. Obviously, we will find no easy answers. Both of us want a substantial cut to start our new life with our best foot forward. While discounting a continued friendship over financial issues seems petty and spiteful, the financial ramifications of breaking up are often most contentious.

To consolidate debts, or to underwrite a Bahamas cruise, partners sometimes apply for—and receive—second mortgage loans, or other types of loans where lenders consider our incomes jointly. We agreed, in good faith, to sign for the loan, although the money was targeted to pay off the ex's credit card debt. Or we celebrated our fifth anniversary in Nassau, blowing the money on cruise tickets, entertainment, and food. Although it should be our ex-partner's responsibility to pay off the loan in the first example, and our mutual responsibility in the second, we are, unfortunately, at his mercy once we break up. Our only leverage is to remind him that a default will blemish both credit records.

If both of us are gainfully employed when the breakup occurs, we can eventually land on our feet again, even though we may face months of struggle. However, most debilitating are the splits between partners who have a large discrepancy in their incomes—particularly if the divorce occurs on less-than-civil terms. If a couple has lived extravagantly, or in a manner aligned with the means of the more affluent partner, then the other may be left in a precarious financial dilemma. With no way to make ends meet, he may be forced to move in with his parents (if they are still alive), sell cherished possessions, risk foreclosure or eviction, have his car repossessed, or any number of humiliating consequences.

One man was promised by his ex-partner that he would continue to send half of the mortgage payment monthly. Neither wanted to sell the house. It would "come in handy" at tax time; besides, who knew when one or both men might need an equity loan? After three months of religiously sending a check for his share, the ex-partner stopped. "He told me that he was behind on his car payment, and his other expenses had drained him financially," the man said. "For six months, he continued to make excuses why he could spare no money. He *promised* he would stick to the arrangement. When we broke up, we pledged to remain friends. We both wanted this connection—this business partnership, which was the way we regarded the house. Or so I thought. We decided that even if I met someone and moved away, we could still find someone to rent the house. That way, we'd be able to split the extra income, and also use the equity for a loan. He seemed so sincere when we talked. Finally, I stopped calling him. I got tired of hearing his fucking excuses. I'm still unsure of what I'm going to do, but I'll be damned if his name will stay on the mortgage if he isn't paying. My problem is that my credit is ruined. When he moved away, I could scarcely afford to buy groceries or pay the utilities. What lender in his right mind would consider writing a mortgage solely in my name?"

The bad news is that we, as gay men, don't have a prayer when we are treated unfairly. Since marriage is a privilege denied us, along with its inherent checks and balances, even legal action would probably yield unsatisfactory results. Our best course of action is prevention—i.e., hiring an attorney to draw up a legal agreement protecting us when our relationships end. Unfortunately, what feels like a legal business partnership destroys any feeling of romance. Besides, such an agreement does not guarantee us serious consideration by the courts. For most of us, what we *should* have done offers little consolation. That's why we should strive to maintain an open line of communication with our ex-partner, no matter how unpalatable that may seem.

As agonizing as dealing with money matters can be, dividing possessions we have accumulated as a couple is a significant emotional challenge. These "things" are the landmarks of our history together. Unless we hate the man whose life we no longer share, we created many cherished memories together. When tempers rise while dividing up the stuff, we can avoid ill will by first analyzing our anger before expressing it. As always, communication remains the key to resolving conflicts—particularly when deciding who will keep the sensuous gold leaf sculpture of David and Jonathan purchased in a La Jolla art studio whose proprietor was *obviously* a brother.

In "splitting up the goods," we are forced to consider the sentimental, the financial, and the practical values of each item. Maybe it's easy to part with the ugly, vinyl-coated recliner, but a much more difficult decision involves who gets the giant-screen rear-projection television. If one of us moves in with another man whose home is technologically well equipped, then the decision should be easy. If we purchased an item jointly, to insist on keeping it just because it's nice, or "my idea," is malicious and petty.

A more difficult decision might involve the same television. Yeah, it's true we're moving across town with our new lover. It's also true that he has an adequate television and sound system. So what's the problem? We leave the entertainment system behind with the ex, right? Not necessarily. What if, together, we decided to buy the system, yet we made all the payments? It is hardly inconsiderate to take stuff that we paid for. But if we don't need the television, perhaps we could exchange the scaled-down model for the newer set. Or we might offer to sell it for a reasonable price. No matter our determination to make a civil break, we will always encounter situations where no decision will be mutually satisfying. Just because we're breaking up doesn't mean we have to be a martyr, or a charity. Whatever our decision, we should clarify that it isn't meant to hurt anyone, and explain our position thoroughly.

Now is the time for a little compromise. If we really feel strongly about deserving the big-screen Sony, is there something else the ex might find appealing as a fair exchange? In settlement matters where nothing is really fair, a little wheeling and dealing will not only make each of us realize that we are serious about being equitable, but it will also make this component of splitting up more endurable. Robert and I made a game out of dividing up our belongings. We joked about items our tastes had out-grown—like the monstrosity of a TV tray, depicting Michelange-lo's painting of God touching Adam's hand. Robert had never known how much I hated that piece. Yet at the same time, we discovered sentimentalities about various items we had never expressed. (He never knew that the plant belonging to his mother prior to her death made me feel connected to her. As a result, Robert insisted that I keep the plant.) In surprising ways, we learned things about each other we hadn't known before. Although getting back together was not a consideration, personal discoveries deepened our friendship.

John and Clay are two ex-partners living in Virginia who fought over who *wasn't* going to inherit their bed. Later, because both were convinced that sleeping in their old bed would be too upsetting for either of them, they determined the best course of action would be to sell the bed at a yard sale—which is exactly what they did, then split the money. Later, just before John moved away, they cried in each other's arms because "the physi-cally intimate part of our marriage had been reduced to money— and a paltry sum at that." (The bed sold for only ten bucks.) Earlier, the couple had gotten dangerously close to a fist fight over jewelry they had exchanged. Clay felt that since the rings were gifts, neither had any obligation to return them. John felt the rings were symbolic of their loving commitment; now that the commitment was broken, the rings should be returned. Ulti-mately, the conflict required mediation. They called a mutual friend to help them decide. John and Clay agreed that, after

Fred considered both sides, they would abide by his decision. An objective outsider might be an option for us when collecting the spoils of our relationship, as long as both of us are willing to relegate the "power of attorney" to him.

Despite the tiring rhetoric purporting our unfitness for parenthood, many of us have children—whether by an earlier heterosexual marriage, through adoption, or other circumstances. Occasionally, we serve as surrogate fathers to kids having a rough time with their biological parents, or to gay and lesbian kids who have been kicked out of their homes. Regardless of how we got them, those of us filling parental roles regard these children as members of our families. More than likely, even when one partner is the biological father, the child regards the other partner as a parent. Invariably, the connections between the child and the men are strong, even intense. Kids, particularly adolescents, have an uncanny knack for sensing (and being incensed by) injustice. As a result, familial bonds are strengthened by the child's perception of social injustice toward gay people. Almost as readily as any gay militant, young people close to gay and lesbian families will assume an "in-your-face" stance when confronted by screaming homophobes and ranting bigots.

While appearing both certain and confident when confronting prejudice, children and adolescents can be devastated upon learning their two "daddies" are throwing in the towel. Here are two men who have chosen to live together as a married couple, albeit without social and political recognition. Since homosexuals have been hidden from children and adolescents—usually in the interest of "protecting" them—the existence of gay people in their lives adds an element of uniqueness. Some kids even feel "special" when a gay couple entrusts them with the truth of their love for one another. One young man in Georgia, upon learning that his mother demanded a divorce when his father came out, then defamed his reputation in the community, hitchhiked to Texas to live with his father and his partner. If kids are willing to go to extreme lengths to live with gay parents, or put their own reputations on the line when they defend homosexuals, it is little wonder that news of a gay divorce would reduce a sixteen-year-old boy to tears. "My family situation really sucked," says Thomas, who lives in Springfield, Missouri. "I became friends with my karate instructor, and later found out he was gay. At first, I was shocked. I got over that in just a few days. Then, when my father got pissed at me for calling in sick to work so I could attend a football game, he punched me and threw me out of the house. I went to Troy's place, and didn't leave for six months. When I heard he and Brandon were splitting up, I went for a visit. Tried to talk 'em out of it. But they said they'd made up their minds." He shakes his head sadly. "Their house didn't even feel the same. I loved visiting them, even after I got my own apartment. Their house was always full of people and laughter. That night, I drove around for two hours. I mean, I was that upset. When I got back to my apartment, my roommate asked me what was wrong. That's when I burst out crying."

Children who have already experienced Mom's and Dad's divorce suffer a double whammy when their father and his partner split up. Some kids, rather than suffering the emotional pain of another broken relationship, choose to withdraw. "When I told Joey, who lives with his mother, that Mark and I were breaking up after ten years," says Bill, "he just shrugged and walked away. I thought, 'Great. I might as well have told him two platonic friends had gotten into a fight.' A few minutes later, I heard choking sounds coming from the bathroom. I listened outside the door, and realized Joey was crying. At dinner, I noticed his eyes were red. But he wouldn't make eye contact with me. I *tried* to talk to him, but he kept saying this had nothing to do with him. His mother later told me he'd written a letter to Mark, but decided to throw it away rather than mail it."

Even when children aren't involved, gay couples usually establish an extended family consisting of a close network of friends, both gay and straight. The longer the duration of our partnerships, the more problematic their ability to cope with the dynamics of a breakup becomes. After all, friends have known us for a long time as a couple. Even when we have coffee with them in our partner's absence, our friends still view us as part of a team. Our lives are strongly interfaced. In turn, our friends aren't certain how comfortable they can be with us as individuals. No matter how much we reassure them, they feel uncertain that we will maintain our friendships with them, uncertain that we will continue to be the same man. To retain our friendships, we must strongly reassure our friends that they are still an important part of our extended family. Yet, no matter our effort, old friends may be so blown away by our misfortune that they gradually withdraw. "I kept calling Joe, but it seemed he was never at home," says David, 28, a car salesman in Madison, Wisconsin. "We'd been friends for over ten years. I just knew he was looking at his caller ID box, so I tried 'Star-67,' to keep my number from being displayed. Sure enough, he answered. He was very guarded. Finally, after doing my damnedest to make him understand that I was handling my breakup with Cal just fine, he was able to make his confession. He said *he* needed time. He said he just didn't know how to relate to me now that I was single again." At first, David was angry. "But I swallowed my pride and told him, as kindly as I could, that I wouldn't call him anymore. I said I wanted us to be friends, and I hoped he would make the decision to call me. So far, he hasn't. And that's all right. You know? I mean, I wish he would, but I understand that what happened to me affects everyone I know."

Another potential trauma that occurs during a breakup involves the assignment of custody of the family pet. Rover or Puffy has grown accustomed to two masters, and the adjustment when partners split up can be difficult indeed. Psychological studies attest to the therapeutic benefits of pet ownership to humans, but research ignores our role in their lives. They, too, grieve when they lose one or both men in their lives. In fact, some men reported symptoms of depression in their pets when their partners moved away. From a human perspective, the security our pets provide after a hard day at work or play can be greatly missed when we have to give them up. Volatile arguments often erupt between partners when they finally get around to the dreaded decision of who gets to keep the family pet, causing even more stress to the animal. "Dan had two cats he had purchased shortly after we met," says Bobby Hanes. "We raised them together, but they were, in essence, Dan's cats. One cat and I had developed a relationship. We were pals. When Dan and I began to sleep in separate rooms, 'my' cat knew something was going on. When the movers came to take my furniture to my new apartment, we had to put the cats on a little side porch. My cat let out the most horrible noise. It was inconsolable. I would caress it, but it knew I was leaving. That just about broke my heart."

When our partnerships approach the breaking point, we may discover the regard our "blood relatives" really had for our partnership. If our parents, siblings, and other relatives accepted our relationship, and were actively involved in our lives, they, too, will feel as though they've lost a close member of the family. They wonder if their relationship with us will change, and if our ex-partner will continue to have any role in their lives. Toward those of us who are not closeted at work, our colleagues might create distance so they won't have to deal with the discomfort our sadness may cause them. Or they may become overly accommodating, filling the role of mother hen proffering advice and, perhaps, romantic prospects. And our children, whether biological or not, will suffer sadness and disorientation because it is the nature of children to feel a friendship fully, and devastation when it ends.

As much as we hurt, we owe it to ourselves, and to those we care about, to make the break as clean as possible. In fact, if we are capable of remaining involved in their lives, we may discover a lessening of our own self-absorption. The pain won't go away, but our reconnections allow us to climb out of the crevice of self-pity and self-blame, into an "other orientation" that lightens our mood, clears our mind, and reaffirms our worth.

How can we prepare for such a challenge? We solicit our ex-partner's support and sensitivity, as hard as such a gesture can be, and attempt to become his ally, not his enemy. Then, our loved ones will breathe more easily, knowing that while ending a partnership, we haven't lost our humanity, or the operative core of our identity.

New Vows to the Old Partner

Only the details differ. The essential experience is all the same, whether we live in Chicago, Little Rock, New York, Los Angeles, or Atlanta. This breaking up, this discontinuation of the social and sexual construction of our love, this desire to go on but knowledge that we can't—it's all the same. The emptiness we hope will soon fill up again, the teetering on the brink of loneliness, the feeling of having lived a story whose end we will never know—it's my experience, it's yours. It belongs to us all. We struggle to regard what has happened as an opportunity for a better change, perhaps even a better man, but the act of resistance against intense emotion reminds us that life has dealt us a lousy hand. We wonder whether we'll ever win again. If we can't, is there a point to it all, a point to carrying on? A point at which we will look at our lives, with the realization of happiness, or at least a subtle contentment?

We follow a route that leads toward such introspection, but it involves some travel through unsavory neighborhoods. Some willingness to stand in front of the mirror, with a critical, insightful eye. And courage to face the monster of a man whose inability to sustain what we started brought us to this impasse. Yet, while harboring the image of him as a monster, we are struck by guilt, and knowledge that what we would like to convince ourselves is a lie. But face him we must, if only in a figurative sense. Even if facing him means conjuring from our best dreams and worst nightmares a man with and for whom we can find words again. Because we have to talk, to paraphrase an acerbic Joan Rivers, whose actual words are more to the point. Can we talk? We can because we have to.

Do we want healing? The all-too-obvious answer means that we have to be friends again even if we never speak, or have coffee together, or dance together in the club where everyone goes to be seen. We must have a reconciliation of hearts that will never come if we harbor the resentments and shun the neutrality that's still too deep in our souls to feel. But the question remains: How do we position ourselves for friendship when we have hurt each other so? Each of us has his own answer, and only one place to look. The bravery is in the looking, the self-examination, the culling of all the bad components of the relationship so that what we have left is the good.

If we reach that point too early, we haven't reached that point at all. A danger lurks in that delusion, the delusion resulting from an inability to give ourselves enough time. Skin heals much more quickly than the heart. We can easily mistake the need for wholeness again for healing; our minds are set on regaining balance, and are quite capable of tricks. We are gullible enough to play the mind's fool. If we aren't careful, we might attempt to enact the fantasy that we could be lovers again when we know nothing is farther from the truth. The truth we want to believe is that the easy step of getting together again beats the hell out of starting over; at whatever stage in life we are, it's much too far for starts. We thought we were done with stops and starts. We thought we had found a man with whom we could enjoy that journey toward something called fulfillment. He knows us better than most; his is not a place to be taken. Not a place to be taken lightly.

An insightful friend might say we're given to idealization of our relationship, and we would wonder, wisely, whether that friend was right. In this lost-and-alone feeling that has become symptomatic of existence, how easy it is to question ourselves, to wonder whether we made a mistake, to know that the new body in bed beside us, no matter how exciting, is no match for the old one we've given up. Temptation escalates. We crave the comfort of familiarity. Because of that desire, we may become blind to all that was uncomfortable about our lives with the ex-partner. No matter how cold our partnership had grown, no matter the doubts of whether silence or conversation was better, at least here was a man who knew us, and whom we knew. It's like parting with the old pair of athletic shoes for the newer model, only to find that breaking them in requires a different, less comfortable gait. The raggedy pair—now those were *serious* running shoes.

But as comfortable as they are, we aren't totally aware of the damage that's being done. The soles are thin and no longer protect our feet from the constant impact. The shock absorbers built into the heels have already absorbed more than their share. The arch supports do a sloppy job. We've begun to notice a soreness that lingers long after we've removed the shoes. We *know* we have no choice but to give them up, but even the thought of parting with them reminds us of the pain of the new pair. Did we *truly* get as much out of them as we might have? Should we have hung on to them awhile longer?

Once our decision to move on is made, we stick to it. We've weighed the evidence. We've made the lists of pros and cons.

We've talked and cried until we had no words or tears left. So what's the point of turning back—unless we weren't honest with ourselves before? But assuming we were, let's recognize any inclination to get together again as a bad response to the numbness we feel. Numbness is part of the grief which must be endured and processed. Circumvention invites a recurrence of misery. Often, moving forward feels like no movement at all; it's best for us to know, so we don't attempt any shortcuts. Time is what we need.

Most likely, we've talked over our problems and determined that this divorce is the only healthy way of coping with our unhappiness. To help in our healing, it's time to examine the possibilities for forgiveness. It's a step best done together. If we aren't in a position to meet our ex face-to-face, then we might imagine him sitting across the table from us. Let's pour him a cup of coffee. Set the ground rules that while we'll be nothing but honest, we'll try not to be cruel with the honesty, or to lose our tempers, or to walk away. Let's place ourselves in one another's shoes, acknowledging that we've hurt each other, but we want more than pain to be the legacy of our relationship. Perhaps we will find ourselves willing to confront circumstances, issues, and feelings now that weren't even a part of our self-awareness a year ago. We know, when we've come only this far, we've arrived at the beginning of growth, of transformation. Autonomy can't be too far from our reach.

What we know to get on with our lives—what we *have* to know—is forgiveness. Without forgiveness, we say goodbye to freedom. Without freedom, we can't see our way clear to love again. At the very least, an unwillingness to forgive both ourselves and our partner means we are forever sorry we never sought revenge, or took steps toward retribution. Nonforgiveness imprisons us; it makes us cold, obsessive, bitter. Without forgiveness, we relinquish most chances to connect with other people, with other love potentials, with ourselves. How can we get to ourselves when bitterness buries us? How can we free ourselves to love again, when retribution—or a remorse for never achieving it—drives us?

With those realizations, we are ready for healing.

Just How Bitter Are You?
Determining Your Bitterness Quotient (BQ)

So your decision is made. It's time to throw in the towel. While establishing clarity is a necessary step toward recovery, you can't experience clarity until you're able to eradicate the bitterness that probably resulted from breaking up.

The activity below establishes your Bitterness Quotient (BQ). If you make a high score, breaking up has taken a high toll indeed. That's okay. At least you'll have a few tangible goals toward which to work—like turning bitterness into hope and optimism.

Read each statement carefully. Then, in the table, write the number which corresponds to your most accurate response.

3—Oh, yeah. This is very, very true of me.
2—Well, this statement is largely true of me.
1—Although not often, I sometimes feel this way.
0—Absolutely not! This statement is never true of me.

1. I feel sad when I see a gay couple having fun.
2. I don't believe in the "power of love." In fact, what does that mean anyway?
3. I plan to get revenge for my ex-partner's leaving me.
4. It's not unrealistic to say I hate my ex.
5. The quality of my life will deteriorate without my ex.
6. There's no point in going out anymore.
7. I wish I wasn't even gay.
8. Casual sex is a good way to get even with other men. I even refuse to give them my telephone number.
9. I feel life really sucks.
10. I've noticed that I don't smile anymore.
11. My idea of fun is cutting other people and/or their ideas down.
12. When I'm with friends, I spend time trashing my ex.
13. I never go out with friends.
14. I've already experienced the great love of my life.
15. I'm too old to fall in love again.

16. I'm very angry because I didn't get the fair shakes from my ex.
17. I'm very down on my parents for their shortcomings as care providers.
18. When something reminds me of my ex, I get angry.
19. Whenever someone tries to talk with me about what happened, I quickly change the subject.
20. I think my life isn't worth living.

1.	5.	9.	13.	17.
2.	6.	10.	14.	18.
3.	7.	11.	15.	19.
4.	8.	12.	16.	20.
Add 1-4:	Add 5-8:	Add 9-12:	Add 13-16:	Add 17-20:

Now, calculate the sum of the boxes of the bottom horizontal row.

The total is your BQ. Write that sum here:

What Your Score Means

If your score fell within the 48-60 range, you're experiencing a lot of bitter feelings resulting from your breakup. Try to inject some positives into your life. In fact, turn directly to the Strategy Building Activity found below.

If your score fell within the 30-48 range, bitterness is a problem for you, and may get in the way of your recovery. However, you don't have too far to go before life seems rosier.

If your score fell below 30, you're well on your way to turning your life around—at least, your attitude toward it is definitely positive. You're doing a great job at moving on!

Strategy Building: Turning Bitterness into Optimism

The statements which follow are positive interpolations of the earlier BQ assessment. You know you'd make a pretty lousy score if you used the same criteria utilized in the first activity. But let's do something a little different here. Let's look at how far you have to go to turn your attitudes and disposition around.

Of necessity, this activity will be somewhat arbitrary, since you're utilizing a graph. On a scale of 1–10, respond to each of the following statements. A score of 1 indicates that you're as far as you possibly could be from attaining the indicated attitude. A 10 indicates that you've arrived! Anything in the middle approximates the distance you are from eradicating bitterness. Let's begin.

Place the appropriate number in the space next to each statement. Don't take too long to make a decision. Your first instinct is probably closest to the truth.

_____ 1. I'm happy and optimistic when I encounter gay couples enjoying each other.

_____ 2. I believe in the power of love. In fact, I believe that I will experience "true love" again.

_____ 3. I look forward to socializing with close friends.

_____ 4. Although my relationship with my ex was often good, I believe I have yet to experience the "great love of my life."

_____ 5. The quality of my life will improve without my ex.

_____ 6. I look forward to going out again, and possibly meeting new people.

_____ 7. I feel very positive about being gay, and about the opportunities being gay provides.

_____ 8. Sex is a wholesome way to feel close to another person.

_____ 9. Life is full of wonderful opportunities.

_____ 10. My life is wonderful. I do everything I can to make it exciting.

_____ 11. I can never be too old to fall in love.

_____ 12. When I'm with friends, I never speak disparagingly of my ex-partner.

___ 13. When I think of my ex-partner, I feel only good will toward him.

___ 14. I feel affection for my ex. I always will. What happened was unfortunate, but the best thing for both of us.

___ 15. When something reminds me of my ex, I acknowledge it, then go on with my life. It doesn't screw up my day.

___ 16. Although my ex wasn't always fair, it's a waste of time and energy to get angry about it.

___ 17. Whenever someone tries to talk to me about my former partnership, I'll respond as honestly as possible, without assigning blame to either myself or my ex. I regard such opportunities as good therapy.

___ 18. When conversing with others, I listen a lot, and talk assertively and politely.

___ 19. My parents had their shortcomings as care providers, but they did the best they could. In fact, they equipped me well to handle life's travails.

___ 20. When I leave my house, I leave with a smile on my face. People are genuinely glad to see me.

Now, get out your multicolored pencils and make a rainbow flag out of the following graph. For each numbered row corresponding to the statements, draw a colored line extending to the value you assigned to the statement.

First of all, take note that the graph is divided into three sections. Numbers 1–11 indicate how well you're dealing with the world at large. Numbers 12–17 indicate your regard for your ex-partner. Numbers 18–20 indicate how well you're relating to and feeling about other people.

Second, examine your chart closely. Notice in which areas your scores are low and in which areas your scores are high. Categories receiving low scores should be listed in the "Needs Work" section. Categories receiving high scores should be listed in the "I've Arrived" section.

Finally, cultivate an awareness of where you need work in order to eradicate bitterness. With that awareness, move on to Chapter 4, "Toward Healing."

Statement	Assessment Values									
	1	2	3	4	5	6	7	8	9	10
1.										
2.										
3.										
4.										
5.										
6.										
7.										
8.										
9.										
10.										
11.										
12.										
13.										
14.										
15.										
16.										
17.										
18.										
19.										
20.										

Needs Work   **I've Arrived!**

Needs Work	I've Arrived!

CHAPTER FOUR

•••••••••••••••••••••

Toward Healing

Beyond Angst

The house has never seemed emptier. The smell of him still lingers, and reminders of our lives together are scattered about. A music album he left behind. A photograph he didn't have room to pack. An old shirt he no longer wore that we had been using as a dust cloth. His voice on the answering machine, repeating, "Please leave your message at the sound of the tone." We cringe every time the phone rings but feel an optimism, too, that maybe the caller has a quick fix for happiness. Maybe it's Ed McMahon with news that we have the lucky number. Of course, it's not. It never is. Chances are, it's someone out of the loop calling for *him*, and it's left to us to tell.

Lucky us.

Here's a good idea for the gay tabloids. In addition to those tacky personals, a "divorce column" would be nice. We can publicize our misfortune, and not have to repeat the news to everyone we encounter who predates our misfortune. "Bill and Ted announce their divorce, June 13, 1998, after twelve happy years of partnership. The cause of their breakup is unknown, but everything is okay. As you know, both men are survivors. They welcome your phone calls as long as you agree not to ask the hard questions." Maybe we can scoop up enough copies to distribute to all our friends.

He left Rover behind. We thought the dog would not only be good company, but also an effective treatment for loneliness and anxiety. Where did we get *that* crazy idea? Oh, he's all furry and snuggly, but petting him now just doesn't yield the same satisfaction we derived from his soft coat when he was the product of a two-parent family. Rover's a stranger, too. We know him as the pet of two masters; he's not a one-man dog. Never has been. In fact, he seems a bit depressed lately. Always wanting to snuggle up, or play, when we just want to be left alone. Adding to our quite considerable guilt, we've considered putting him up for adoption.

Motivation is a problem, too. We just don't feel like doing much of anything, except feeling sorry for ourselves. We've become very good at that. Going to work is such a chore, even to a job we once loved. We keep wondering, "What's the point?" Ironically, we don't like coming home from work either, because a "home" isn't what we have anymore. That house is a place to eat. A roof over our head. Something else we're responsible for, when we don't want any responsibility. Why can't the world allow us the hiatus we need? A little time and space to lick our wounds, to regroup, to wallow in the unpleasantness of singlehood again? One is the loneliest number, goes the song we used to like when we hardly knew what the lyrics meant. It is. God knows, it is. Too bad the lyrics have already been penned, because we could write them ourselves. Hell, we could write them better.

The workday ends. If anyone calls, we talk awhile, then tell them we'll have to get together soon. Thank God "soon" is a relative term. We've finally convinced Rover to play alone with his annoying toys. Why do manufacturers insist on those squeaky implants? After reading four pages, we toss aside the novel we've been reading for two weeks. We tune into the news—same old shit. Don't we feel bad enough? Finally we listen to Madonna as Eva Peron sing "You Must Love Me" over and over again, grateful that compact discs are impervious to scratches. We pray for a time when we never want to hear Madonna's voice again.

Then, we light up a smoke, pour a glass of wine, or a cup of coffee. We sit in our favorite chair—or maybe his. We lean our head back, close our eyes just as Madonna repeats, "You must love me." Yeah, right. That word—*must*—is a problem. For years, we thought we had a sure thing going. He *did* love us. The experience of romance and passion drove him—it left him no choice. He *had* to love us. Then, the love stopped. We thought his love was our only permanence in an impermanent world. His passion for us was a profound, philosophical construct—the core of our belief system. So when he proved us wrong, we lost more than a man. We lost something much more fundamental. We lost a belief, a trust, one of the few things in which we had faith. Our bodies translated that loss into an emptiness, a numbness extending to the bones. This loss and its resulting emptiness are symptoms of our loneliness and disorientation. Like gout, they induce the sublimest pain—a pain which must be suffered alone. There is no easy or quick fix. We realize how hard healing will be as we try to define our illness—try to sort through our symptoms. We feel lost. Sad. Defeated. Worthless. Guilty. A failure.

If we had done something differently, would we be sitting alone in this room now? Were there ever correct things to say, but we were never smart enough to figure out what they were? And if we're suddenly struck by a much-needed intelligence, would anything we say now be too late?

We feed the dog, start the dishwasher, read the newspaper. We think of the relationship that ended—it still seems like yesterday. We think of *him*. We can see his face as clearly as we can see that the dog is losing weight—just like us. Just like the time we first met, when love was more than an adequate substitute for food. We wore a perpetual smile, because we were in love. That experience not only constituted the center and apex of our lives, but it also colored our perception. Everything was all right. *We* were all right.

To revisit our former relationship is not only a common experience for us, it is, in many ways, an essential one. After all, the years we spent with our ex-partner provided long-term stability, a sense of belonging and family, and a love transcending even our most exciting sexual experiences. That time allowed us to understand the most poignant theme of the best love poetry— to fall in love is to taste eternity. We perceived no end to our partnership; it provided for us in adulthood what our parents' affection provided (or should have) in our childhood. The difference was that our love was a love grown up, a love that allowed us to be individuals (or should have), to be true to ourselves, without the judgments issued by Mom and Dad. We experienced the delightful paradox of freedom and commitment, and understood that in the maturity of love, our willingness to commit was yet another act of freedom.

So what are we without that freedom now? To admit to ourselves the end of our partnership is, in effect, a fundamental loss of identity—an identity we worked long and hard to cultivate. In view of that hard work, we demand to know where we went wrong. Because if, in review, we can determine what we did right—*and we did so many right things*—what could possibly have blinded us to everything that was going wrong?

Depending on our level of tolerance, the stage of emotional self-mutilation lasts for various periods of time. Later, when we are "over" these events so close to us now, in time and emotion, an evaluation will help us to ensure we don't screw up in similar ways with another relationship. Now, we take the punishment for what it is—part of the process of grieving. Eventually, this pain will lead toward healing.

Throughout the grieving process, we must take one responsibility very seriously. We commit to the goal of making friends with ourselves once again. The path toward friendship with ourselves includes self-affirmation—the validation and celebration of self. As down on ourselves and on life as we are, cultivating sturdier self-love might seem damn near impossible. It means identifying those traits and qualities we find commendable and redeeming about our lives. It means building self-esteem in many possible ways, rebuilding and renovating the man we once were, and imagining the man we can be in the future. It means finding comfort in being alone again. Comfort in being alone—in being ourselves—doesn't mean soaking in an antistress bath, joining a gym, or visiting a tanning salon once a week—though the ways we pamper ourselves positively influence our feelings of self-worth. Being ourselves entails a willingness to identify what we like about ourselves, what we have to offer other people, and the ways we grow emotionally and spiritually. To make progress toward recovery, we search for clarity within the confusion, sadness, anger, and pain—a clarity that demands of us to open our eyes to who we really are. We must be willing to experience aloneness. We must find enjoyment in peace and solitude. We must live in the midst of self-awareness.

Inevitably, as the clouds of disorientation subside, we will begin a redefinition of ourselves, but not without guilt. If we had made this strong effort to change while we were still together, we might still be together now. But some driving force declares an independence, in the absence of our ex-partner, to grow. Some inner voice frees us to try new things and cultivate new interests. Perhaps we even attempt a revival of old interests that defined us a decade ago. Despite our boldness to try on different hats, we can expect feelings of uncertainty and moments of regret. Perhaps we will feel a fleeting desire for our ex-partner to see us now. We want him to feel sorry for not giving us the chances we deserved. We *can* change, damn it. We *can* discover new ways to live, to think, to feel.

At times, we will feel as though we're living an unfocused life. But trying new experiences and taking bold opportunities are necessary steps out of stasis. Simultaneously we experience excitement and fear. We need a way not only to experiment with life's novelty, but also to analyze those subtle things that have begun to happen to us. Conversation with a trusted friend—whose insights resonate with us—is one way to move beyond mere experience into new life. We might also try keeping a journal. Right now, we can easily fool ourselves that we have stumbled into recovery. It's an easy delusion, but one from which we could fatally crash. "Talking it out" and journaling are effective means to trace the act of becoming, a way to process the grief. After breaking up, we experience a cacophony of motives, drives, urges, emotions, and attitudes. Our emotional landscape feels like a battlefield. One side wants to destroy us. The other side wants to drive out all unhappiness. As the internal battle of wit and emotion is waged, our mind cultivates an uncanny propensity for deception. While we try on different roles and live life as though on a stage, we must try to stay grounded. Groundedness cannot be maintained by a man who is not self-aware. Conversation with a friend, a therapist, or through the pages of a journal can help us grow toward self-awareness.

In taking both tentative and bold steps toward healing, what is it that we are looking for? We strive to discover precisely what *we* want—not what we *should* be. We want change, but not the capricious variety. We want a bold revolution of self that provides opportunities, not to regress into patterns predating our relationship, but to face the demons of our past. We want to face the insecurities, paranoia, codependencies, and aggressions that characterized our former partnership. But we must extend our view even farther back. The way we behaved with our ex-partner, the way we treated him, the way we regarded ourselves, were to some degree determined by life's early experiences. If we have been out of the nest for a while, we began an assessment of parental influence on our personalities long ago —an assessment that continues for the entire human life span. The greater our awareness of Mom and Dad's influences, the better our ability to overcome negative lessons they taught us. But what of other influences during our childhood and adolescence? Few men recovering from a failed relationship will place blame on an invalid lesson from their past. But our behaviors are stubbornly shaped not only by our parents, but also by other relatives, friends, peers, and adult caretakers.

What can we say about the man still nurturing that internal/ eternal little boy who was mercilessly called a "sissy" or "fag," and for whom no adult was willing to be an advocate? How has he been equipped for a partnership of two equals? What of the man whose memory still haunts him of a fundamentalist minister condemning all homosexuals as evil, predatory, reviled by God? How is he equipped to grow spiritually in a relationship when part of him cannot escape the hold of this misguided cleric? What of the man whose admired and respected teacher approached the literary work of a gay author by condemning his "lifestyle," then undermining the value of his writing because of its gay content? How is he equipped to bring a heightened degree of self-respect to a relationship? And what of the man whose parents "accepted" him as a member of the family while concurrently condemning his sexual orientation? How is he equipped to understand the validity of a relationship when that part of his identity enabling him to experience love was dismissed by those who gave him life?

All of us must deal with these issues on the path to self-actualization. In the process, we often discover unresolved inner conflicts that surface when situations reminding us of negative childhood experiences occur. Those emotional skirmishes also remind us of how intrusive early experiences were on our growth and development because they occurred when we were most fragile. When we break up, that fragility returns. In its midst, we reexamine personal circumstances and experiences that have influenced who we are.

If, in our vulnerability, we are willing to face all the issues that have undermined our self-esteem, we can anticipate heightened success in recovery. A breakup is no less damaging than the death of a loved one, or a serious illness that puts us at the brink of mortality. Such experiences provide opportunities for a life review. In truth, we have no choice. We *will* look back, reliving those times that affected our identities, our self-esteem, our goals. In that examination, we will interpret those events anew. We may find that old analyses are no longer valid. Then, we become motivated to start working on ourselves. If we stick with the task of healing, we will complete the renovations, clear away the refuse, begin the polishing, and apply the finishing touches. None of it will be easy. In fact, this work we do on ourselves will undoubtedly be one of the most uncomfortable periods of our lives. But stick to it we must. We begin the act of reclamation— a reclamation of our lives, ourselves, who we are. We are of little use to anyone—including ourselves—until that happens.

No More Men Who Don't Live in My Zip Code

Saturday morning, September 5, 1997. Atlanta. David, white, 47, a physician doing research at the Centers for Disease Control. Duncan Teague, African-American, "born during the Kennedy administration," a research coordinator at Georgia State University. During their partnership, which lasted for more than two years, they were invited to all the best parties. David, the healer. Duncan, the activist. When we talked, Duncan had, the night before, received an award for Community Activism at Atlanta's "In the Life" celebration.

"I met David at a potluck dinner," Duncan begins. He has a friendly voice, an easygoing manner. Being the center of attention is no problem for him. "Brook, a friend of mine, had been telling me, over and over, that she had a friend she wanted me to meet. She dropped the delightful information that he was a doctor."

It was Brook who engineered David and Duncan's first meeting. "We were partying in this crazy man's backyard," Duncan continues. "I was there with Brook. At the time, I had a lover whose name was Norm, but I didn't bring him to this particular event. Actually, Norm lived two hours away from here. When I met David, both of us were involved with men from out of town. I didn't realize I was supposed to be impressed by him; he was, after all, so quiet. Other people would talk nonstop for two hours, and David would barely say a thing. We *did* say enough to each other so that we could have a weekend thing—which didn't even compare to Thanksgiving six months later."

David mildly objects to Duncan's portrayal of him. "I wasn't as shy as Duncan makes it sound," he says. "I was chosen to be the presiding Clerk of the Quaker congregation. I had to visit with the other members of the Quaker meeting at other tables, and didn't have time to chat with Duncan. I *did* notice that he was kind of cute. Yeah, he was at the Quaker meeting house, too, and I invited him to cut in line. I was also quite attracted to his irresistible sex appeal."

Soon, David and Duncan began to discuss romantic involvement. "We didn't move in together," Duncan says. "Still, we tried to be monogamous. That was the hope: that we would be monogamous. But we differed on how we felt about that issue."

"I would say so," David interjects. "I found the idea of monogamy less unappealing than Duncan did."

On a deeper level, David was drawn by Duncan's activism. "There's an integrity and intensity there, which I admired," he explains. "Besides, he's very smart."

Duncan admired David's sense of humor. "Besides, I thought he was rich, being a doctor and all," he jokes. "Listen. In the past, I dated a number of men who were crazy, to put it politely. When I met David, I had just come out of a very good relationship that ended because of circumstances beyond our control. David had a civility about him that I was attracted to. That was unusual for me. Once, I had a fantastic, but unstable romantic affair. We would get vehemently mad, make up, then have fantastic sex. Then, we'd wait for the next go-round. Simply, I was not looking for that kind of excitement anymore. I was not looking for people who had not done any work on themselves, or who were struggling. I think people felt David and I were good for each other, because we enjoyed quite a bit of support. People were mournful about our split."

David agrees. "I have only been in Atlanta for five years," he says. "When Duncan and I started seeing each other, I had been here for an even shorter period of time. My circle of friends were to a certain degree work-related, or Quaker-meeting related. Both [circles] were supportive of our relationship. They *still* say they like Duncan, and they still ask about him. My brother met Duncan. My cousins knew all about him. They were all very supportive. Duncan's sister-in-law and I got along really well."

Duncan segues into an issue made even more significant by his and David's relationship. "I know that in both the gay and straight press, there's the misconception that black people have a harder time accepting gay people than whites, that black people are more homophobic than white people," he says. "That's a load of crap, and I think our relationship is indicative of that fact. I haven't seen a bunch of white folks running in the streets who are supportive. Before desegregation, where did they think black gays and lesbians were? The idea that we all left and went to the white gay community is ridiculous because there wasn't one. We couldn't go where the white folks went. Even now, there are lots of same-gender-loving blacks who never intersect with the white community. Somebody's going to tell me that white folks are so much more embracing of their gay and lesbian children? Why do we have runaway teens in Los Angeles? Or, heaven forbid, San Francisco? Where is this bastion of white folks that are jumping up and down and having parties once they find out their kids are gay?"

After David points out that Duncan's position about black homophobia is indicative of his intensity, they wander back into the arena of their relationship. "David's always been a rather quiet person," Duncan says. "But a couple of months before we broke up, I sensed a distance in our relationship that was different than just his customary quietness. It was as though he was always thinking about something—and not wanting to talk about it. Then, I felt a real sense of dread that our relationship was going to end. It was never anything he said; it was that he didn't say *anything*. So, we went to couples therapy."

Duncan characterized the early sessions as the battle of the loudmouth versus the quiet warrior. "Sarcastically, I asked if David could possibly talk about his feelings before a week passed by," Duncan continues. "He asked me if I would shut up a minute, so he could think about his feelings."

David, however, has a different perspective. "It wasn't just a matter of my being quiet, and not being as open with my feelings," he explains. "Some of the things that attracted me to Duncan were also the difficulties in the relationship. He really likes to be involved socially. At times, I need more solitude. Duncan gets his energy from large groups, from being an activist. But a big issue was the difference in our attitudes toward monogamy. It became clear to me that it wasn't going to be easily resolved. I was the one who stepped back. We talked about this in our sessions. I was the one who first felt like this really wasn't going to work as a committed relationship—that it wouldn't work for us to be lovers. It was real hard, this realization, because I never stopped loving Duncan. It hurt a whole lot for me. It was obvious that Duncan was in fully as much pain as I was over the separation."

Could the fact that Duncan and David did not move in together have contributed to their breakup? Duncan doesn't think so. "I saw him every time I could get my hands on him," he says. "We spent four or five nights a week together—except when he was occasionally traveling on the weekends. One of my criteria for the relationship had been that we would be able to spend the nights together. I told him I'm not dating another man who's not living in my zip code." He shrugs. "I compromised. I took a man who lived in the *next* zip code."

When the warning signs occurred, both Duncan and David searched hard for solutions. "I had a lot of friends who were very supportive of our relationship," says Duncan. "They felt I should be monogamous. It's true, monogamy was a pinnacle issue, but it wasn't the only one. The other issues made it difficult to deal with monogamy. I just don't view monogamy the same way as David—or as many other people. It's important, but it's not this golden ram that will save a relationship. There are worse things you can do to your partner than be with someone else sexually. There are times when the other partner should ask for monogamy and receive that kind of commitment. There are other times when you should be able to ask for something other than monogamy and work through it. I think many people feel the way I do, yet they give the other party line."

"Throughout it all," David interrupts, "he was very honest about this. I respected his opinion. I don't want monogamy to be presented as the only issue in our breakup, or the one beside which everything else pales into insignificance. For me, what I said before about basic personality differences played a part. This was continually difficult for me to deal with, and was a source of contention."

Finally, both men realized they were not going to make it as a couple. "We were no longer sexual with each other," Duncan says. "David was being more and more introspective. I was trying to clear myself out of his way. That took about a week. I have the benefit of having gone through way too many divorces. I knew that I wanted to preserve a friendship with David. It got really uncomfortable for me to be at David's place. I started to separate. I didn't want a long, agonizing, drawn-out process. When you drag it out, you're acting ahead of your healing. I *wanted* to stay, but I knew that wasn't going to work."

It was on a Sunday afternoon that David and Duncan decided to go their separate ways. "I came over to his apartment to drop off some stuff and check on him the next day," David says. "Then, a few weeks passed before we had a couple of new sessions after we broke up. We had several individual sessions, then one or two together. After that, we didn't really see much of each other for a few months. I didn't even go into that part of town."

Duncan remembers the breakup the same way. "I avoided Ansley Square, the area where David lives," he says. "I avoided David at first—except at counseling. Counseling helped preserve our friendship. I'm prone to drama, and counseling helped me to understand that David was not a monster. He was not out to destroy my life."

However, David would have desired a friendship with Duncan regardless of counseling. "I'll admit, counseling allowed us to communicate with each other better. It's true; Duncan would have made up his own story to interpret the split if it had not been for counseling," David says.

What about finances? "David is very businesslike, so it was very simple," Duncan relates. "He was considerate, and also very generous. Before we broke up, David had told me he was going to buy me a computer."

In fact, Duncan's sister-in-law chastised him. "You idiot!" she said. "You broke up with him before you got a computer?"

But when David returned some of Duncan's belongings, he also wanted to talk about the computer he had promised Duncan. "I didn't want to use the computer as a theme," Duncan explains. "I guess, in some ways, it took me a long time to decide what computer I wanted because I was hanging on, and maybe avoiding the issues. Four months later, we were able to conduct the business of buying a computer. I admire him for that. Many men would have said, 'Fuck it! No way!' Particularly considering the fact that I'm horrible with my money. I already owed David some personal loan money. We resolved that."

Other issues exacerbated the way both men dealt with the breakup. "For better or worse, I spent a few months with too much solitude and too much brooding," David explains. "Life went on, and I had plenty of things to do at work, and at Quaker meetings. There were also various family concerns."

In fact, they broke up on the day Duncan's father had surgery and his mother was diagnosed with cancer. "And David's mother, who was eighty-seven, had undergone an endoscopy, which had ruptured her esophagus," says Duncan. "We were both having serious complications in our families. That made our first attempts to express our concerns about our relationship to each other, as well as being supportive, somewhat more difficult."

"I was aware of Duncan's father having surgery," David says. "My parents kept my mother's diagnosis from me."

"David's like the medical dictionary," says Duncan. "In spite of the fact that we recently broke up, I went to him for advice about what was going on with my mother. I don't think it hurt to go to him. There was more connectedness, particularly since we were dealing with someone else's hardships. Increasingly, I was able to ask for more assistance after that."

While Duncan is "very out" to his family, David didn't come out until he was thirty-nine years old. "My self-awareness went further back," he explains. "Acceptance and acting on my gay sexuality didn't come about until I was thirty-nine. I thought it was too late to come out to my mother. I'm out to my brother, who's ten years older than I.''

Duncan came out to several friends in high school, but waited until his sophomore and junior years in college before coming out to his parents. "Actually, I should say my mother yanked me out of the closet. I had been on the *McNeil-Lehrer Report* and was grand marshal of the Gay Pride Parade. It was ridiculous for me and my folks to ignore the issues. So I asked, 'Can we talk about it?' They said, 'Hell, no.' I was pretty sad that I couldn't share my relationship with my family. They have a 'don't-ask-don't-tell' policy. I'm convinced my family talked Clinton into it.''

When David's brother heard about the split, he and his wife traveled from the West Coast to cheer him up. They took David to a popular restaurant in nearby Savannah. David was surprised to find Duncan dining at the same restaurant.

"Our tables were very close together,'' Duncan explains. "When David's brother sees me, he invites me to join them. It was very uncomfortable; it was weird. But I was really grateful to his brother for extending himself like that.''

David insists that he and Duncan are comfortable in their friendship. "We're still there for each other,'' he says. "Things have settled down, and we're going to continue to be there for each other. We get together every two weeks—sometimes more often than that. We call each other even more frequently. It's gotten so much easier.''

However, Duncan admits having been afraid of what might happen to David once they broke up. "I have all kinds of queer family that I could depend on when I broke up with David. I was afraid for David because he didn't have that. I always felt that part of my role was to help David feel more comfortable around all three hundred of my friends. Sometimes it worked; sometimes it didn't.''

Later, during an emotional moment following their split, David asked Duncan if he could remain a part of his gay family. "I'll be honest,'' Duncan says. "I didn't like it when he first asked. So I told him: 'You *had* the prime spot, and you didn't want it.' Later, I was touched that he asked me that. I feel totally different about the question than I did before.''

Where are David and Duncan now on their road to recovery? "I've been to social functions with gay men, but not sexual interactions," David says. "I had a brief romance last summer following the breakup, but that's about the size of it for me."

"The fates have been kinder to me," says Duncan. "I am now in a new relationship. I've been dating him for four months now. And I am in absolute terror because of the breakup with David."

Reconnections

The work we do on ourselves can never be fully realized until we have reconnected to the world around us. No matter the insights into self, the growth of self-esteem, or level of differentiation and autonomy we have achieved, we cannot begin the recovery process without getting involved once again with people. Even if we are shining examples of Ralph Waldo Emerson's edict to "know thyself," satisfaction with our lives increases when we know ourselves more moderately. With the involvement of other people in our lives, we can more easily overcome self-obsessive tendencies. Often, self-analysis becomes self-indulgence, a condition we can lick if we pump up our social calendar.

As we begin to feel better about ourselves, an inner drive will compel us to take advantage of opportunities for socialization. After all, the degree of exposure to others we afford ourselves makes our redefinition public; indeed, part of our makeover occurs because of social diversification. One man in Birmingham, Alabama, whose relationship ended after twelve years, attended therapy sessions six months before the split became official. He had the foresight to "read the signals," he says. Although James *could* speak eloquently for hours about his psychological motivations and personality traits, he seldom talked about anything for two months after his ex moved away. When he finally managed to get out of the house, friends saw a man preoccupied with himself and his plight; his facial expressions of perplexity, anger, and even disgust distanced him from human contact. Eventually, James began reaching out to people, one by one. His affect changed; he seemed more cheerful, more self-assured, more approachable. "Although I was still hurting from the breakup," he explains, "I could feel the pain subsiding the more often I planned stuff with my friends."

How do we manage to reconnect to the world—particularly a world that doesn't seem as enticing as it once did? Our world lacks appeal because we lost our connection through, with, and by our ex-partner. When we discover ways to reactivate involvement, the world becomes a friendlier place.

Some of the least threatening ways to "make contact" can be found on the Internet. Gay men have, perhaps more than any other group, utilized the Information Superhighway to establish a sense of community in a society which perceives our very existence as a threat. Besides providing access to news about gay issues, gay retail outlets, gay bookstores, and even gay porn, the Internet provides ways to socialize that are less threatening than the bars. Considering our vulnerability after dissolving a long-term relationship, our computers are an easy step back into the world. Gay mailing lists, or "listservs," provide anonymous places to pour our hearts out, and usually to receive some sympathy. "Chat rooms" provide us with instant conversation with other men who may be (more than) willing to give advice or share their insights into matters of a broken heart. According to *The Advocate*, at least six thousand gay men and lesbians at a time may frequent AOL chat rooms during peak hours. We can also find a wide variety of "dating services." Even if we're not ready for a new romance—realistically, it may be too soon at this stage of recovery—quite a few men have related stories of close friendships developing through their access to gay dating services. One word of caution, however. Some of us can too easily grow attached to our computers. Contact via the Internet should never become a substitute for real companionship. If that happens, our computers become an impediment to our recovery, a pathological symbiosis that keeps us living inside the box—as evidenced by one New Yorker who sometimes stays online from dusk to dawn.

Another way of sustaining human contact occurs through altruistic service. Many organizations in our communities welcome volunteers who can spend time or provide support to those in need. Men frequently cited involvement, after their breakups, in AIDS service organizations, "soup kitchens," gay youth support groups, and other projects. They also reported tremendous feelings of satisfaction, of experiencing a renewal of self-worth. New friendships are also established through community service. Several men stated that while they had envisioned their involvement as short-term, their feelings of satisfaction ran so deep, they committed themselves to long-term service.

A selfish but enjoyable path toward recovery is to plan a vacation, either alone or with companions. However, a vacation alone should take us to the center of human activity, compelling us to interact with others. If we can afford it, inviting a close friend to accompany us and offering to pay for his or her expenses will deepen our connection to that individual. After ending a long-term partnership, we often experience a strong need to get away, to interrupt the routine of our lives by escaping to a new environment. Pampering ourselves with a vacation encourages us to filter out the anxiety, depression, and sense of loss we may be feeling. Upon returning home, we are likely to enjoy a totally new perspective of our lives.

Many of us still in mourning avoid even the poshest soirees. Who feels like hours of repartee, loud music, and loudmouths when we've recently administered the last rites to our most cherished relationship? However, while a good bash won't transform us into happy, self-assured men, it can certainly provide positive social encounters to get us back on the circuit again. Nothing better than a party interrupts our self-pity and forces us out of withdrawal.

For many of us, a big question remains. How do we reform ourselves so that even strangers are magnetized by our intelligence, our charm, or our good looks?

First of all, what's wrong with playing into vanity's hand and trying to make ourselves as physically attractive as possible? Nothing like a good diet and challenging exercise to make our bodies leaner and meaner, as well as to build our self-confidence. As unfair as it is, people gravitate more readily toward those individuals who have taken care of themselves—or at least have a little pride in the way they look. And speaking of appearances, as far as money will allow, we might replenish our wardrobe. What's wrong with adding a little sparkle to go with the new build? Soon, we notice people are smiling at us more, initiating conversation and maybe issuing a few invitations—or even propositions. But can we logically attribute a change in *their* attitude to our fashion sense and muscle tone? Probably not entirely. But even superficial changes have the capacity to open us up. Our facial expressions, as well as the way we carry ourselves, communicate social receptivity and self-confidence. While once appearing tentative, discouraged, and timid, we seem to have a new grip on life. Of course, the stylish duds and the hard muscles are facades. They don't begin to provide a glimpse into who we are. But that's okay. The social contacts they generate will eventually result in our willingness for personal disclosure.

Once we stop learning, we stop living. We don't want to ignore the opportunities before us for self-improvement. We are in a unique position to reshape our lives and expand our minds. Whether we choose to read a book a week, enroll in college courses, or restrict our social contacts to the local intelligentsia, intellectual growth is a big turn-on for our potential social contacts. All of us have met individuals who talk a good talk—at first. Then, the better we get to know them, the more obvious it becomes that after they yanked their degree from the dean's hand, they never bothered to learn another thing. These people quickly grow tiring. Eventually, we stop returning their calls. Who wants to be bothered by such major drains? We also know individuals who can spout a wealth of information on demand. In their company, we notice they are constantly soaking up everything they hear, read, see. These are the people who fascinate us. We look forward to seeing them again. Well, imitation *is* the highest form of flattery. Let's waste no time following their example. We don't have to become the community sage, but how nice it would be never again to be considered a bore.

We can't afford to ignore our spiritual growth either. A man's spirit can be defined in many ways; each one of us must determine what needs healing when our spirit is sick. Perhaps all of us can agree that whatever our spirit is, the concept can be partially defined as the "life force," or the "energy that pervades our lives and propels us toward a meaningful search for the unknowable." When our spirit is healthy, we feel a sense of harmony with the world, and confidence that whatever our lives are, they have meaning. Eventually, that meaning will be revealed to us. Or as one man having a difficult time during recovery puts it: "I'm just so tired of waiting to be home. In my heart. You know?'' If a journey toward spiritual healing sounds like overindulgent self-pity, we might remember that spiritual growth reaches a plateau when pursued in isolation. When we accompany other individuals on their spiritual journey, we can all help each other grow. We are able to share our yearning to be home, in our hearts, and perhaps assist one another in finding that peace.

Some people give up on their spiritual journeys. They have tired of the long trip and finally turned around, resigned to the height they've grown. They appear unwilling to reach any higher, or travel any farther. Often, they strike us as pathetic creatures, content to watch television all day, or to overindulge in work. Then, they spend their waking hours talking about nothing. They are empty people confused by life.

During recovery, if our world shrinks rather than stretches, it's easy to conclude that what we already know of the world is all that's needed. But we don't want the easy way out, do we? We don't want to stop growing, even if we can conscionably blame our stunted growth on the ex. Even if we could really and honestly believe that lie.

At this stage in our recovery, we might try searching for something healthy to obsess about. Sometimes, we're tempted to consider another partnership. But it's simply too soon. That's not to say we shouldn't date, but we need to apply the brakes against infatuation. We're learning to live with ourselves now, to identify what makes us strong, to learn what needs repair. To fall immediately in love, then set up housekeeping with another man would probably have disastrous results. Yet some of us have done just that, and have suffered for our actions. What could be more demoralizing than hooking up with another lover after ending a long-term partnership, only to have the new one go rancid in three short months?

However, we can find other interests and activities worthy of our commitment. Perhaps we can find a new hobby that stretches our talents and abilities. We don't fancy a halfhearted involvement either. We dedicate ourselves to it, lock, stock, and barrel. Or perhaps another obsession might be education. For years we've wanted to return to college for an advanced degree. Now the opportunity arises. But let's set our goals even higher. Let's graduate in the top ten percent of our class.

The most important obsession for us now? Discovering new ways to look at ourselves and at the world around us. Concurrently, we reach both inwardly and outwardly. We can't socially withdraw while realistically hoping to grow as a human being. By the same token, we don't become a social whore, driven to avoid opportunities for introspection. Happy balances—that's what we work toward. A Janus vision, where we can see in two directions at once.

Once we commit to work on ourselves, we'll eventually experience a resurrection. We've felt like slugs for so long. We aren't sure what's been driving us to eat, drink, and sleep. Up here, in the brain, there were times we didn't care whether we lived or died. But *something* kept us shoveling food down our throats. S*omething* forced us to survive. Now that we see what to do, we feel a stronger motivation rekindled by greater energy. We experience spurts of joy and sensations of well-being. Maybe happiness is too much to hope for right now. But we realize we can't eschew human support. We've *got* to accept what's given—like warmth, acceptance, love, friendship, even sympathy. We must give back in kind. How can we receive fully that which we cannot give? We must strive to *be* warm, to accept others openly, to offer sympathy, friendship, and love. The more positive energy we can circulate, the more open we are to healing. The time for complete recovery isn't right yet. But it's coming. It's coming.

To Be Who I Am Today, I Had to Go through That

Erik Fischer, a library assistant in Philadelphia, met Andrew, his partner of four years, at a party hosted by a mutual friend. Andrew, nine years younger than Erik, was drawn to Erik partially because of his age. "But he also liked the fact that I could party as much as he, even at my age," Erik adds. "The guy he was living with then was about my age, but felt he had outgrown partying. He wasn't a real social guy. Andrew liked that about me."

When Andrew asked if he could move in with Erik, Erik said no—at first. "Finally, I relented. Once he moved in, my apprehension drifted away. We lived together really well. Both of us felt strongly that we should be monogamous, and that's the kind of relationship we had."

After about a year, Erik began to wonder if their relationship was on a growth track. "Part of it was me," he explains. "I'd lived in the area longer. I had this whole group of friends. My life, though, had begun to revolve totally around Andrew; I wasn't paying attention to my friends. We hung out with people we met as a couple. I ignored the people I knew before I met Andrew."

One day, Andrew made a comment that disturbed Erik. "You don't have any friends of your own. They're all *our* friends."

Erik knew then that Andrew was beginning to feel smothered. "And rightfully so," Erik admitted. "There was another warning sign, too. Earlier, he had said we needed to examine our relationship more closely. I felt there was nothing wrong with it. Understandably, his comment confused me. He was being vague, I thought. Shortly after, he would tell me he was staying with his friends for a few days. I think he knew me well enough to realize that I was pissed off about it. But I never called his friends to check up on him."

However, Andrew's absence grew more frequent. Finally, Erik confronted him.

"You have to tell me the truth," Erik said. "Are you seeing anybody?"

"Well, whatever I'm doing, it doesn't have anything to do with you," he replied. "But no, I'm not seeing anyone sexually."

Finally, one night, Erik went out to a gay club. "Andrew was there, with one person in particular," he says. "I was pretty devastated about it. What made it worse was that when I talked to my friends—the ones from before I met Andrew—I found out they already knew that Andrew was being unfaithful. In fact, he had been seeing this guy for three months. My friends had frequently seen them together. Andrew was telling our mutual friends that we had already broken up. I went through a real hard time."

What made the truth even tougher is that Andrew and Erik had signed a lease for another year. "Basically, our apartment soon became nothing more than a place for him to store his stuff.''

But other circumstances complicated their breakup. "We were still having sex, although he was seeing someone else. I told him that he couldn't come over for sex, then sleep with someone else.''

Despite Erik's posturing, he couldn't bring himself to refuse Andrew's sexual overtures. "I started going to a therapist," he explains. "She couldn't believe it. I mean, we weren't having sex a whole lot less than when we were living together. I told her I didn't want him back, but sex with him was easy and available. Besides, I wasn't seeing any other men at the time. In all that time, I might have had two one-night stands—maybe three. I wasn't feeling good about myself while this was going on. But Andrew and I had always been very comfortable with each other sexually. Sex was always good between us. Comfort with his body and with him as a person were the reasons I tolerated his visits— as well as the continued sex. It was more than merely wanting him back. I knew I wasn't going to get him back.''

Essentially, Erik needed to feel that everything was all right— at least, until he could wean himself from the sexual intimacy. "Sex was very nice," he says. "That's what I needed to feel, and felt. I convinced myself that I needed this intimacy. My therapist, of course, thought he was using me. And part of me thought that continuing sexual relations with him wasn't very smart.''

Besides the lack of communication and socialization in Erik and Andrew's partnership, different sexual standards may have contributed to the rift between them. "Andrew once said that having a relationship with someone had little to do with sex," Erik says. "I'm beginning to understand what he meant. I have visited Andrew and his new partner since. The dynamics between them are right. That's obvious to me. They maintain their individuality, and are still able to be in a relationship. It's interesting how their relationship has evolved. Even more interesting is the fact that I've become a friend of theirs. Through their example, I've come to understand that I relinquished a lot of my identity to be involved with Andrew. And it wasn't at his insistence.''

Several months after their split, Erik talked with Andrew about their experience as partners. "I told him how hurt I was that he started seeing someone else before our relationship actually ended," says Erik. "He didn't seem overly concerned about my observation. I interpreted his stoicism as meaning he had suffered no remorse about what happened between us. During a subsequent conversation, I continued to moan and groan about what had happened. Finally, he interrupted me."

"You don't think I feel any sadness about what happened to us?" he demanded. "Well, you're wrong."

"That was a big shock to me," Erik says. "I had never considered that he was affected by the fact that we were breaking up. My concept of the whole thing was that he fell in love with another guy, and was just leaving me."

In one sense, Erik felt he drove Andrew to search for someone new. "I had gotten to the point of depending on him to fulfill my emotional, social, and sexual needs," he explains. "No one can be that responsible for another human being. It's interesting, because I see now that I have a tendency to lose myself in another person. That's what really damaged our relationship. Even now, I think I would gravitate toward a similar kind of dependency. Here's an example. I met someone this summer. I was really interested in him. When we first met, we talked on the phone a lot. When I wasn't talking *to* him, I was talking *about* him."

"Erik, you're obsessing about this man," a friend told him. "He's not showing *that* much interest. You need to back off."

"Backing off was really difficult," Erik admitted. "It took a while before I was able to look objectively at the way that guy was treating me. It's something I need to always be on guard about."

To help himself deal with the breakup, Erik read self-help books and became involved in the local AIDS Project. "That helped me a whole lot," he says. "At first, I just went to the meetings thinking I would get to meet lots of other gay people. Actually, only one other gay man had volunteered. The others were lesbian or straight women. Even so, I went through the training. I'm happy to say I'm still involved. I've been involved for eight years. It's a very rewarding experience. In fact, I got to know myself through this project. I could see myself in a different way. I saw myself as less weak. I have lots of strengths. I was lacking self-confidence and self-esteem that first year. My involvement helped me to build that.''

Now, Erik has relegated the breakup with Andrew to history. ''When I think about it, I don't feel hurt, regret, or pain. I recognize the fact that I wouldn't be the same person I am today if I hadn't gone through all that. That's important. Because I like where I am today, and wouldn't be there if I had never been involved with Andrew.''

Erik also takes himself less seriously. ''I'm more relaxed. Things don't have to happen right away, or be explained right away. I'm much more patient. I stay informed about things. I'm not afraid to talk with other people about issues in my life, even if something's not going right. I've been involved in several short-term relationships since the breakup.'' He chuckles. ''Once I'm with a guy for several months, I tend to be afraid to talk about the relationship. I'm afraid I'll jinx it.'' Erik sighs. ''But it's not a bad thing if they don't stay for the long haul. I tell myself that's as far as that particular relationship was supposed to go. I'm not hard on myself if it doesn't go any further than that. I'm not hard on the guy either. If I ran into anyone I've been involved with, I could easily invite him for coffee and be comfortable with him.''

Filtering

Before we begin the process of healing, we must be capable of recognizing those qualities about ourselves we want to keep on display in our ''trophy case,'' where everyone can see, and those traits we'd rather place in the ''junk drawer,'' where our dirty little secrets remain. In ''The Trophy Case,'' indicate the positive traits you want to keep—those things that make you feel good about yourself and make others consider you a desirable friend. In ''The Junk Drawer,'' jot down the negative traits of your personality—those things you wish you could get rid of. Then, when you can think of no others, move on to the next step.

The Trophy Case

The Junk Drawer

Now that you've placed the undesirable traits in the "Junk Drawer," close it. Try to access only those qualities you admire about yourself—those you've placed in the Trophy Case. When you become aware of a junk trait creeping into your day-to-day life, shove the drawer closed again, and take down one of the trophies you've earned. Those are the hard-earned prizes of your personality that draw people close to you.

Managing Self-Esteem

The following activity allows you to determine how good you feel about yourself. If you respond honestly to each statement, you'll wind up with a score that accurately reflects your level of self-esteem. Use the items below as responses to each self-esteem assessment statement.

3—I feel strongly that this statement is true.
2—I feel this statement is often or moderately true of me.
1—I feel this statement is infrequently true of me.
0—I feel this statement is never true of me.

1. Dressed in my finest clothing, I am handsome and desirable.
2. Others seek me out for conversation.
3. Stark naked, my body is sexy and appealing.
4. I know a lot about a wide variety of subjects.
5. I have many qualities that another man would find appealing.
6. In public, I feel confident and self-assured.
7. Learning new things is very important to me.
8. Finding employment doesn't bother me. I can always find another job easily.
9. When people talk about me, they say mostly positive or complimentary things.
10. When I'm alone, I easily find something that occupies my mind.
11. I find other people very interesting, and love to hear what makes them tick.

12. I'm a very intelligent guy.
13. I feel strongly that people close to me love me.
14. The quality of my work makes me proud.
15. I wake up feeling energized.
16. I can laugh at myself very easily.
17. People are genuinely interested in what I have to say.
18. I see something good in everyone I meet.
19. Social interaction is easy for me.
20. I possess strong and well-defined moral values.

1.	5.	9.	13.	17.
2.	6.	10.	14.	18.
3.	7.	11.	15.	19.
4.	8.	12.	16.	20.
Sum 1–4:	Sum 5–8:	Sum 9–12:	Sum 13–16:	Sum 17–20:

Now, add the numbers in each column and place the sum in the empty block beneath the columns.

Add those five numbers in the bottom horizontal row, and place the answer here:

What the Responses Mean

A score of 40 or higher means that your self-esteem is in pretty good shape. You're moving on toward recovery.

A score between 25 and 40 indicates that while you don't consider yourself hopeless, you do have some room for growth. Before retiring each evening, read the entries in your trophy case until you *believe* them.

A score below 25 means that your self-esteem has been considerably damaged as a result of breaking up. But just think. With this room for improvement, you'll be able to take advantage of many opportunities to change your outlook.

CHAPTER FIVE

•••••••••••••••••••••

Remembering Our History Without Repeating It

Perceptual Shifts

We awaken to an ordinary day. We gravitate to that part of the house receiving most of the morning sun. We wonder what steps can be taken to enhance the qualities of the house. We surf the television channels in search of Bob Vila, but he's not to be found. Not this morning. He would know what to do. He would know how to capture those energizing solar rays—which part of the house to open up to make it more welcoming.

As we flip through the newspaper, we drink our traditional morning beverage. The same stale issues dominate today's news as well. Still, we read as though half-expecting a test on current events later in the day. The force-fed reading causes the word *vacuous* to come to mind. We haven't thought of that word, or a synonym, lately. At least, not since applying it to our lives upon breaking up.

The day progresses. We think of our old lover only fifty times in two hours. We smile at the gradually improving record, though we can't quite shake the low-grade anxiety accompanying our thoughts about him. We have to admit, happily, that our depression has a lighter touch these days. We've been told—by a therapist or a friend; sometimes, it's hard to tell the difference— that we're traveling through an emotional evolution, a gradual shifting in the way we experience our lives. Glibly, we say we're glad it's a shift, rather than an erosion. In fact, we may have experienced a perceptual shift a while ago, when reviewing a report our supervisor expects on his desk in less than an hour.

What we felt was like a blow to the back of the head, more violent than a eureka response. Then, a calmness grew out of the realization—calmness, satisfaction, and assurance. Because of what we've just experienced, our lives will never be quite the same. We won't *feel* life in quite the same way.

Usually, we experience these mystical moments without much effort. Effort at mental and emotional changes usually encounters resistance. As an example, a parent attempts to micromanage a child's life. The child simply rebels. We have become that particular child now, resisting restraints because restraints prohibit growth. A mind in search of itself is like that child. We want to allow his freedom, even if that allowance means the child must endure pain. We accept mistakes and embarrassments. An occasional faux pas has seldom killed anyone. We try to be forgiving of ourselves because we can, at least, see our goal clearly. We want to be over it—to heal the wounds, to stop the tears—to *deal* with it. For so long, our mind has been searching for itself. Now it has become a mind finding itself. It doesn't even take a close reading of Carlos Castaneda to figure that eventually, we have to *let it go*.

If we find ourselves finally slipping away from that ubiquitous relationship, it's because we're committed to putting some distance between ourselves and the pain. Forgetting will never be an option, but a perceptual shift reveals that we possess the power to turn negatives into positives. Maybe we've been wearing ashes and sackcloth for far too long. They're a lousy fashion statement anyhow; might as well break out of the guilt, and make a copy of the key to our souls, if not our hearts.

But now, revisiting the relationship is even more important, while our perception seems to be shifting more frequently. We're able to get a handle on what went wrong, perceive our mistakes in hindsight, and resolve never to repeat them. We have to take another look if we expect the wound to leave nothing more than a faint scar. If we want to reclaim equilibrium, we have to face the ex once more, stare into his face, knowing quite well that we are simultaneously looking at ourselves. In some ways, this second (or third, or fourth) look may be even harder because the healing we've already experienced is so tenuous. Just one look, and we might think all that hard work we've done on ourselves is shot to hell, but it's a look we have to take. Otherwise, our ex-partner will intrude on our lives somewhat later. It's necessary to confront the ex *now*. We know it must be done because the musical, *South Pacific*, mandated it. Rogers and Hammerstein don't lie when they advise us to "wash that man right out of our hair." Even if we want to maintain a friendship, we must scrub away residual feelings that sealed what we once had, but can have no more.

If we harbor ill-will toward our ex, we move ourselves farther from the possibility of regaining mental health. Essentially, good mental health means having the capacity to love and relate to others, the ability to work productively and the willingness to behave in a way that yields personal satisfaction while not encroaching on the rights of others. If we're still hung up on a death wish toward our ex, we erect substantial road blocks to emotional well-being. Harboring negative feelings is an easier task because we understand the negatives so much better. Positive feelings defy explanation and logic. If we allow ourselves the journey out of negativity and toward affirmation of both our lives and his, we become capable of confronting our loss and the grief accompanying it.

Many of us recall from psychology classes the research of Elisabeth Kübler-Ross on dying and bereavement. The same five stages of mourning a loved one's death occur when a long-term love relationship ends. The process isn't fast or easy; in fact, the pain, anxiety, and frustration of the process often hinder us from fully letting go of the ex. In the final analysis of what our relationship has meant, we experience the stages of grief more fully than when we first decided to call it quits. Why? Because, by now, reality has set in—what we perceived as possessing the capacity for everlastingness has indeed ended.

When our relationship ended, we probably entered a stage of denial. Unless we've already worked hard on ourselves, we may still be trapped in that stage.

Oh, sure, he'll come to his senses, we're likely to believe. *He just needs a little time and space to be himself.*

When we finally realize that he's probably never going to come to his senses, we enter a healthier stage of anger. *That son-of-a-bitch*, we're likely to feel/say/believe. *After all the years of my life I've given to him, he treats me this way?*

From that sentiment, we entertain the most refreshing possibilities of revenge. Before rigor mortis sets in, we look anew at the relationship. Perhaps we actually confronted the ex-partner, in an attempt to negotiate a reconciliation. That's the stage Kübler-Ross calls "bargaining."

C'mon, we may say, *let's work on the problems. I've got a therapist lined up who specializes in gay couples counseling.*

An insidious part of the bargaining phase occurs when we *express* willingness to make concessions that we know we aren't capable of keeping. If *you come back to me, I'm willing to let you see as many men as you like. If you come back, I'll pay all the household expenses. You won't even have to buy any groceries.*

When bargaining doesn't work—except to dehumanize and humiliate us—then depression ensues. Depression is the destructive storm before the rainbow. After finding ways to alleviate depression, we accept the end of our relationship. Finally, we are ready to get on with our lives.

A month after Robert and I said goodbye, Brock, my close friend of twenty years, was diagnosed with pancreatic cancer. Ten years older than I, Brock was a closeted gay man who divulged his orientation only to the few gay and lesbian acquaintances in his life. Coming out to straight people was, in his mind, tantamount to acknowledging a sex life that wasn't their business. Brock told me how he felt about his homosexuality as he lay in his hospital bed. I was shocked and angry. I couldn't imagine any self-respecting gay man relegating his orientation to the level of his "sex life." But because of Brock's rapid physical deterioration, I kept my objections to myself. I pitied my friend who was so fearful of discovery that he had never established a long-term relationship with another man. Now he was going to die having never experienced that joy.

Part of the reason that I plunged into denial about Brock's imminent death was that he and I had discussed ways to bring him out of the closet following his hospitalization. Brock was scared (and so was I). He pledged that if God allowed him to recover, he would never again live in fear. I was scared for quite another reason—a selfish one. Brock was my biggest ally after my split with Robert. He would patiently listen to my pain. Although he could hardly speak from experience, he was capable of giving sensible advice whenever I requested it. Brock's dying was a double-edged sword. On one hand, my role as his principal caretaker kept my mind and my heart from obsessing about breaking up with Robert. On the other, dealing with my feelings about his terminal illness made me recognize how out of control of my own life I had become. Additionally, I was dating a man whose mother had died just four years earlier of lung cancer. Possibly, my only connection to sanity was a weekly appointment with my therapist who, once Brock's illness yielded a prognosis, allotted two hours per session rather than one.

Just two hours after Robert pulled out of the driveway, a U-Haul trailer attached to his Jeep, I drove the five short miles to Brock's house. Neither of us had any inkling of the horrors the next six months would bring. All I knew was my life was in shambles, and Brock was empathic enough to feel my pain. The image of the trailer ambling out of the driveway kept replaying in my mind, like a crazy scene from a Sartre play. I kept thinking of a line from *No Exit*. Finally, I understood what it meant.

"Hell," Sartre wrote, "is other people."

Or more specifically to the point: *Hell is Robert—leaving me.*

Brock was just what I needed. His backyard was beautifully arrayed with numerous varieties of flowers and shrubs, a vegetable garden in the back and meandering paths through all the foliage. The scampering squirrels and chattering birds gave the yard a Disneyesque appeal. How could anyone not feel a sense of comfort here?

Graciously, Brock brought me a fresh cup of coffee and sat beside me on the Charleston park bench. In his gentle, soothing voice, he pointed out the varieties of plants and flowers in his yard, and disclosed what he planned to grow in his vegetable garden. (While his veggies grew lush and plentiful, the birds benefited most. While they feasted, Brock's body was nourished by liquids funneled into his frail body through tubes.) At first, I was impatient at what I interpreted as his callous disregard of my pain. In short order, however, I understood Brock's purpose. He was comforting me in the best way he knew how—to help me understand my connection to nature, and its healing capacity. For a while, I visited Brock almost daily, helping him keep his yard manicured, taking the edge off what I later realized was his incredible loneliness. Guiltily, I thought of my fifteen years with Robert. Most of them were happy years. We had a history. We had memories. Much of who we were could be attributed to our lives together. And here I was, in Brock's gorgeous yard, feeling sorry for myself when it was obvious that Brock would have given *anything* to share his life with a man he loved. Despite Brock's closeted status, I admired his romantic instincts. Part of my recovery encompassed a dedicated effort to convince Brock that there was someone "out there"—that huge, nebulous space of hope—for him, but he had to take the initiative for the search. Constantly, I reminded him of all the admirable qualities he possessed—tried to convince him of his selfishness in remaining cloistered in his beautiful but lonely yard.

As we began to make some progress, the blow came. Quite suddenly, Brock suffered severe stomach pains whenever he ate—so severe that he skipped an entire day of eating from time to time. Finally, his neighbors and I convinced him to make an appointment with his physician, who referred him to a gastroenterologist, who referred him to an oncologist. His life became a series of journeys from doctor to doctor. He spent more nights in hospital beds than he did in his own. He developed abnormally close relationships with medical personnel; at times, he seemed more interested in them than in family and friends. Later, he came to know other cancer patients well. Toward the end, Brock greeted me with the news of another cancer patient's death each time I came to visit.

Just three weeks before Brock took his last breath, he instructed me to pull my chair close to his hospital bed.

"We have to talk about some things," he said. "I'm counting on you to hang in there after I'm gone."

I scowled dismissively. "Don't talk like that, Brock."

"Look, Dann, the doctors have already told me that I need to make preparations," he explained in a voice that sounded slightly annoyed, yet slightly relieved. "Things don't look good. You have to be ready."

I nodded. But I couldn't maintain eye contact. Instead, my eyes wandered to the television screen and a rerun of *Frasier.*

Minutes passed in silence. Discomfited, I looked again at Brock. He smiled gently. "I'm not afraid, y'know."

I swallowed hard. "Of what?"

"Of dying," he replied. "I'm ready whenever my time comes."

Brock's will stipulated that no funeral service would be conducted, but that didn't keep me from reflection. I remembered the trip home from my last hospital visit before his death, when I was struck by the unfairness of it all. Driving along the Interstate, I burst into tears.

"It's just not fair! It's not fucking fair!" I shouted into the windshield.

I had lost a very dear, generous, kind friend. My grief was logical. I mourned what his death had taken from me, but felt grateful for what I had learned from him about relationships—about being human. Somehow, surviving Brock's death—dealing with his illness—allowed me to regard the end of my partnership with Robert with renewed strength. Robert and I had broken up. But I was still alive.

But what of those men who must surrender their long-term partners to death? Perhaps we have something to learn from them, not only about loss, but also about living. Perhaps they can bring a perspective to breaking up not possible for those of us who lose our partners to circumstances, or to another man.

With those possibilities, Bud Robbins and Michael Drennan tell us their stories.

Cherished—and Maintained

Bud chatted casually on the phone one Sunday afternoon from his Russian River home in California. At seventy-one, he is more alert and conversant than many men half his age. He's eager to tell about his life with the man with whom he spent thirty-three years.

"At the time we met, I was teaching on the Southshore of Long Island, New York," he says. "Frequently, when I finished grading papers, I would go to a bar located close to the school where I was working. One day, while I was waiting for my drink, someone put a cold glass against my neck. I turned around to look into the face of a very handsome man."

According to Bud, the bartender knew the scoop on everyone

who patronized his bar. However, he didn't know much about this man, who came in very rarely. It was up to Bud to fill in the gaps. "What bubbles up to my mind, he was Irish," Bud continues. "I have always liked Irish men. He had auburn hair, and was clever and witty. He was very attractive, and hirsute, which is important to me, and very masculine. He was a happy, friendly man. At the time, he was dating women, which I found appealing, because I was not looking for a relationship. I was about twenty-eight at the time we met. He was between jobs. Before, he had been working for a supplier to NASA in a situation where he had to be fairly closeted because he was in a high-security position."

But Joe had decided to take some time off, and was heading to Florida for a vacation. "Some of my family lived there," Bud says. "I gave him the phone number of my sister, in case he wanted to meet women. I also gave him the phone numbers of several gay friends, in case he wanted to meet men. During a phone conversation from Florida, he told me he was enjoying the good weather, but was looking forward to seeing me when he returned. And that's how everything began with us."

Bud wasted no time introducing Joe to his relatives. "Joe and my father got along very well," he explains. "Joe was a likable person. My father said he was one of the nicest friends that I had. I told him that I was a pretty nice guy, too, and that all my friends were nice people. As you can probably surmise, my father and I didn't have a very close relationship."

Bud came out to his parents when he was in high school. "My marks had been slipping, so we had a heart-to-heart chat," he says. "I told them that something wasn't right about me. I was aware of having feelings for male friends, while realizing those feelings were not reciprocal. I joined the Navy, thinking that I would be put right. At the same time, my mother hoped that I would get married, and provide grandchildren for her. Dad was disappointed that I was a sissy. Joe, on the other hand, was never regarded negatively by my father. In fact, they even played golf together. Hell, I don't know of anyone who didn't appreciate Joe's charm."

Around 1960, Bud and Joe were financially able to purchase a house in San Francisco, regarded then as the Great Gay Mecca. A couple of years later, they purchased a summer home on the Russian River. After the two men moved in together, Bud recognized a trait of Joe's that would prove to be a problem. "He was much more closeted than I, and much more fearful of being openly gay," he explains. "I couldn't give a shit about that—about what people thought and said. I had made up my mind about that issue when I moved west. The first Christmas in our new home in the city, we threw a party for gay friends. We hosted a separate party for our straight friends."

Bud told Joe the idea of two parties was ridiculous. "If people are going to like us, they will like us for who we are. I don't want to go through this charade again."

Soon, Bud was out at the school where he taught. "You see, an art teacher—a colleague of mine—came over to help me patch up some holes and repair a few rough edges while we remodeled our house. Shortly after, I was no longer introduced to single female teachers. Each time the school sponsored social events, I was told to bring Joe along. Everybody knew that I was gay, and it made a very easy relationship with me. Some teachers were opposed, of course, but I was a good teacher, and people either accepted me or left me alone. No one caused any trouble for me."

As a result of Bud's openness, the Bay Area Network of Gay and Lesbian Educators (BANGLE) used him as an example of an "out" gay teacher. "Some members would speak of me in awe as though I were among the first teachers who ever came out," he says. "I was never known as 'the gay teacher,' but my partnership with Joe was acknowledged. Joe and I had a monogamous relationship for many long, intense years—almost twenty-five, I would say. We didn't see anyone else. He was still very charming with women, but he didn't date them anymore."

However, Bud has a difficult time applying the word "marriage" to their relationship. "Friends of ours asked us if we had an open 'marriage,' " he says. "We didn't consider what we had a marriage at all. Our relationship was something very good that happened with us. We never had a commitment ceremony, or any kind of formal acknowledgement. Our families, however, became very good friends. Strangely enough, one of his nieces and one of mine both grew up to be fairly decent professional artists."

Despite the discomfort of applying traditional terminology to their partnership, Bud says that "both of us appreciated the twosomeness of our relationship. Joe always remained much more closeted and conservative than I. He would always caution me to be careful of my openness because of my profession. We both felt relief when the relationship was no longer monogamous. I think, after twenty-five years, our sex life had diminished and we weren't very physical anymore. I had become interested in community theatre, and he spent more and more time with Asian people. There was nothing secretive about our situations. He brought young Asian men to the house. Often, they would cook for both of us. I felt strangely uncomfortable about that. Then, as Joe became more and more immersed into Asian culture, he began to study Buddhism. As a result, we grew apart, although socially we remained together. We always went together as a couple to the River. But we began to look for others for physical relationships."

However, neither man was at all interested in falling in love. "What we had established for ourselves was so comfortable," he explains. "It worked so comfortably, our partnership, that I was never expecting to fall in love again. It wasn't something I wanted. Finally, I went back to straight men for sexual intimacy—to make sure I would not have emotional entanglements. Joe, on the other hand, became a bit promiscuous, and had many Asian men coming and going. He was never looking for an affair. He simply liked hairless and smooth younger men who often seemed to gravitate toward him. I liked hairy chests—the more hirsute the better. I never looked to disrupt our relationship by finding someone else to live with. And it never happened."

In fact, neither man regarded their loss of sexual interest as an indication of trouble in their relationship. "It just happened. We moved into separate bedrooms. After twenty-five years, we saw this as part of the evolution of our relationship."

Then, when Joe got sick, everything happened incredibly fast. "No one appreciated how sick he was," says Bud. "Not even me. I didn't know his doctor. I knew nothing about his medical personnel. At one point, the head nurse came into Joe's hospital room. My niece, Judi, was there with me."

The nurse looked at them with concern. "I think we need a

reality check with Joe," she said, then turned to Joe. "Joe? Can you tell me where you are now, dear?"

"Paris," he replied.

"I knew he was joking," Bud continues, "although his nurse thought he was serious."

In the meantime, Joe's family came to visit. Everyone sat around the men's living room, chatting about old times. Then, one evening, the head nurse called, and told Bud to come to the hospital. "He expired—just like that," Bud says sadly. "It was shocking to me. Constance stepped in, and was very efficient, as lesbians often are, and contacted the Veterans Administration. She made other arrangements, as well. I was able to grieve because Joe's family took care of everything. We had a party to commemorate Joe's memory."

At the party, Joe's sister, a mother superior from New York, told Bud: "You know, the whole family knew of the love you and Joe had for each other."

Bud chokes up for just a moment. "I always felt very welcome in that family."

After Joe's death, Bud worried about money. "After all, I was retired, and living on a pension," he explains. "My finances were of urgency to me. I couldn't maintain both the house in the city, and the place on the River. I just knew I'd have to put the Russian River home up for sale."

Bud didn't want to forfeit either house, but especially not the Russian River house. After all, he and Joe had bought it as partners. "It had meant so much to us," he says. "I told Judi that I would have to get rid of the River house."

"Let me talk to Steve [her husband]," she said.

"They decided to purchase it," Bud relates happily. "In fact, they paid fair market value, and gave a significant amount to Joe's niece. It's no longer a cabin. It's very elegant now. They created two new bedrooms and a bath."

After the remodeling, they led Bud into one of the new rooms. "This is your room," they said. "In fact, the whole cabin is yours. The only thing that isn't yours is the bills."

"It just worked out like a miracle," says Bud.

Once financial matters were settled, Bud began to examine his life, and his relationship with Joe. He needed to understand what both had meant. "People wondered if I had AIDS," he says. "They thought for sure Joe had it, but I don't know. The death certificate says he died from pneumonia. So, I think he *may* have had it. However, I'm not infected. Maybe being so close to death was meant to make me realize my ultimate mortality. I mean, I never expected to see seventy, and here I am at seventy-one."

So now, what is the focus of Bud's life without Joe? "My focus is three-pronged," he explains. "First, I intend to see the ban in the military lifted. I also want to see all schools made safe for gay and lesbian students and teachers. The issue of aging is also of interest to me—particularly those of our community whose families have rejected them. I am also active with the Alexander Hamilton Post of the American Legion—gay and lesbian veterans. Presently, we're suing the Legion for fifty million dollars for discrimination."

As an illustration of the significance of Bud's life in his golden years, he relates a particularly moving incident. "I was marching in a gay pride parade, wearing my Legionnaire's cap," he says. "A cluster of eighth-grade girls—all former students—came out from the sidewalk and hugged me. They told me they were proud of me. I perceive that my life is special and gifted. It was very touching, this incident at the parade."

Even earlier, Bud received, via the postal service, a photo of a very handsome man in cap and gown who identified himself as a former student. "I just graduated from Stanford with honors in two areas," he wrote. "I attribute my success to my eighth-grade year with you."

Bud's satisfying relationship with Joe contributed to his deep sense of fulfillment in his life now. "I think openness and honesty are the best foundations on which to base a relationship," he explains. "There are times when you're going to have ardent disagreements, but you maintain a sense of commitment—an innate sense that the two of you work together on problems. You understand, the two of you, that the relationship needs to be cherished and maintained. If *that* is the agreement between you, then the other things can be shaped and maintained." Bud sighs. "But I really don't like to give advice. Joe and I occasionally got angry with each other, but we cherished each other so very much. My mother once said, 'Your father and I never went to bed angry.'

Joe and I always talked things through so that, like my parents, we didn't go to bed angry either."

Bud and Joe also respected each other a great deal. "We reached a high status in our professions. We were very proud of each other. That helped a lot, too."

Although he misses Joe, Bud no longer grieves. "I'm certainly glad we had all that time together," he says. "I don't think I feel a sense of loss now. Rather, I feel an appreciation for what we had. I'm not sure what would have happened had we continued. I felt a sense of closure. We had over thirty-three years of each other's lives. We both grew and the mutual pride was beneficial. We cultivated such a marvelous wealth of friends, both straight and gay. I don't know why I deserved all that, but I have it. And I'm grateful."

Recently, several straight friends asked Bud to have dinner with them. For a moment, he hesitated.

"That's the anniversary of Joe's death," he told them, out of the blue.

"I asked myself: Why did I have to mention that? Of what relevance is it? I just have October twenty-fourth in my mind as an important date. But I needn't have chastised myself. My friends loved Joe, too, and as we all age, most of us have lost intimate partners along the way. But we have to keep active. We must have interest in living. Life moves on. If we sit home and grieve, we're not getting anywhere."

Loving the Questions Themselves

Although Freddie and Michael were partners only for the last seven years of Freddie's life, they were platonic friends for the previous twenty. "And for those twenty-seven years of Freddie's life, I want to honor his memory," says Michael.

Their happy life together changed dramatically in September 1990, shortly after buying their new home. "I don't understand why I don't have much energy anymore," Freddie told Michael.

"I thought he was doing so much that he was wearing himself out," Michael explains. "I kept telling him to pace himself because he was working two jobs. He was also doing volunteer work, and running a private business out of our home. Whenever people asked for help, he obliged. By the time I got home from work, he'd be asleep. Finally, I convinced him to have a physical.

"On my way home," Michael continues, "I had a feeling something was wrong. I saw his truck in the driveway. He had left the doors open. The truck was parked strangely. He was standing in the kitchen. His eyes told me that something had happened."

On Halloween 1991, Freddie gave Michael the bad news. He was HIV-positive.

Their relationship changed immediately. "I became this gung-ho, we're gonna fight this, we will beat this type of person," Michael says in his crisp Australian accent. "Freddie went through all the stages of anger, frustration, denial, and eventually, acceptance. Finally, he had a peace about it all that I'm still working on. I haven't reached the peace that he did. I've lost so many friends, you see. I could not show him that. I was the cheerleader. I wanted him to keep fighting. He humored me through all that."

The day after Freddie died, his family became extremely hostile. Before, Freddie's family had seemed quietly accepting of their relationship. Soon, he would discover their silence had been misinterpreted. "Admittedly, they didn't spend a lot of time with him," Michael says. "Being Latino, he had a tremendous sense of duty to his family. They all knew that he was gay, though he had never discussed his homosexuality with them. The day after he died, they came by to loot my home. If it had not been for my neighbors, they would have succeeded.

"It was difficult, and so expected," Michael continues. "It was bad enough dealing with Freddie not being here, yet having to watch out for hostility that could break out any moment."

What about Michael's family? Could he count on them for support when Freddie died? "My parents and I dealt with my being gay when I was a teenager. When I was in high school, they came home and walked into my room, where they caught me with one of my classmates. Of course, they worried that I would be hurt. They were concerned that my life would be a tough one. But they were never judgmental. In fact, about two weeks later, they started making jokes about the 'interesting position' in which they found me. Dad even said it looked like I was hurting the boy."

All of Michael's family lives in Australia. When Freddie died, he wrote to his brothers and sisters. "They didn't even answer my letters," he says.

From Michael's friends, he has wonderful support. "After Freddie died, I felt quite isolated. Four weeks after he died, my back collapsed. They rallied around me just wonderfully."

Still, the finality of death struck Michael hard. "It's horrible knowing I will never see him again," he says. "With the other partners in my life, well, they are a part of my life now. But Freddie and I were going to grow old together. We would still be together. I won't ever see him again, and that's so hard to take."

How has Michael dealt with the loss? "I'm still dealing with it," he admits. "I think, because I ended up in hospital so soon after he died—I had two back surgeries—I had to put aside a lot of feelings about his leaving and deal with the physical pain. I had to learn how to walk again. At first, it was hard, living in the same house. I couldn't move out, because I was in a body cast. It's easier now. But it's important to know that Freddie died in our room. I was holding him when it happened. The house is full of him. Everything of his is around the place. His workplace is still in the garage. Once I finish college, I may be able to move into the city. I don't know."

Despite the intensity of his loss, Michael is ready for another relationship. "I'm ready, but I'm really awkward about dating, and about meeting people, and being intimate with someone else. I went to Washington for the quilt [the AIDS quilt]. The neighbors wanted to construct a piece for Freddie. I went to see it last October. I thought it would be nice closure."

While in DC, Michael met a "wonderful man from Montreal. We hit it off. That was my first sexual experience with someone else since Freddie died. I just opened up."

"It's been a while since you were able to do that, hasn't it?" the man asked.

"You have to realize that, after losing the man you loved for so many years, intimacy with another man will open up all kinds of things in your heart," Michael explains sadly. "I'm ready to be held again—to do that again. But I'm just so awkward about meeting people. When I move to San Francisco, things might be easier."

Michael takes relationships very seriously. "I don't entertain the idea that there are thousands of people out there, just waiting for me. Finding a partner won't be easy," he explains. "I'm very focused now when I look at people. Everything about people is important to me now. I try to understand them. The guy from Montreal and I talk via e-mail every day. He's been HIV-positive for fourteen years. He's just now having some health problems. He doesn't want to move to the States, and I don't want to live in Canada. However, if we were living in the same town, something would happen. We are that close."

While Michael's HIV status is negative, another man's positive status would not eliminate him as a potential partner. "What is more important right now to me is loving someone, and being loved in return. Whatever length of time it lasts. That is what I miss so much about Freddie."

Michael thinks the most important component of a relationship is good communication. "I cannot stress that enough," he says emphatically. "Honesty of feelings, of needs—you need to find time to talk to one another. You need to get over the thought that by saying something honestly, you might end the relationship. It's best to take that risk rather than finding out in a much more painful way. Three of my relationships ended because of a lack of honesty on my partner's part."

Michael feels he has much to offer now. "I've matured a lot," he says. "I've become more passionate—more physical with people. In the past, I tended to have a Victorian attitude toward touching people. I'm a lot warmer now. I also have an incredible sexual passion built up in me. I have an appreciation for a relationship and for what it can do—for what it can do for both men, and for how enriching it can be. I actually look forward to it happening."

Meanwhile, Michael cherishes a quote from poet Rainer Rilke—"something that has been helpful, along with going back to college at my age. It's a marvelous experience." The quote resonates with the mystery of love and life. Michael, whose beloved Freddie is buried on the property they jointly owned, reads in his quiet, refined voice. "I beg you to have patience with everything unresolved in your heart, and to try to love the questions themselves, as if they were locked rooms, or books written in a very foreign language."

The comforting sentiment of the poem has encouraged Michael.

"Could you leave him behind?" someone asked him. "His ashes are here. Could you really leave?"

"Yes, I could," Michael says. "This is his home. This is where he should be. Finally, I'm able to leave him behind, but it has taken me a long, long time. But I *have* been able to let go of him. Still, I would love to see his smiling face come through that door."

Looking Back

Tragic circumstances forced Michael and Bud to assess their lives. The termination of relationships will force us, like them, to examine our history, laugh at parts of it, cry at others—but all the time learning from our stories. History is nothing more than biography. It is our biography that we must scrutinize to determine what works in our lives, and what doesn't, and proceed to make essential changes. The unexamined life, Socrates said, is a life not worth living.

After Michael and Bud passed the initial stages of the grief process, they reviewed their own biographies—their own histories—and made some important observations about themselves, their personalities, standards, and decisions. They understood how their partnerships not only influenced their identities, but also synthesized their individuality—their differentiation—with the individuality of their partners. In a way, their reflection on their partners' lives permitted them to grow even more as gay men, even to regard life more poetically. Additionally, they grew more poignantly aware of their capacities to love and of what they wanted to take from life as they entered a new personal era. They effectively responded to one of life's greatest paradoxes. From any great loss, we achieve the freedom for great growth, as well.

Theirs is a recognition we want for ourselves. No matter how painful our separation has been, we should open ourselves to the lessons our history has to teach us. While living with him, we probably devoted little thought to how we were growing, or in what direction. Our energies were focused on preserving our happiness as a couple. Perhaps we even grew to worship the status quo. Our overriding goal may have been to clock in those forty hours to maintain the lifestyle we found so comfortable, and to which our close friends had grown so accustomed. As long as civility characterized our relationship, why worry about passion? Why worry, indeed! Life had become so easy. We lost our knack for introspection. It took the slamming door, the growling sound of a moving van, and the desolation of a lonely house to demand attention. *Attention must be paid*, Willie Loman's wife shouts to her sons in *Death of a Salesman*. It is with a similar sense of urgency and desperation that we regard our own histories now. To deny attention to our lives imposes a sentence to live according to the earlier patterns. Change, no matter the discomfort, is essential.

So we see, in looking back, the mistakes we made, the strengths we cultivated, even our neuroses. We find this retrospective surprisingly free of hostility. Perhaps resentment is not completely licked, but we have moved somewhat closer to forgiveness. When examining ourselves, we are able to take a loving look. We step outside ourselves, take ourselves by the hand, and travel through our history, pointing out the ways we fumbled. We have to expect a little regret every now and then, seeing as we do truths that should have been seen before. Then, if we had a clearer eye, our ex-partner might be here, next to us, now. But we are doing something right. The process of healing seems on course. While looking with a touch of sadness at what we relinquished, we can gladly anticipate our future gains.

The future, we know, has a way of dissolving into the past. We have to make some decisions now, take some time for healing, before time speeds up again. Did jealousy impair the easy trust of our relationship? Was his flirtatiousness designed to activate our jealous nature? Did we regard him as a subordinate, always barking orders or offering criticisms for his life's improvements? Was he a Type A to our Type B, and was neither of us willing to make any concessions to our intimacy? Were we cold fish, keeping our hands always to ourselves when we knew he craved hugs and kisses?

What can we do to change? It is a question we have to ask ourselves along with an equally important query. How do we avoid the same mistakes in the future? No longer can we use the excuse that because Daddy was a macho man, we never learned that real men hug. We're adults now. Partners tend to have precious little patience with guys who, at 40, are still using their lousy childhood to justify their pathologies. Nor can we attribute our insecurities to a mother, perpetually dissatisfied with her marriage, who threatened to leave hubby and all the children for an exotic escapade. We realize we're on our own now, baby. If we need to relive past traumas, or even return to the womb, the aftermath of our breakup is probably a good time. When we meet that new man—and we will; it's only a matter of time—we don't want to realize, after several months of passionate, intense involvement, that we're slipping into a macabre journey down memory lane, and we're taking the new beau along for the ride.

Still, pathologies, those embarrassing artifacts left from childhood, can hardly be predicted. Who wants to spend forever whining about the fabulous guy who got away? The longer our previous partnership, the longer it'll take to recover. Some say we'll never *fully* recover. But aggressive remediation is the key to avoid slopping around in an alphabet soup of neuroses. History always takes bizarre twists. Our personal histories are no different. The way we (try to) avoid the past's mistakes is exposure. We tell the stories, then hope humanity is smart enough to avoid repetition. What happens when we fail to listen? Second verse, same as the first.

We should follow the same pattern with our personal histories. No one wants to pull skeletons out of the closet in the presence of a man we're trying to impress, win, or woo. As intimacy grows, sure, we'll tell each other the juicy stories, while creating even more. But now is not the time.

However, we have to tell someone. We have to get the monkey off our back, the chip off our shoulder, the thumb out of our butt. The clouds and the scowl have to go. It's time for an attitude adjustment.

And that's what friends are for.

Relationship Assessment Quotient (RAQ)

Now, you can see in black and white the quality of your former relationship. How compatible were you and your ex? Had you established the kind of relationship where happiness could grow?

Rank each statement with a number from the list below. Place each number in the Values Chart below the list of statements. Be honest as you regard your former relationship when you first realized it was in trouble.

4—Absolutely! All the time!
3—Mostly I felt this was true.
2—This is how it was frequently.
1—This is how it sometimes seemed.
0—This is never how it was.

1. My partner and I avoided shouting at each other when we argued.
2. When we disagreed about plans, we usually ended up in an argument.
3. We talked openly of our sexual needs and desires.
4. My ex-partner often said that I didn't communicate well.
5. In public, my ex-partner and I were able to show affection to each other easily.
6. I tended to smother my ex-partner because of my extreme jealousy.
7. I avoided criticizing my partner behind his back.
8. I was willing to tell lies, no matter how large or how small, in order to avoid arguments.
9. If we discovered we could not meet appointments with each other, we always called to let each other know.
10. When we saw another man to whom we were attracted, we frequently pointed him out to one another.

11. Both of us felt we were evenly matched intellectually.
12. At some point in our relationship, I discovered that I did not fit the typical profile of the man to whom my ex-partner is generally attracted.
13. When we encountered problems, we discussed them rationally and calmly.
14. I was always afraid my ex-partner was cheating on me.
15. I'm sure that guests in our home felt as though my ex-partner and I loved each other.
16. I found myself concealing information from my ex-partner, beneath the ruse of protecting him from something he didn't want to know.
17. During conversations, we spoke assertively, not sarcastically.
18. My ex-partner threw away money like it was nobody's business.
19. I was quite comfortable expressing my feelings to my ex-partner.
20. I felt as though my ex-partner was either ashamed of me, or was afraid my presence would identify him as gay.

The Values Chart

1.	5.	9.	13.	17.	A.
2.	6.	10.	14.	18.	B.
3.	7.	11.	15.	19.	C.
4.	8.	12.	16.	20.	D.

Add up the numbers in the horizontal rows, then place the totals in the lettered boxes at right.

Add the numerical values for A and C, then place that sum here: (1) _____

Add the numerical values for B and D, then place that sum here: (2) _____

Now subtract the number in line 2 from the number in line

1. Please note that this number can be negative or positive. The more negative the number, the less compatible you and your ex-partner were. The more positive the number, the more compatible you were.

Put your values on the number line below. See how the reality of your relationship compares to your vision of a successful relationship.

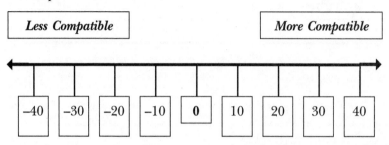

Less Compatible						More Compatible		
−40	−30	−20	−10	**0**	10	20	30	40

My Vision of a Successful Relationship

In this activity, you'll use your multicolored pencils or pens again. Below each category, you will notice a vector. The far left end of the vector corresponds to the value, "Not Important." The center of the vector corresponds to the value, "Somewhat Important." The right end of the vector—the end with the arrow—corresponds to the value, "Very Important."

Here's the way you should envision each vector:

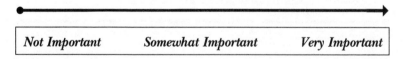

Not Important	Somewhat Important	Very Important

Use a variety of colors to indicate where your vision of a successful relationship will fall on your vectors.

Monogamy

My partner and I will have no sexual encounters outside our partnership.

Age Congruence

My partner and I should be within the same age range.

———————————————————————————▶

Intellectual Compatibility

My partner and I should have achieved an equitable level of education.

———————————————————————————▶

Income Potential

My partner should make at least the same amount of money I do, or at the very least possess the talents and abilities to demand a high salary.

———————————————————————————▶

Appearance/Build

My partner should meet my standards of attractiveness.

———————————————————————————▶

Fashion Consciousness

My partner should always dress in trendy attire. I get embarrassed by fashions that are out of style.

———————————————————————————▶

Social Status

My partner should be invited to all the "best" parties, and know all the "right" people.

———————————————————————————▶

Family Background

My partner's family either enjoys a lot of respect in the community, or treats their son with love and respect. In other words, I don't want involvement with someone who has a lot of family issues.

⬤─────────────────────────────▶

Professional Prestige

My partner should be a "mover and shaker" in his profession, and have the respect and admiration of others in his field.

⬤─────────────────────────────▶

Political Views

My partner should have the same political views as I, and be a member of the same political party.

⬤─────────────────────────────▶

Religious Views

My partner should share my belief system. In all conscience, I can't relate to a partner who adheres to a different set of religious principles.

⬤─────────────────────────────▶

Out Factor

My partner must have not only acknowledged to himself his homosexual orientation but also asserted his gayness to friends, acquaintances, and family.

⬤─────────────────────────────▶

Sexual Compatibility

Since I have recognized specifically those erotic activities I find most pleasurable, my partner must enjoy sexual activities which complement my preferences.

●————————————————————————————————▶

Now that you've graphed your honest reactions to those components of a relationship that influence your compatibility as a couple, write a paragraph of no more than five sentences which summarizes what you cherish in a loving relationship. Refer back to this description frequently so that your vision drives your actions in your daily life.

CHAPTER SIX

•••••••••••••••••••

You Got to Have Friends

Friendship Closes Its Eyes

After breaking connubial ties, we often withdraw from the most important component of our lives—our friends. In a way, it makes sense. Who wants to be surrounded by people whose lives are on track while we're caught in a tsunami of confusion? What a downer. Besides, we may be a little embarrassed by our misfortune, particularly if we delivered a feverish sales pitch to convince our friends that our relationship with a man they never liked was for keeps. Now we share the title of Fortune's Fool with poor Romeo of Verona. Our friends may have more class than to say, "I told you so." But hanging out with them feels a lot like eating crow. After all, our friends are often the first to notice when our relationship's gone awry. Maybe we can even recall, once we broke the news, our friends saying: "I saw it coming, but I wasn't comfortable saying anything."

When we silently and secretly withdraw from friends, we are guilty of second-guessing those who mean the most to us. Why would they want to hang out with a heartbroken old sod? we wonder. We're too depressed to have any fun. Of course, they'll be liberal with all kinds of advice, which we don't want to hear. They never liked us as much as they liked what's-his-name anyway, so why pretend? Besides, we don't have the energy to make the call. Even less to make the drive to their house.

Maybe there's a shred of truth to any excuse we devise for not contacting friends. We have lost the most significant connection to humanity and to our hearts. We're still licking our wounds.

To withdraw from friends only exacerbates our sense of being alone in the world. It's true that friends won't always respond to our loss the way we would prefer—or in the way we need. But friends are people we can count on.

What can we do to correct this self-destructive tendency? First of all, regardless of the noble sentiments surrounding the institution of friendship, we have to know when we need solitude and when we need companionship. When friends call during our moments of solitude, we must be honest. With grace and gratitude, we simple say that we need to be alone tonight. Better to be honest than to have a miserable time. If *we're* having a rotten time, chances are the rest of our friends are, too.

However, there will be times when we would prefer wallowing in our self-pity, but we know we should go out. The easy solution is to make excuses. The easy solution is the wrong one. Eventually, our friends will grow weary of our excuses. When we establish an unhealthy balance between solitude and socialization, we have only one choice to make: Go out! Even the most highly qualified shrink can offer little help in the area of motivation. Our only option is to force ourselves out of our chair, escape television's vast wasteland, put on our favorite clothes, and even if we can't *fully* enjoy the evening, we *can* put on a convincing performance.

What about friends who withdraw from us? Friends have many reasons for experiencing discomfort when we're around, some of which they aren't fully aware of. Difficult though it is, we have the unenviable responsibility to be sensitive to their feelings, and perhaps even try to understand their hang-ups. Maybe they don't know how to relate to us anymore. Maybe our plight is a painful reminder of the failure of a relationship in their past. Maybe they never really liked us, and only tolerated us for the partner's sake. Maybe it's simply a matter of bad timing. Our split might have occurred at the busiest time of their lives. They're afraid if they're *too* encouraging, we might cling to them like white on rice.

If we cherish our friendships, we try to determine the reasons behind the cold shoulders, then attempt to rekindle what we had before our breakup. That means doing something about which we feel the utmost discomfort. We have to open up. We have to initiate contact. Human nature leads us, when we're subjected to someone's freeze, to deal with the resulting hurt by wiping the culprit out of our lives. But human nature doesn't always provide the healthiest alternative. We might try swallowing our pride, repeating a mantra of peace a hundred times, then making contact. Although there will be an occasional exception, most friends will appreciate our reaching out to them.

Cal, an architect in Indianapolis whose relationship ended after nine years, was concerned that an old friend kept giving him the slip. "Finally, I got up the gumption to call," he relates. "I told Kenneth that I was worried, since I hadn't heard from him after leaving three messages on his machine, that I had done something to upset him. At first, he sounded very cold. He denied that I had done anything. I was tempted to hang up. He sounded as though he'd rather be whipped than talk to me, and he's never been into that scene. But I stuck it out—tried to be my charming and sensitive self, y'know? Finally, he admitted that my split with my ex-partner had shocked him. He noted that we seemed to have such a strong partnership. What happened to us made him a little shaky about a new lover he started seeing almost a year ago. Jokingly—though we both knew he was more serious than he would ever admit—he said he and his new partner were afraid I might be contagious. Maybe I would jinx their relationship. We still don't see each other often, but we talk a lot over the phone. There's never anything other than warmth in Kenneth's voice. I know we're okay now. He's just wrapped up in the trappings of being in love."

Once our partnership ends, reconnections to old friends will require some effort. To ignore the repairs that dependable relationships need will put our lives in danger of emptiness and nihilism. Breaking up brought upon us depression, loneliness, and fear. We felt like a stranger among strangers. The solid foundation of our lives began to move, shake, and collide like crust platelets during an earthquake. Friends have the capacity to stop the tremors. Reconnection to old friends requires honesty, openness, and vulnerability. If they *know* we're hurting, they will have a hard time trusting us while we pretend we've suffered no damage at all. If we equate honesty and intimacy to weakness, we try to make our friends believe that we didn't even stumble once the bastard left us. Friends won't believe that kind of nonsense. In fact, it will erode their confidence in our capacity for recovery. We return to our past friendships with honesty, integrity, and vulnerability. It takes far more bravery to admit we're hurting than to pretend we're tough guys who don't scar.

How do we establish new intimacy with old friends? We return to the fold with a full expression of our needs. We don't throw ourselves a pity party and invite all our friends. In fact, pity parties make us more miserable, more hopeless. Self-pity lowers self-esteem, and prolongs healing. Instead, we assert our needs to our friends in clear terms. For example, we may need our friends to kick us in the shins each time we allude to our ex. We know it's a tedious and boring habit. But we may need a little help to break it. "I've noticed that I keep mentioning Steve during conversations," we may say. "I need to move forward—not live in the past. I've got to get beyond this torch-carrying phase. Will you point out to me, when we're together, the times I mention him?"

For Cal, Friday nights were, without exception, reserved for him and his ex-partner to spend "quality time" together. Usually, they spent a night at the theatre, had dinner in a nice restaurant, or spent quiet evenings at home. "After we broke up, I had a hard time filling those Friday evenings with enjoyable activities," Cal explains. "When I spent them alone, I would almost go crazy. Sometimes I would break into uncontrollable tears, or get irrationally angry. Finally, I called a couple of close friends, and told them about the problem I was having. Without my having to ask—that's what wonderful friends they were—they volunteered to spend Friday nights with me. We'd take turns determining the evening's activities. Now, this has become as much a tradition for me as those evenings spent with my ex. I thought I'd never look forward to Fridays again."

As much as our good friends want to help us through our grief, their generosity has limits. Nothing taxes their good intentions more than our taking them for granted. To keep our friendships intact, we must show how much we care for our friends. We demonstrate our concern by asking about their lives, involving ourselves in their pastimes, and steering conversations toward topics to which they can relate. On the surface, these steps seem embarrassingly simple. However, in our emotional state, we may not care at all about their lives. In fact, the temporary solace we derive from interaction is often the only reason we continue seeing them. If they didn't permit our self-indulgence, we'd probably stay at home and simmer in silent suffering. Just as wearing a happy face will affect our moods positively, feigning interest in the lives of our friends will pave the way to genuine interest.

"There were times I listened to Nita rant on and on about her problems with her adolescent sons," said Donovan Cane, 37, a jeweler in Olympia, Washington, whose relationship ended after five years. "I often thought I would explode if she didn't shut up. Then I would remember how she had listened for hours as I processed my feelings after breaking up with Latrell. A couple of times, these conversations lasted into the wee hours of the morning. She never seemed to tire of me, although she had to report to work by eight o'clock. My realization of her generosity and concern made me mellow out pretty quickly. I began to pay attention to what she said about those brats of hers. Soon, I found I really cared, to the point of offering some advice based on my own adolescence. We've never been closer."

Soon, we may desire to hear what our friends think about our breakup. We might even cherish some advice. Frequently, friends are reticent to do much more than listen. Understandably, they don't want to be an influence in a decision that may increase our suffering. After all, no foolproof answers or quick-fix cures exist for the questions we are confronting now. What works for our friends might not work for us. But let's say we have a friend known for his sensitivity and insightfulness. More than anything else, we would love to hear his take on our "situation." Yet his modest nature compels him to keep the lid on his opinions. How do we draw him out?

Once again, communication is the key. First, we assure him of our respect for his opinions. In fact, we would appreciate hearing how he might deal with a particular dilemma confronting us now. Perhaps we can't shake feeling angry about the breakup. Or maybe our ex owes us some money and he's taking his precious time paying it back. Regardless of the problem, we should let our friend know that we really value his opinions. We don't want his advice. That request is both unfair and uncomfortable. No friend in his right mind wants the responsibility for our lives as well as his own. But to ask for "practical empathy" establishes an even closer bond, whether we act according to his hunches or not. We listen carefully to what he has to say, *without argument.* He tells us what *he* would do under similar circumstances. Graciously, we thank him for his feedback, saving it for closer consideration later on. Above all, we don't argue with him. Once our decision is made, we should let him know how—or whether— we used his information. If we responded according to his insights, we let him know how things turned out. If we didn't, we tell him so, with a brief explanation of why his hypothetical solution wasn't quite right for us. Usually, friends don't care all that much whether we agree with them. But they *do* like to know we're listening, and that we respect their opinions.

A sticky issue regarding the maintenance of friendships after breaking up pertains to friends we shared with our ex-partner. Frequently, these individuals feel they have to choose between two loyalties. If we've conveyed this message, we need to set the record straight. Our friends can hardly be expected to maintain a split allegiance, listening to us dish our ex, while our ex rants on and on about us. If they have been good friends to us both, it's unfair to put them in such a position. We might inform mutual friends of our desire to sustain relationships with them apart from their relationships with our ex-partner. In no way will we place them in a tug-of-war between loyalties. Once these ground rules are established, we stick to them. If we can't utter the name of you-know-who without hostility, or bursting into hysterical tears, then we restrict the topics of conversation until we can regard our ex-partner with more neutrality.

On the other hand, we face a particular danger in maintaining mutual friendships—a danger that could easily take us by surprise. If our ex-partner has dumped those friends, they may be tempted to express their distaste for him. We should consider two issues here. First of all, our friends, who probably feel a heightened sense of our ex-partner's rejection, are responding out of their own injured feelings. Second, in our present vulnerable state, we don't need to hear any forensics, no matter how eloquent, about our ex-partner's copious faults. While *we* reserve the privilege of chewing our ex a new asshole, no one else has that privilege. In fact, when a friend takes such liberty, we feel the value of our partnership has been questioned. As a result, we may even doubt its value. Nothing is more demoralizing than the suspicion that we have wasted the years we spent with our ex-partners. "While it was okay for me to talk shit about David from time to time, I didn't like hearing it from people I thought had been friends to us both," says Tony, 56, dean of curriculum at a technical college in Albuquerque, New Mexico. "I felt very uncomfortable when that happened, and doubted whether this person had ever been a true friend to either of us. I also wondered if my friend might be right—that maybe I should abandon all my efforts at sustaining a friendship with my ex. I mean, it was a constant mindfuck."

Yet those same friends—the ones we shared with our ex-partner—have a capacity not possessed by other friends and acquaintances for helping us though recovery. If we can establish an understanding that our ex-partner should never be subjected to hostile criticism (*constructive* criticism is another issue altogether), neutral friends can be wonderful sounding boards. They have a handle on what we and our ex-partner meant to one another. To the extent that we allowed them into our lives, they are also familiar with the dynamics of our relationship. Because of their familiarity, they may provide enormous support and insight in helping us come to grips with issues directly related to our broken relationship. In a sense, they shared our history. They can accompany and assist us in its exploration and interpretation.

Take Gary, for example. After twelve years, he and Jonny went their separate ways, primarily because "we just grew apart. We had lost the ability to meet each other in the middle. But don't get me wrong. Our breakup hurt as much as it would have under any other circumstances." While Jonny moved to the Midwest, Gary stayed in their Key West condo. As a result, Gwen, a mutual friend, processed the split with Gary more often than with Jonny—although she remained his friend as well. "Gwen was wonderful," relates Gary. "She had known both of us for almost ten years. When I expressed my grief to her, she understood as much as I did—sometimes it seemed she understood more." When Gary informed Gwen of Jonny's revelation that he had not received the emotional satisfaction he needed, she nodded sagely.

"She reminded me that Jonny was the 'baby' in his family, and needed more nurturing than I had been able to give. What she said made sense to me. I just wish I had thought of it before. I am the oldest of four sons in my family. I was sort of forced into a position of independence. I never considered that Jonny might have interpreted my independence as emotional distance."

In addition to reliance on "old friends," we can't discount the necessity of cultivating new friendships. Granted, the quality of depth—the psychological sense of being fully and unconditionally accepted—will take time to achieve. That's why we never relinquish old friendships. But new friends refresh us. They allow us to look at ourselves with new eyes. They don't have the insight or the prejudices that our personal history would provide. With them, we compose new chapters in our lives, with new dynamics, a new cast of characters and new themes. With friends we've known for a while, we expand old themes. In fact, to the extent that we can manage, and to the limits of our friends' tolerance, "mixing" old friends with new ones creates a dramatic new *oeuvre* for us. Exciting new clashes and alliances will continue to define us, delight us, and titillate us through our misguided conviction that we had entered the Dark Ages of our lives.

Grieving over Broken Dreams, Then Sharing with Friends

Keith Schrag, 59, a licensed marriage and family therapist living in Ames, Iowa, broke up with his 40-year-old partner with whom he'd lived for almost three years. "I met Art during a monthly lesbian, gay, bisexual, and transgendered support group meeting at a folksy bar," Keith relates. "We really got to talking. Within six months, we decided it was time for commitment. The story goes like this. I had gone to a naturist conference. When I got back, there was a romantic message on my answering machine. I called him back. He came over, and that was it." Keith chuckles. "Don't tell *me* that old guys don't try new things."

Unfortunately, theirs was a case of two men involved in a relationship more fulfilling when they lived apart than when they moved into the same house. "Most of our issues dealt with expectations," Keith continues. "And to be honest, maybe things would have been better if Art had been more adept at what I call the common courtesies—particularly in the area of communication. For example, we might attend an event together. Often, we would predetermine the time at which we would leave. If Art changed his mind during the event, he would totally disregard the plans we'd made, with no consideration of my feelings. He saw the whole matter as a control issue. Mind you, this was not a matter of perspective dependent on our age difference. If the tables were turned, the same expectations would be there."

Keith had also embarked on a spiritual journey leading him away from Art. "I needed less and less assurance from him, and less reinforcement from him of my okayness or consistency," he explains. "In the past, I had been heterosexually married after two years of dating. Getting married was a way of feeling affirmation that I was getting over the temptation to be with men." Part of Keith's need to "get over" his attraction for men was attributable to his twenty-year service as a pastor in the Mennonite Church. He wasn't sure how the Church would react to his homosexuality. "However, even as a married man, I had an eight-month long-distance relationship with a psychologist who lived in Ohio while I lived in Iowa. He was also married at the time. So, we'd spend a weekend a month together, and a lot of time on the phone. The relationship finally ended because neither of us was ready to move. The relationship was good, though. Don't get me wrong about that. We both did a lot of neat growing."

In fact, Keith perceived his ex-partner's behavior as a threat to the growth that began during his affair with the Ohio counselor. "Sometimes, it was a matter of two or three days that Art wouldn't speak to me," he says. "Perhaps I didn't like something about his behavior. When I commented, he would give me the cold shoulder. Then, there was the issue of monogamy. We had mutually agreed that our relationship would not be monogamous, but he would rather it had been."

In the beginning, sex and touch had been common components of their partnership. "Touching and sexual intimacy were integral to our interactions for the first year and a half," he says. "But Art had a lot of back problems. He had trouble sleeping in our bed. He decided he wanted to sleep on the floor in our living room. After that, we had some sex, but not much. This was such a departure from the beginning, when there was frequent sex."

In contrast, their relationship began on a very positive note. "A significant person to both of us—Betty—always asked Art to do her hair, since he's a cosmetologist," Keith explains. "Additionally, she and I shared leadership roles in many spiritual education workshops. We work together with mutual clients. A couple of years ago, I asked her about monogamy—you know, to get her take on it. Throughout my life, I have had such a hell of a time dealing with monogamy issues. Anyway, Betty performed our commitment ceremony in our back yard attended by seventy-five friends, both gay and straight. The ceremony was sanctioned by our very unusual Mennonite group. Our local newspaper even carried the wedding announcement. But even then, I asked: How is this commitment on my growth path? How is this struggle part of my own spiritual growth? How can I be direct about who I am? These questions didn't just originate from my identity as a gay man; they were also related to past life issues I was working with."

Eighteen months into the relationship, Keith and Art broached the subject of breaking up. "Increasingly, there were some things I simply could not tolerate," Keith explains. "For example, the way he expressed himself. He was extremely disrespectful in his interactions with me."

In very clear terms, Keith told Art that he could not remain in a relationship where he didn't feel his partner respected him. "Finally, Art signed up with a psychic spiritual leader," Keith says. "That gave me cause to think that there was the possibility of continuing the relationship. While he studied with the psychic, I had to do some extensive traveling. When I returned, Art told me he was ready to break up. In fact, he had been dating someone for three months."

This "someone," a counselor, was actually a friend of Keith's. "I also thought he was a hunk," Keith says. "The night I returned from my trip, he was at the same bar that Art and I frequented. He grew really sensual with both Art and me. All three of us went to his place. It was fairly clear that it was more of a two-way than a three-way. Art and Randy were in love with each other, and I was the odd man out."

Which really didn't bother Keith all that much. "I was always glad when he found people he could get involved with," he explains. "He's more of a homebody than I ever was. When people called me at home, Art would get jealous. If Art were seeing someone, I reasoned, then he wouldn't be upset when someone wanted my time."

In retrospect, Keith recalls many good times during the course of their partnership. "We traveled a lot together. We had meals together. He would bring me coffee while I read the paper—sweet things like that. He was very much a soul companion. That was very much the case, especially during the first year."

When their relationship ended, Keith spent five months grieving over broken dreams. "I have an image of myself as flexible in many ways," he says. "I felt that I could deal with changes. Yet, I couldn't always do that. When he crawled into bed with me in the mornings to talk, for example, he said I couldn't touch him because his back or his leg hurt. It almost killed me not to touch him. We were so affectionate before he stopped sleeping with me."

Keith has grown stronger in terms of who he is and what he wants. "I've become so much clearer, and talking with close friends helped me achieve that," he explains. "From them, I got a new twist on some of the things we were dealing with. My view of myself improved, too. In the relationship, I realized, I had grown as much as I could. And so had he."

Now, Keith misses the companionship. "I'm ready for another companion," he says. "I'm expecting Mr. Right to come into my life anytime. I've had a couple of contacts in the last few months. As a naturist, I go to bare-skin events. I enjoy nudism around the house. I make contacts in fairy and naturist gatherings. Because I don't observe the usual barriers between sexuality and spirituality, I make friends more easily. Unfortunately, I spend more time with straight guys than with gay guys."

Nevertheless, Keith does not feel encumbered in his search for another relationship. "Recently, I met a guy whose energy was similar to mine. We figure we've been intimate in various past lives."

On a practical level, Keith looks for similarities on some level with a potential boyfriend. "I've been an activist all my life," he explains. "Women's issues. Antiwar issues. I've been a war-tax protestor. I don't have to have issues in common with a companion, but each partner should have his own significant core issues. This can be helpful in establishing a relationship with me—because I have to be involved with people. I get energy from them. I grow spiritually because of my human connections. Don't get me wrong. I'm very grateful for this relationship with Art. It will always be very significant in my life. Yes, there were times when I felt real anger toward him, or disrespect. Now, I really have a lot of respect for him. He's finally working on himself. He's growing spiritually, and I'm finding it easier to maintain a friendship with him. I don't like ending relationships with people. My former wife and I still have contact, and that's the way I want it."

"Does contact with ex-spouses mean living life in reverse?" Keith asks. "I don't think so. I feel better than I ever have. I'm ready to go on. The next twenty or thirty years can be the most exciting years of my life."

My Friends Told Me to Disengage

Personal values have more than a little effect on the success of a relationship, and Allen Williams, a professor in Boone, North Carolina, found out the hard way. He fell in love with a closeted assistant to a local correlative to Jesse Helms, who not only supported the conservative politician's philosophies and politics, but also held a deep fundamentalist faith. It took Allen's friends to help him wrench free of the partnership.

"Another thing that helped was that we never got to the point of moving in together," Allen explains. "We would discuss it and then get into some sort of fight. We *did* commit ourselves to each other; we dated from the time we met. We were very much a couple. I had met someone else, the night before I met him. Although we had gone on just one date, I told the other guy that although he was really nice, I met someone who really clicked. David and I had a strong understanding that our relationship would remain monogamous."

Allen admits, however, that both partners occasionally cheated on each other. Because neither respected the other's religious beliefs and personal standards, being unfaithful was easier. Still, they tried to work things out. "Yes, we talked," he says. "We tried to make compromises. As our relationship reached crisis proportions, we arranged to see a couples counselor. We broke up before the appointment. David finally decided that he just wanted it to end. In truth, even though he often pursued more commitment from me, he got cold feet when I finally committed one hundred percent. Maybe my falling for him was his victory. Or, maybe the reality of what he wanted frightened him too much."

On a deep, inner level, David was still dealing with self-hatred and hatred of gay people in general. "By nature, he never expresses many of his true feelings," Allen explains. "He keeps them bottled up. Some of his feelings erupt in passive-aggressive ways, or in manipulative behavior. He's not entirely comfortable with his homosexuality. After we broke up, he moved in the direction I had been pushing him. He changed jobs. He no longer works for the Helms wannabe. As far as I know, though, Christianity remains a strong part of his identity. He meets other Christian gay men. He's also found an outlet through music, and is even a member of our local gay men's chorus. Through that organization and while attending their national conference in Florida, he began to feel good about himself. Before, I think he felt all gay relationships were doomed. Maybe he thought it was natural for us to break up."

Allen and David stay in touch with each other, though not on altogether friendly terms. "I can honestly say I'm friends with every ex I have, except for him. It's strained. I think we both have strong feelings. The other week, when I won an award, he came up and hugged me. Then, I saw him out a weekend ago, and he dissed me. The following weekend, he e-mailed a joke, thinking I might find it amusing. I wondered why he behaved this way—snubbing me in public, then making contact in private. He's done shit like this before. He implied he was moving in with someone else, to see if I still cared." Allen shrugs. "Yes, we are still in contact. My friends would prefer that I had no contact whatsoever. I would like that we would become civil."

However, that desire might be impossible to attain. "He's burned a lot of bridges and, in the process, rebuilt his life," Allen explains. "Fortunately, I think he's passed that stage of tug-of-war between heterosexuality and homosexuality. Early on, he had realized he was gay, then repressed it. He entered Crossover Ministries. Personally, I don't dislike transformative ministries. I just don't think they're effective. But for him, he could never have walked into a gay bar if it hadn't been for Crossover. Crossover was his first step toward coming out. People who go through these programs learn about gay life through people at the ministry. Six people I knew went through Crossover's program and became sexually wild. It's a balancing act. 'Graduates' don't look at Crossover with resentment at all. They see ex-gay 'ministers' as individuals who are supportive of them. Even so, these organizations don't work. Fundamentally, they can't change a gay man into a straight one. Basically, these ministries are very conservative gay support groups for very conservative evangelicals. They perpetuate the closet, but don't turn men straight."

Essentially, Allen and David broke up twice. "I thought I had given it my best shot, and tried to get on with my life," Allen says. "Then, he came back. My friends were surprised, but I knew it would happen. I got back into the scene with David, only to set myself up to get hurt twice as badly. Yes, it was rocky, but I was comfortable. He stayed for a while longer, then left. This time, I felt hopeless and really down on relationships. Maybe there was something wrong with me, I thought, or with the men I attracted. Maybe all gay relationships face a difficult time. Maybe society makes it difficult for any gay couple to make a success. After all, men are socialized to conquer one another. They're not expected to indulge in any kind of emotional changes. I felt his breakup was inevitable. And yes, there was someone out there for me—just like my friends said. But who I really wanted was David. Even if he wasn't perfect, I wanted him. After almost two years, I've reached the point where I don't dream about him every night, or wonder where he is. Sometimes—and I swear this is true—I can feel his presence. When I look around, I see him passing me in a car. When Christmas comes, I have no one to shop for. God, how I enjoyed shopping for him! I just came out of a long depression. During that time, I did some unsafe things. I know why. I really didn't care about myself. Maybe I thought that if I got sick, he would come back. I've talked to my friends a lot. Many of them never really liked David very much. Even before we broke up, they were at odds with him, his actions, and his viewpoints."

Allen's friends were forthcoming about their opinions of David. Some hated David. Others said he wasn't a "bad person," but he wasn't right for Allen. "Others were supportive of me, and said that I needed to find someone better," he continues. "But when they came down on him, I found myself defending him. I would even ask them to call him, and check on him." Allen laughs. "You can imagine their reaction to that request."

"You're obsessed," one friend told him. "You're bad for each other. You need to disengage. It's time you stop acting like Farrah Fawcett in *The Burning Bed*. The man is insecure. He's manipulative. You need to avoid him."

Allen tried his friend's advice by hopping into bed with a stranger. "I thought that would ease my pain," he says. "It didn't. It made me feel even lonelier. Sex was good, but something was missing. Then, the following June, I met someone. We dated, but he was younger—just coming out—and I was on the rebound. I liked the person, and respected him. But this couldn't work. I would rather be good friends than bad boyfriends. I've decided I'm not emotionally ready for a new romance; I'm still in love with my ex."

Lately, aided by the insights of friends, Allen has taken another perspective. "I think the right long-term relationship has great value," he says. "But I'm not going to get involved right now just for the sake of having one. I've talked to many long-term couples. I asked them what made their relationships work. My parents, for example, said you need to have common values. You can love someone, but you may not be able to live with him. He also needs to be on the same intelligence level. If, after a year or two, you still want to be with somebody without touching them, that's the true test of a relationship, my grandmother said.

She told me to watch other guys—watch them with other people, with their families, and see how they treat each other. The way they treat others—that's how they'll treat you.''

During a conversation with a good friend, Allen confessed that since he was fourteen, he always longed to meet his soulmate. ''I wanted someone I could trust, and know that person was always going to be there,'' he says. ''I have retained this romantic hope. This is what I want, yes, but I'm not sure it's achievable. I want a good, long-term relationship. Something that's easy. Something you don't have to slave at every day. In the gay community, it's not unusual to hear someone say, 'Let's go out. I'm gonna look for a husband tonight.' I compare that silly attitude with searching for friends. Now, if you move into a new city, you might meet some new friends. But you don't say, 'I'm gonna wake up and meet my best friend.' That's not how life works. You make friends; then, maybe someone will become your best friend. This idea of deciding to *find* a best friend in such a contrived way is odd. It's crazy. But we don't think it odd or crazy when somebody goes to the bar in search of a husband. Yes, I want a long-term relationship. But it's more about having somebody to talk to, and share things with, and have a regular love life with. A partner is useful, in a sense. And I want to be useful to him. I'd love to be swept off my feet. We would understand each other, do community work together, watch movies together, and grow old together. But who knows? If it happens, it happens. If it doesn't—I'll be miserable the rest of my life.''

Allen is convinced that once we establish partnerships, we replicate our parents' marriages. ''Our views of how we love, and how we react to each other, are played off our parents,'' he says. ''The problem with gay relationships is that they are like an inverted pyramid. Often, they start with sex, followed by companionship, then true intimacy, rather than the reverse. There tends to be unreasonable value placed on sexuality among gay men. If we want to just talk, or to cuddle, what do we think? We think our relationship has encountered a big problem.''

Allen has also noticed several paradigms of partnerships among the gay community. ''Some gay couples meet, then quickly drop out of the gay scene,'' he observes. ''They lead their lives like any other couple. Those are the couples that seem to last longer. But the flip side is that if one leaves the other, they don't have a strong support network, or the legal resources they need. The second type of gay couple is seen at all kinds of social functions, rather than in bars. Typically, you don't see them in places you wouldn't see a heterosexual couple. Then, the third group goes out to the gay clubs a lot. They have a difficult time because there is so much temptation. If someone sees a long-term couple, he may think: 'This would be a good boyfriend because he's stayed so long with this guy. And I need that kind of commitment.' "

Allen would love to know the answers to two simple questions. "What is real love?" he asks. "I'm really curious about that, and another issue as well. What, I wonder, should a gay couple be like? I wish someone had the answers. I wish someone could tell us all how to survive, to live life wholly, and to invent for ourselves a dream that would be great to follow."

Unprecedented Intimacy

Here's the pattern. Before meeting that "special man," we regularly fraternize with our cadre of friends. In fundamental ways, they comprise our family. We show up at the same dinner parties. We dance at the same clubs. We shop at the same boutiques. Perhaps we even read the same books and magazines. We are, in many ways, like lovers, without the sexual component. In terms of communication and personal knowledge—the sharing of issues and concerns that are most important to us—our intimacy is unprecedented.

Then, along comes Mr. Right—or, as is often true, Mr. Goodbar. We begin thinking with our penises. Our almost physiological obsession with the new lover leaves little time for anything—or anyone—other than our job and a few meals. We think of no one else but Mr. Right. He's the leading man of our dreams. Our highest intellectual exercise revolves around the question of whether he thinks as often of us, or cares as deeply. Our most significant fantasies embrace scenarios of a life with Prince Charming—Fantasyland tunes crescendo in the background—a happily-ever-after proposition which often diminishes the quality of time spent with close friends who once meant the world to us.

And make no mistake. They still do. Often, we just don't let them know how much we care. We hope they understand the monopoly our new partner has on our lives. Then, our relationship moves into Phase Two. We're talking commitment. Maybe we call to tell our friends how happy we are. Even before we openly acknowledged our homosexuality, there he was, in our hearts and imaginations, the man of our dreams, the one who would sweep us off our feet. We just didn't know how long we'd have to wait for him to show up. And now that he has, we want to do absolutely nothing to jeopardize our relationship. Our friends seem genuinely happy for us, though we may detect their subtle familiarity with this pattern. They suspect their friendship with us will change. Indeed, it has already become less important, though we're damned if we'll admit it.

For most, commitment translates into setting up housekeeping with our lover. We channel our energies into learning how to interface with Mr. Right—determining his idiosyncrasies, allowing him to discover ours, moving slowly toward a comfortable fit and a pleasing harmony. Such an accomplishment takes time—lots of it. Besides, we want nothing more than to spend every minute we can with Mr. Right. Hell, this catch was hard enough to lure; we don't want to lose him. Meanwhile, our contacts with friends grow more sporadic. In fact, just yesterday, a good friend commented that we never get together anymore. Now, "let's do lunch one day" means "don't hold your breath."

Once the honeymoon period of our partnership has ended, we make a superficial attempt to rekindle our friendships (though some of us still feel that our partnership should answer all human needs). We discover that our friends' lives have changed dramatically. They're busier; they have established new friendships. The last time we declined their invitation was the last straw. Perhaps they, too, have fallen in love. Of course, we still *like* one another. We recall past experiences that make us laugh, that bring tears to our eyes—that even inspire us. But the nature of our past friendships can't be recalled. Furthermore, our partner's opinions of our friends may influence our feelings, or cause us to reexamine our friendships. Maybe we have gone overboard to make friends of *his* friends, and sacrificed our past friendships in the process. Whatever we've done, we feel we have misjudged. Our friends contributed to who we are; how could we give them up just like that?

When we suffer the misfortune of a failed partnership, it is with this scenario that we must often contend. We want to reestablish our friendships. That's true. We *need* them to make us feel better. Initially, we made our friends freely. Now, because of our neglect, a battle with guilt begins. By the same token, our friends may wonder if our new efforts at friendship might be exploitation. "You called only because you need me," a friend might think, even if he has too much class to say it. When we make that call, let's declare ownership of "friend neglect." Let's say we're sorry. Before we unload, let's spend some time acknowledging what a louse we were to take them for granted. Humble pie never tastes good, but it's the dessert we've made for ourselves. Although we can't expect to wipe away all the damage our disregard has done, honesty should make a friend's heart soften.

Sounds pretty selfish, doesn't it? To a degree, it is. However, if we genuinely want to re-establish our friendships, the fact that we are up-front from the beginning puts the ball in their court. They are certainly empowered to say fuck off. "I know I've been out of touch," we might humbly say. "I was totally involved with Mr. Right. As you've probably heard, he turned out to be Mr. Wrong. I'm sorry. I neglected our friendship while we were together. That was wrong. Now, I'm hurting, and I need your friendship more than I ever did. I hope you're willing to give me another chance." To admit having made a mistake might incite a mild tongue-lashing for our negligence, but the result will be a renewal of their support and empathy. Besides, their tongue-lashings are mild compared to the abuse and heartbreak we've taken from Mr. Right.

But we must take care not to short-change the friendship. Our pain-ridden self-indulgence can grow tedious if friends suspect we're using them for their sympathetic nature alone. Even if we have to pretend for a while, we should strive toward other-orientation, inviting them to share important details of their lives. If, at first, we don't feel all that interested, we later welcome the chance for involvement in their lives. It leaves us less preoccupied with our own pain.

A word of caution is in order. We have an obligation to apply the lesson we've learned. When we fall in love again, we will busy ourselves correcting the mistakes we made before. We will desperately hope the new partnership will take root. However, we must also nurture our friendships. With relatively little effort, friendships generally have the longest warranty. Why risk losing our close friends by exploiting them? If keeping our friendships means having a serious chat with our new partner to let him know we aren't giving up our friends, then it's a talk we should have.

"Depending on the security level of your partner," says Dwayne Smythe, a Vermont native who became involved with another man about a year after his three-year partnership ended, "he may feel threatened by your close friendships—perhaps to the point of jealousy. It's hardly a waste of time to reassure him that while your friends mean the world to you, he's still the core relationship in your life. Even if you have to revisit this theme several times, you should not lose your temper with him, or appear annoyed. I've also found that including your partner in activities you have with friends removes the mystery from your other relationships. He sees he has nothing to worry about. Of course, if your partner and your friends hate each other's guts, that's hard to do, but they should at least know each other. Something else I always do, as well. If I visit a friend without taking Justin along with me, I let him know when I intend to return home. And if I can't meet my own self-imposed deadline, I call to tell him I'm running late. I know a lot of us don't like to regiment our personal lives, but it's no big deal to take that extra step to build a little extra trust. Everybody has a telephone.

Qualities of Close Friendships

This activity will determine if you can count on your close friends to empathize with and assist you through your recovery.

Respond to the statements about the friend with Y for "yes," and N for "no." Because it is likely that several friendships are involved, a chart has been included to keep the scores organized.

	Score On	
Friends' Names	**Compassion**	**People Skills**

Compassion Statements (Reminder: Your responses are Y for "yes," and N for "no.")

_____ 1. Friend can discuss touchy subjects without withdrawing from the conversation.

_____ 2. Friend uses humor to diffuse situations that can be painful.

_____ 3. Friend never judges my ex-partner or my relationship unless his opinion is solicited.

_____ 4. Friend understands what it means to lose a true love; how it feels to have a relationship end.

_____ 5. Friend is capable of keeping things in confidence.

_____ 6. Friend supports me in my decisions.

_____ 7. Friend possesses nurturing qualities.

_____ 8. Friend offers advice in a gentle but assertive way.

_____ 9. Friend is intellectually stimulating.

_____ 10. Friend recognizes my self-destructive behaviors and attempts to intervene.

People Skills Statements

___ 1. Friend is a good listener.
___ 2. Friend invites me to go out with him for social activities.
___ 3. Friend is available whenever I need him.
___ 4. Friend tends to lighten my mood when I'm around him.
___ 5. Friend includes me in his social circle.
___ 6. Friend doesn't push me to speed up my recovery process, such as hurrying me to find someone new.
___ 7. Friend has other friends to whom he can introduce me, some of whom may become my friends, too.
___ 8. Friend continues to come around even when, in my deep anguish, I lie and say that I would prefer to be left alone.
___ 9. Friend knows when to confront me about my self-pity.
___ 10. Friend involves me in his personal life.

Total the number of "Yes" responses for each section, Compassion Statements and People Skills. Enter these numbers in the chart for each person you've screened.

After the chart is completed, place a mark on the graph for each person, using their compassion and people-skills scores as coordinates.

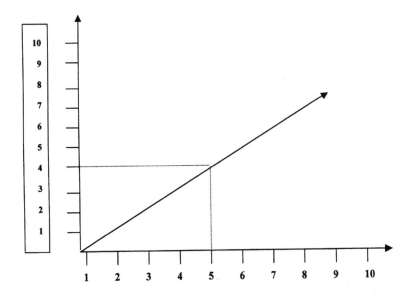

Plot each friend's score on the same graph. Be certain to write the friend's name next to his "dot." The diagonal line represents the "perfect friend" (in terms of his ability to empathize and help you process). The friends who are closest to the diagonal line and farthest away from the origin (meaning, "O") are your best choices to share your innermost feelings about your recent breakup.

A point occurring in the dotted box indicates a deficiency in the skills necessary for your friend(s) to help you through recovery. While you might look to another friend for more support during healing, you shouldn't discontinue your friendship with this individual. After all, he may be a wonderful companion at the movies or a rock concert.

CHAPTER SEVEN

•••••••••••••••••••••

Family Ties

Family Fascists

Young Henry Teale never felt a part of anything. First of all, he lived in a small Southern town, where the locals' idea of fun involved climbing into a pick-up truck and driving around the Wal-Mart parking lot, looking for action. He'd heard that fights over young women frequently occurred beneath the bright neon lights illuminating the lot. A suggestive glance from the wrong man could easily kindle a jealous rage in the heart of the young man who had originally laid claim to her. Henry liked neither pick-ups nor girls—at least, not in "that way." Second, in elementary school, most boys tended to ignore or ridicule him. Once, when Johnny called him a "little queer," he noticed his third grade teacher hiding a smile behind her hand. She said nothing. She didn't even chastise Johnny for calling him a name—an offense in Miss Boldeware's classroom. It wasn't that he particularly liked playing with girls all the time, but often they were the only peers willing to offer him any companionship at all. What he couldn't force himself to tell anyone was his terror at going to the rest room during breaks and at lunch. There, the other boys often ridiculed him, called him names, and even suggested that he had trespassed into the wrong rest room. Once, when he unzipped his fly, John peered at his crotch, then said: "Well, I'll be damned. Hank *does* have a pecker, after all."

At home, he felt as though he were an extraterrestrial placed on this planet through a celestial mistake. Surely *this* mission had been intended for a comrade. His earthling parents were marginally educated people who worked together in the same factory. Lately, local rumor had it that because of diminishing demand, the company was seriously considering a plant closure. Once the rumor started, his parents, who had never been overly warm or supportive, grew more apprehensive, taking their anxiety out on Hank and his two sisters. They weren't physically abusive— just impatient. No dialog occurred between them—only parental questions requiring abbreviated responses. If the kids tried to elaborate, Mommy and Daddy would quickly remind them of their proper place.

Hank was only nine years old, but he wasn't blind, and he wasn't stupid. While his parents were usually impatient with all their children, he sensed another response when they related to him. Though he didn't have words for it then, his parents seemed to regard him with a certain nervousness—as though afraid that Hank might pull out an automatic weapon and blow them away. Or, as he later realized, they worried that another adult might criticize their "funny" kid, or cast aspersions on their parenting techniques. As a result of his parents' inability to relate to him, Hank began to regard himself as a displaced space traveler—a fantasy extending to his adolescence.

Partially to placate his parents, Hank asked for a GI Joe for his birthday. He was acutely aware of the relief and pleasure in their eyes when he made the request. Later, in therapy, he was empowered to say that this single incident communicated that he was more likely to receive his parents' acceptance while pretending to be someone other than who he really was. Back then, all he knew was that he had chosen a toy acceptable to his parents. What his parents didn't realize was Hank's attraction to Joe's military prowess and his pursuant machismo. He had constructed a complicated scenario for Joe in which Hank, the hero, rescued Joe from prison camps, and comforted him as mortar exploded around them. Hank even had "conversations" with the doll, who understood him better than anyone else—including his own family. Their friendship was unshakable, their intimacy unbounded. Later, Hank's shrink would express glib surprise that he could get all that from a doll. "Well, where else could I get it?" Hank asked.

But there was more. Hank admired the plastic bulkiness of

Joe's torso, and the high-impact plastic muscles of his arms and legs. In fact, his "attraction" to Joe inspired Hank to pay closer attention to actors on television and in the movies. Before long, he developed crushes on stars similar to those of his sisters. When he told them about the young heartthrobs to whom he was attracted, they didn't seem to think their brother weird at all. At school, when each student described, then identified, someone they most admired, his class almost hooted him out of the classroom when he sang the praises of Michael Douglas. Later, in the clarity of hindsight, he realized he had sounded too intense, too enamored of the actor. His classmates probably detected the reverence he felt for his rising star, and knew it wasn't "normal." But just like Hank, they didn't have the words to describe what they were hearing.

The following year, he wanted to join Cub Scouts, primarily because a couple of guys who were occasionally nice to him were joining. But Mommy and Daddy said no. Their adamant refusal to grant permission befuddled him. What the hell was wrong with being a Cub Scout? He was taken aback by his parents' refusal, when he had anticipated encouragement and enthusiasm. In a voice full of disgust, his father said: "Ordinarily, I would say it's okay. But not now. Not in this town. I heard, down at the barbershop, that the Scoutmaster of the troop you want to join has a nice boat. He invites his troop to go out on the lake with him, where he makes them give him massages. I'm not having that pervert turn my son into a queer. So just shut up about it."

His comments were like a slap in the face. Although he had not worn the label yet, something about what his father said seemed to fit. In fact, he was remotely excited by the prospect of touching another male the way his father described. What was wrong with massaging someone anyway? he wondered. His parents made it sound so dirty.

Besides, when he had met the Scoutmaster, he knew he wanted to be this man's friend.

Several days later, after throwing another tantrum, he demanded an explanation from his mother. "Your father just doesn't have any use for homosexuals," she said. "When he was in the Navy, stationed in New Orleans, one of those boys came on to him. You see, your father had been drinking and stayed out past curfew. Rather than returning to the ship, he accepted another man's offer to spend the night in his apartment. Once they were in bed together, the man placed his arm across your father's bare chest."

"What did Daddy do?" Hank asked, feeling strangely titillated.

"What any normal, red-blooded American man should do," his mother replied indignantly. "He punched him in the mouth, threw him out of his own bed, then went back to the ship. He'd rather spend time in the brig than spend the night with a pervert."

Before he could stop himself, Hank asked another question. "What would you and Daddy do if one of your kids turned out to be a pervert?"

She looked at him strangely, her head cocked to one side. "That wouldn't fly with me," she said. "No child of mine is gonna turn out like that. I'd throw them out first."

Then puberty hits with the shattering force of a wrecking ball. Hank's innocuous crushes are intensified by the onslaught of hormones. At school, he is drawn toward his handsome physical science teacher who shatters Hank's fantasies when he mentions his loving wife and adorable children. He longs to spend hours with the sensitive new boy who just moved into town, and who has not learned that to hang out with Hank is to risk getting a "reputation." Hank dreams of embraces and kisses, of sleepovers, of touching the young man's naked body. He has no idea how two boys might give pleasure to one another—although he is grateful to the new boy for the fantasies he has enjoyed alone in his bedroom. Hank wonders if the new boy thinks of him in the same way.

Finally, it happens, but not with the new boy. Quite unexpectedly, while John and Hank are working the same shift during an evening school fundraiser, John asks Hank to accompany him to the deserted second floor, where the English classrooms are located. Persistently, John attempts to find a classroom door that the custodial staff has left unlocked. Though delightfully intrigued, Hank sweats nervously. Laughter comes from the cafeteria where band members serve barbecued chicken, rice smothered with hash, and coleslaw. The Band Parents Association prepared the meal to raise funds to send the band to march in the upcoming Mardi Gras parades. As Hank utters prayers that their band director won't miss them, John finds the open door he has been looking for. He grabs Hank's hand and pulls him into the room. Instantly, John is all over Hank, his hands exploring every part of his body, his lips pressed against Hank's lips. Suddenly, John pulls away, grabs the teacher's chair, and positions it beneath the doorknob, the way Hank has seen on television crime shows. They sink to the carpeted floor. They kiss and paw at each other. Soon, their hands find each other's genitals.

Hank returns to his post in the cafeteria. John disappears into the night. He's dreadfully afraid that diners can tell what happened just by looking at him. But even more frightening is the realization of how much he enjoyed touching John—although all they did was jerk each other off. A sinking despondency accompanies his realization. He is a pervert—the kind of man his father despises, the kind of kid his mother throws into the street.

What about John? John continues to be the asshole he's always been, but mercifully, he never mentions the incident. What could he say, without implicating himself? Hank speaks to him on several occasions, but John either glares at him with disgust, or turns his head away. Hank's sense of isolation—of being different, a pariah—increases. He even considers suicide. But each time he thinks he has enough courage to kill himself, some positive snippet about homosexuality appears on the TV news or in the newspaper, providing hope that he can be both gay and happy.

Each fleeting moment of hope is countered with plenty of negative moments. At a recent Sunday church service, his fundamentalist Baptist minister used his bully pulpit to denounce gays and lesbians as bearing the blame for the inevitable fall of civilization. Hank is struck by his minister's stupidity. He cannot see how homosexuals pose any threat to families. Mothers like his are willing to disrupt a family when one child comes out as gay, but that's a threat posed by mothers, not by their gay sons. He has also heard an uncle crack a gay joke or two with his father who, while having never told one himself, still finds such jokes hilariously funny. If the opinions of his classmates are any indication, perhaps Hank *should* exercise the "suicide option." Not only are homophobic jokes frequently told on his high school campus, verbal taunts are used to put down any student perceived as different, or who expresses an opinion not in line with the provincial attitudes of the rest of the student body. In fact, the most positive comment Hank has heard about gays came from the new boy. "I guess the world would be boring if we didn't have queers," he said one day while sitting at the lunch table. "After all, who would we laugh at then?"

One evening, when Hank joined his family for dinner, his parents were all wrapped up in the latest town gossip. What he heard made him want to lash out, to scream, to strike his parents with a fatal blow. Weren't the rumors about this man bad enough without incriminating an entire group of people? Besides, he had not been charged, let alone brought to trial. Hank had met this man when he substituted for the high school band director when she was out for surgery. He had never met a more charming, or funnier, guy.

The blacklisted man was a music professor who, while making his home in Hank's hometown, taught at a university located an hour's drive away. Even Hank would readily admit his eccentricity—he owned a dog named "Bugger" that he spoke of and treated as his child—but he seemed only moderately strange. Hank sensed nothing sinister, or criminal, about him—at least, not during the week of his band director's absence. Her surgery had been scheduled near the winter holiday, when the university had a more generous break than the local high school. Hence, "Chief," as he was affectionately called, had extra time to extend his friend and colleague this favor. While applying the same tough university standards to the high school musicians as he did to his own students, Chief's manner was so relaxed and gently humorous that even the most cynical adolescent liked him.

Which is one reason Hank found his parents' story so incredible. Privately, they accused Chief of inviting teenage boys to his house to swim in his pool, to shoot billiards and play computer games. After earning their trust and affection, Chief would offer them a small fee to appear in his "home movies." This celluloid opportunity had nothing to do with nostalgia. Instead, for money, Chief expected the young men to disrobe, then to be sexually intimate with each other beneath the scrutiny of his camcorder. According to Hank's parents, the films were used for Chief's sexual pleasure once the boys left. His father said the kids would probably have "beaten the little faggot's ass" if he had tried to touch them. While details of the rumor ended there, his parents offered their own analysis and shared it with several close friends and factory workers. The teenagers weren't the only boys Chief wanted. His parents were convinced that, once the police completed their investigation—which, by the way, never occurred— the town would discover that Chief had committed vile sexual acts on small children as well.

The story's "truth factor" was of little relevance to Hank. What impacted him most was the hostility and hatred toward all gay men his parents expressed. If Hank came out right then, at the dinner table, he was certain his own parents would have killed him.

That dinner was pivotal in Hank's regard of his parents. He grew more and more distant. When forced to interact with them—like discussions of his college plans and of his decision to stop attending church—he could barely conceal the hostile sarcasm in his voice. His parents sounded bored and detached; he knew they would prefer not talking to him at all. In fact, he had grown to hate them as much as they hated homosexuals. Several years earlier, he had relinquished his fantasy of being an extraterrestrial mistakenly placed on a primitive planet. Lately, he wondered whether a mistake had been made at the hospital at the time of his birth. Surely he could not have been born to such hatefully stupid parents. His *real* parents probably claimed the baby that rightfully belonged to these people posing as his mother and father.

Hank was fond of his sisters, however. Just months after that fateful dinner, he came out to them, strongly cautioning them never to tell their parents. They were shocked at first, but came around quickly—as he thought they would. His sisters asked him about his feelings and experiences—and listened to his answers with an open mind. Their only disagreement occurred about the manner in which he related to their parents. His sisters implored him not to be as sarcastic—that if Mom and Dad ever accepted his homosexuality, they would still have to grapple with the way he related to them. He promised he would try to correct his behavior, but he never managed it.

While attending an out-of-state college, Hank felt a refreshing sense of liberation. In college, he first fell in love, then destroyed the relationship in short order. With the help of psychoanalysis, he understood why. The reason could be traced back to Mommy and Daddy. Because they never accepted him—never even wondered why he expressed little interest in girls—he suffered from a chronic case of insecurity. As a result, he never learned about intimacy. Little wonder Hank had never learned how to sustain a romantic relationship.

A year after receiving his undergraduate degree, Hank came out to his parents. His college costs had been largely covered by scholarships. After all, because he had very few friends in high school, he had plenty of time to study. He had also landed a promising job. No longer was he worried that he might have to rely on his parents for financial support. Coming out was a way of exacting revenge for all the ways he had been hurt during his childhood and adolescence. It wasn't a way of establishing a more honest relationship with them at all, and his sisters told him so— after the screaming, the shouting, and the tears had subsided. In fact—and this fact hurt him most of all—his sisters suggested that he not come around for a while. They reminded him—both were college students now, one a sophomore and one a junior— that adulthood should be a time for healing, not opening old wounds. Besides, without outing Hank, they had recently engaged their parents in civilized discussions of homosexuality. While his parents weren't as enlightened as Hank would like, their opinions weren't quite as hardcore as Hank had presumed.

Years passed. Neither Hank nor his parents were willing to meet in the middle. He easily detected their aloofness whenever he visited them. On the other hand, his parents *never* came to see him, though he and his partner lived only two hours away. After a while, his contact with his parents grew less frequent. Honestly, he was tired of them. Every time he mentioned his partner, even during phone conversations, his parents would quickly change the subject. During his last visit, when he spoke of his local activism, his mother wondered aloud why "you gays" had to be so vocal about their sexual orientation. "I mean, we straight people, as you call us, don't go around talking straight, straight, straight all the time," she said.

"Yes, in a way, you do," Hank replied. "Each time you mention your husband, or put that wedding ring on your finger, you're being vocal about your orientation."

His mother scowled while his father turned up the volume on a rerun of "All in the Family." There was nothing for them to talk about, really, and his sisters wouldn't arrive for at least another two hours.

Family Liberation

Let's place Hank in a dramatically different family environment. Since his awareness of his life as distinct from his mother's, he has felt different, quite a cut apart from the other kids. Despite this feeling of "terminal uniqueness," his parents have never made him feel ashamed. In fact, if Mom and Dad hear a pejorative comment directed toward him, regardless of its source or context, they intervene immediately—either by confronting the perpetrator or applying psychological salve to Hank's damaged self-esteem.

Hank and his family live on the West Coast, close to a metropolitan area with a large and politically vocal gay and lesbian population. Mom and Dad have several gay and lesbian friends, and are keenly attuned to sexual minority issues. Although ultimately deciding in favor of a young heterosexual couple, they seriously considered a gay man and a lesbian to be Hank's godparents. By their own account, the only reason for choosing the straight couple was that the gay man's job required frequent travel, and the lesbian friend was embroiled in an ugly custody battle with her ex-husband.

Hank's parents are well-educated, career-minded individuals who express a vocal moral outrage when injustice confronts them. Several years earlier, although both had been raised by devout Catholic parents, they denounced their Catholicism because of the Pope's stubborn stance on birth control and women's issues. They felt he had begun to lean dangerously close to the blathering lunacy of fundamentalism. Determined not to have their faith in a higher power undermined by bad theology, they searched for another congregation to join. Ultimately, the openness and spiritual curiosity of the Universalist Unitarian Church resonated most with their values.

Meanwhile, they noticed that Hank wasn't cultivating—or even exploring—many interests of other boys his age. While his parents weren't particularly concerned, they encouraged Hank to socialize frequently with his peers, even if he didn't want to play sports, or war games, or any other rough-and-tumble pastimes. Hank's dad had never been that big on sports, either, but he couldn't recall being quite as introverted as his son. It was at this stage in Hank's development that his parents broached their biggest parental issue: What if our child is gay?

After much introspection and several conversations with homosexual friends, they decided to retreat from Hank's inter-personal relationships, but to be as supportive of him and his interests as possible. They rejoiced when he announced his desire to play trumpet because they knew he would have to relate to his peers during band rehearsals and performances. Admittedly, his increasing solitude and depressive personality concerned them. He always looked as though he'd lost his best friend. When they asked what was wrong, he always answered with his standard shrug and simple reply: "Nothing." When Hank's mother mentioned Hank's serious withdrawal to one of their gay friends, he gave her his best advice: "Doesn't necessarily mean anything, Rachel," he said. "But if Hank is preoccupied with matters of sexuality, you might want to be prepared for an announcement eventually. And if band doesn't bring him out of his shell, you might want to consider counseling."

Fortunately, band helped. In fact, Hank evolved into quite the social butterfly. Not only did he excel as a trumpeter, but other musicians also discovered their genuine fondness for him. His mother frequently set extra places at the dinner table for his friends. While Hank's friends were pretty evenly distributed between male and female, his parents noticed that he seemed intensely more interested in his male guests. Shortly after entering high school, Hank's intense interest elevated into obvious infatuations. Although both Mom and Dad were tempted to pop the question foremost on their minds, they resisted. They knew that if their son was unsure of his sexual orientation, their probes might make him self-conscious, or send him back into his shell again.

However, Hank's own carelessness provided his parents the opportunity for an answer. While Hank attended band practice, his dad assembled a new bookcase for his study. He needed a Phillips screwdriver, and remembered that Hank had borrowed it several days earlier. Obviously, the boy had forgotten to return it to the garage. Mildly cursing the irresponsibility of youth, Henry the First stomped upstairs and into Hank's room. Impatiently, he scanned his son's room twice before he spotted the tool on the boy's desk. Grumbling, he grabbed the screwdriver. He was about to turn away when he noticed a magazine he'd never seen before. Featured on the cover was the Olympic diving medalist, Greg Louganis, smiling at the reader, with a teaser promising a scoop on a made-for-television biographical movie. The magazine's title? *The Advocate, The National Gay and Lesbian Newsmagazine.*

A little numb, Henry carried the magazine into the kitchen, where Rachel had begun preparations for dinner. He placed the magazine on the counter close to the stove.

"Honey, take a look at this," he instructed his wife.

For a moment, the room was silent. Finally, Rachel spoke. "Well, I guess our hunch is finally confirmed," she said in a neutral voice, then looked at her husband. "So what do we do now?"

Henry sat at the table and leafed through the magazine's pages. "I think we give him the opportunity to be honest with us," he said quietly, then returned the magazine to the boy's room.

But when Hank came home two hours later, he was accompanied by a friend who stayed for dinner. Despite the difficulty of the effort, Rachel and Henry engaged both their son and his guest in light conversation. Once or twice, it seemed to them that Hank might have sensed a change in the dynamics of their interaction.

Finally, after an hour of practice for a duet he and his friend would play in an upcoming performance, Hank's guest said good night. Hank scurried toward the stairs, but his father's voice stopped him. "Hank, your mother and I would like to talk with you. It'll only take a few minutes."

Hank stopped, took a deep breath, then walked slowly into the family room.

"Am I in trouble?" he asked.

His mother smiled. "Of course not," she reassured him. "Your father and I just have a question for you."

His father explained about the screwdriver, then confessed he had stumbled across *The Advocate*. "I wasn't snooping," he said guiltily. "You know your mother and I respect your privacy. But you probably know what we're wondering. Are you willing to tell us—honestly?"

Hank swallowed, then nodded. This was the hardest thing he'd ever done. "You're wondering if I'm gay, right?" he asked sheepishly.

His parents nodded.

"I've known for a couple of years," he said. "Maybe longer than that. But the answer is yes. I'm gay."

His parents thanked him for his honesty. "You know your father and I have gay friends," his mother said. "So we don't have a problem with homosexuality. We *are* concerned, however, because a lot of ignorant people may try to make things hard for you. But that, along with the risk for HIV infection, is the nature of our concern. We have no hang-ups otherwise."

His father placed an arm around his son's shoulders, and pulled him close. "If any problems ever arise because of your sexual orientation, and you think they may be more than you can handle, you know what we want from you, don't you?"

"I think so," Hank said, blushing. "You want me to let you know."

"That's right. We'll do what we can to help you out."

Hank's parents never raised the issue again, unless Hank brought it up first. Nor did they treat him any differently—except never to assume again that he would date girls.

Later, when Hank entered college, he won election as an officer in the gay and lesbian student organization. His parents called to congratulate him. Then, after dating a young man for six months, Hank brought him home to meet Rachel and Henry the First. They treated him as a cherished guest. Then, years later, long after receiving his college degree, when he and his long-term partner broke up, he shared his anguish and disappointment with his parents. They were among his biggest supporters. They were also the people who had taught him about intimacy—about the value of honesty in any relationship. They had empowered him to be truthful about his sexual orientation without fear of reprisal. Truth, he learned, was important to the survival of a relationship. When he and his partner broke up, dishonesty was not a factor. They remained good friends largely because his parents had taught him that people can usually overcome any problem, as long as they are willing to deal with it honestly and courageously.

Hank's parents were liberators who understood their child's need to feel protected, honored, and cherished while he went about the important business of self-discovery. Not only did they make no disparaging observations of gay lives, they also affirmed homosexual orientations as merely another normal variation in human sexuality. Furthermore, they accepted Hank's personality characteristics and idiosyncrasies, gently prodding him when he seemed to be closing in on himself, praising him when he let the world in. Finally, they celebrated Hank's coming out. Their exploration of the possibility of raising a gay child prepared them to react positively.

As most mental health professionals will attest, our parents influence our ability to grow relationships throughout our adult lives. If they have condemned us, we often spend an inordinate amount of time dealing with parental issues. Where parents have affirmed our lives unequivocally and unconditionally, we enjoy the freedom to cultivate our partnership and harvest the love it yields.

The nature of our relationships with our parents influences not only the way we relate to our partner, but also the way we break up with him. By extension, past parental forces also dictate the degree of nurturing we can expect from the two people who have loved us longest.

Attitudes, Latitudes, and Platitudes

Often, our experiences with family fall somewhere in between those of our two Hanks. Mom and Dad aren't quite as condemning of us as the first set of parents, but neither are they quite the bastions of progressivism as the second set. In fact, some of us don't even come out to our parents until we have met the man with whom we plan to spend the rest of our lives. Why expose parents—or ourselves—to the stress of honesty until the beau is picked and the knot is tied? The answer is deceptively simple. If Mom and Dad know we're gay before we meet the man of our dreams, they have already cleared one hurdle toward acceptance. Now, they are more likely to perceive our partnership as a natural and logical occurrence.

Let's move into the life of the third Hank, a man of twenty-eight who met Jon seven months ago, and has been dating him ever since. Since entering college, Hank has yearned to tell his folks that he's gay, but he's been scared of the potential repercussions. After all, he has depended on them for a little financial assistance from time to time. He's also heard them make snippy cracks about gays and lesbians which, while not exceptionally cruel, warn him that his parents may harbor mildly homophobic attitudes. So, he opened his closet door subtly and slowly, content to come out to a few cousins, several friends and other gays and lesbians. After all, he thought, why should his parents know of his homosexuality while he was still exploring that part of his identity?

But now Hank has fallen in love. He's already met Jon's parents who, though Jon didn't *exactly* tell them they were lovers, caught on to the truth fairly easily. Jon's parents thoroughly embraced him into their family. Guiltily, he thought he may have misjudged his parents. Perhaps if he introduced Jon to them, they would instantly like him, and his anticipated problems would be no more than futile worry. Shortly after his visit to Jon's boyhood home, he began a letter to his parents in which he came out, not only as a gay man, but as a man in love with another man.

God, was he ever nervous! Eight days passed before he received a reply. Finally, on Saturday morning, he opened his mailbox to find the letter for which he had been waiting. As though the

Postal Service felt he could handle no more, the letter was the only item he received this cloudy morning. While Jon shaved and showered, Hank tore into the letter.

The letter had been composed in his mother's handwriting, a fact that hardly surprised him. "Dear Hank," she wrote. "As you might imagine, it was quite upsetting to receive your letter. Of course, you are our son and we still love you. We always will. Nothing will change that. But we didn't raise you to be this way. Your father and I can't help but think that your telling us about your sex life is a way to hurt us. Did we do something that made you angry with us? Why couldn't you have kept quiet about your orientation? Why did we have to know? Your father is particularly upset by your disclosure. We have agreed on one point. While you are welcome to visit us anytime, I'm afraid we can't extend the same hospitality to Jon. If you are willing to consider our feelings in *this* regard, at least, I'm sure you'll come to understand."

Although Hank feels overwhelming resentment about their attitude—after all, the spouses of his brother and sister are always welcomed—he buttons his lips during his infrequent visits. After two years, his parents finally extend a holiday invitation to Jon. Gradually, both parents grow to like him. Hank's siblings also find Jon delightful company. Whenever Hank is expected to participate in family traditions, Jon is invited as well, though Hank senses that his parents don't esteem his relationship as highly as they regard his brother's and sister's. He is convinced they are playing a role merely to placate him. They're afraid that ostracizing Jon will stop Hank's visits. Eventually, Hank discovers his hunch is accurate—a discovery Hank makes shortly after he and Jon terminate their partnership.

Initially, the sympathy Hank receives from members of his family—including his parents—is both soothing and energizing. Soon, however, some of the statements, intended to comfort him, contain thinly veiled elements of homophobia. "I know you're hurting, darling," his mother says, "but surely you didn't think yours and Jon's relationship would last forever?" He doesn't ask what she means because he already knows all too well.

Hank's brother is more direct. "I hope you've learned your lesson," he proffers. "There's nothing wrong with being single.

But if you decide singlehood isn't for you, please realize you're not going to find marital stability from another man." Hank bristles. He demands an expansion of his brother's comment. "You know damn well what I mean," his brother says.

Once his family convinces themselves that Hank appreciates their frequent advice, Hank refuses to discuss the separation with them at all. Hank is driven to compare the qualities of his family to those of Jon's. The former in-laws had no hang-ups about homosexuality, or about their son's relationship. Hank's every visit to Jon's family felt comfortable. He couldn't remember a single time when he pretended to be straight. On the other hand, he wondered whether Jon was too nice to express the discomfort he *had* to feel in the company of Hank's family. Hell, almost two years passed before his parents were even willing to acknowledge that Hank and Jon were partners. Maybe the discrepancy in the attitudes of the two families bothered Jon more than he indicated. Maybe he was just too tactful to bring it up.

To a degree, Hank blamed his family for the transience of his relationship. Heterosexual couples learned long ago that marriage unites not only two individuals but also two families. If a man's family disdains the union of their son and another man, their disapproval adds to an already significant degree of stress. How could Jon not feel some trepidation because of Hank's family's attitudes? He would know, wouldn't he, that a man cannot eschew all familial influence, no matter how hard he tries. Hell, his family's attitudes, standards, and beliefs shaped part of Hank's identity. How could Jon ignore the possible damage Hank's family had inflicted on his psyche? How could he fully respect Hank when Hank's family was so unworthy of respect?

As Hank grappled with these issues, he withdrew from his family. His parents didn't have the capacity to feel the depth of sympathy, or empathy, they could feel for their straight offspring. His visits grew increasingly sporadic, though his thoughts of his parents did not. He was saddened by the sensation of having been duped. For several years now, his parents and siblings had journeyed toward full acceptance of him as a gay man. Today, he realized they had taken a sidetrip along the way. He had no idea how to get them back on track. He didn't know if he had the energy, even if he knew the way. The distance between them continued to expand. Hank felt increasing sadness that the people who could help him climb out of the abyss into which he'd fallen when he and Jon broke up, he hardly even knew. His parents had loved each other for a long time, but they were unwilling to share any of love's secrets. He soon replaced them—parents, brother, sister—with fantasies of what a better family could be.

In Hank's fantasy, he envisioned parents who could barely stand to see their son hurting. As parents, they recognized that even a full-grown man experienced moments when he longed to be a boy again. Even a man could desire Mommy and Daddy to take him into their arms, and through the magic of their words, make his life sparkle again. What did it matter that Hank was gay? Here was an organism of tissue and bone and electromagnetic impulses and stardust and imagination—in essence, a part of them—whose universe had imploded. They knew how he felt to be in love. Surely, they could imagine their feelings if their marriage ended. Through empathy, they could know how their son must feel. This was no time to philosophize about the nature of homosexuality, of humanity, of men in general. What Hank needed—what we all need when we fall out of love—was a return to a family who understood, and whose understanding would accelerate healing. He longed for his parents to provide space for healing. If that meant revisiting his childhood, then good parents should humor and nurture the little boy who's returned. Maybe there's something to find in this place, where the boy had only faint dreams of manhood. Maybe there's discovery at this site. But Mommy and Daddy aren't helpful. They don't seem to understand. From their mouths come banal advice and predictable prejudices.

But Hank's had enough of bullshit. His mind is set on healing.

How can he purge Jon from his brain cells? How can he think of Jon without a compulsion to scream? How can he tell his parents of the frightening certainty that he can't possibly go on without Jon?

No matter the intensity of our efforts, how can we communicate to the man and woman who gave us life that all we need from them is a sympathetic presence? If they have to proselytize, why can't they save it for Sunday School? We're in no mood for sermons now. We can love them as the Mommy and Daddy we knew before our penises thickened and got us into all manner of trouble. Look at the trouble we're in now. But if they have to preach, we don't need them. They only worsen the damage with preaching, and break our hearts even more. Being there means simply that: Being There.

But how many of us can honestly say our parents are there for us? How many of us can say our parents know how to open spaces for us to be their children again? Can they resist a compulsion to be advisors? What do we do when, as many of us discover, the same parents who can Be There for our quintessentially straight siblings don't know diddley about Being There for a gay son, whose pain is no different?

I Love You, Son, but You're Going to Hell

Particularly vulnerable to the absence of familial understanding when a partnership ends are the young. From their first kiss to the certainty of commitment, they have few models on which to pattern their romance. Unless they live in an urban center with a large gay population, they can count on few people to understand their pain when their relationships end. Even less likely are parents who accept the integrity of their son's sexual orientation and life choices.

Calvin Yeap, a 22-year-old culinary arts major living in Placentia, California, fell in love with a man four years older than he. "Actually, the relationship started when a few of my friends took me out for my eighteenth birthday," Calvin explains. "I met Michael at the club where we celebrated although, at the time, I wasn't really looking for a boyfriend. My mind was on celebrating my birthday. Then, my friends took me home."

The next day, Michael shopped at the pet store where Calvin worked. Patiently, he waited for Calvin to assist him. "May I ask you a personal question?" Michael asked.

"Sure," Calvin replied.

"Weren't you out clubbing last night with a bunch of friends?"

"At first, I'm worried that he's a stalker or something," Calvin says, chuckling. "He actually described the friends I went to the club with. It *seemed* innocent enough. After all, while we talked, he was selecting an aquarium to purchase."

After Michael made his selection, Calvin helped him load the aquarium into the car.

"Are you interested in doing something this weekend?" Michael asked.

Calvin, drawn to the man's charm and sense of humor, agreed. In about a month, they were dating each other exclusively. "Michael used to say he was attracted to me because of the way I dance," he says. "But he would also say that he liked me for who I am. I had been out for a year—maybe two years. I met him when I was a sophomore in college. My relationship with him was the first of any duration. I had been involved with several men before, but those relationships lasted only a week or two."

Despite the fact that Michael and Calvin were lovers, they never actually lived together. "Of course I wanted to move out of my parents' house," Calvin explains. "But they were still a little blown away because I had just come out to them. If I had moved in with Michael, I would have made things bad between myself and my parents. I never even suggested to them that Michael and I might set up housekeeping. Actually, my parents never knew for sure that Michael and I were more than just friends. My sister, who is about a year younger than I, knew about us, but she didn't tell our parents."

Because Michael and Calvin worked the same hours, they saw each other after work almost every day. They also spent every weekend together. "Sometimes, I would go to his place, stay there for a while, then he would come to my house, and we'd do something," Calvin explains. "Sometimes, I wouldn't come back home because it was just too late. The arrangement wasn't so much a problem, as it was just a hassle. I was still having trouble with my parents, and Michael didn't want to get me into any trouble. He understood my situation at home. He was the only person I could talk to about my parents' lack of understanding about my being gay."

Although Calvin's last class ended at nine-fifty, his parents expected him to observe a ten o'clock curfew. "I seldom made it back by ten," he says. "The curfew was unreasonable for a college student, I know, but the whole problem with my parents had to do with my being gay. They didn't want me out doing 'gay things.' That included my having a boyfriend."

According to Calvin, Michael was closeted at work. His employer thought he was single and straight. When an opening for a transfer to Canada arose, his supervisor selected him. "He was the one person who could be transferred that didn't have to worry about family or children," Calvin says sadly. "For a while, we tried a long-distance romance, but it didn't work. Holidays were really rough. We were never able to get together. Our feelings for each other didn't change. To this day, I still love him deeply. He was my first experience with a gay relationship. We still send each other letters. It hurts, this separation, but I had to bear it more or less silently. I certainly can't talk to my parents about it. They would never understand."

Calvin relied on friends to help him cope. "There were some times when I just didn't want to go out," he explains. "They didn't let me sit around and be sad about this. They didn't let me mope in my own sorrow."

Still, losing Michael was sad, just like losing his best friend. "It felt as though someone close to me had died," he says. "I didn't have the physical part of him with me. I was devastated. I was angry with his employers, and angry at Michael because he hadn't come out to them. If he had come out, he could at least have said he was involved with me, and didn't want the transfer. Who knows? Maybe that would have made a difference. When he broke the news to me, I asked him what his options were. He said he had no choice but to either move to Canada, or lose his job. So, I left it in his hands. But it was so hard, seeing him off at the airport."

When Brian, a teacher in Austin, Texas, first met Ben, he was still dealing with issues of self-acceptance. "I had just moved out of my parents' house, and Ben was going to college," Brian explains. "He still lived with his parents. He came down to my apartment, and we hit it off. We rented a movie, but ended up talking all night rather than watching the film."

On their second date, they kissed for the first time. "My mother called the next day," Brian says. "I was really paranoid. I had this feeling that she knew something was going on, though we had done nothing more than a little heavy petting. Ben said he felt like a sixteen-year-old sneaking home that night."

Several nights later, they met for dinner. After dining, they sat in a park and talked. "Things began to smooth out between us," Brian explains. "Our terminology of self-referral was changing. I was at first calling myself bisexual. He called himself just sexual. It probably took Ben six months before he started referring to himself as gay."

Brian recalls several warning signs of impending disaster in their relationship. "Ben figured out some passwords to a computer service to which I subscribed. He read some of my e-mail. I guess he was afraid I was trolling for other men, and he didn't want to be hurt. When I found out, it was a very awkward situation."

Then, Ben accepted a job that he thought would place him on a fast career track. "It ended up flopping," Brian says. "He started to concentrate intensely on graduating [from college]. That added even more stress. He wasn't sharing things with me. In fact, he seemed to be pulling away."

Then, both men discovered the gay side of town. "For the first time, we started visiting some of the bars," Brian relates. "I thought it was fun. Ben, on the other hand, grew a little paranoid. Personally, I don't think there's anything wrong with looking at an attractive man. After all, I knew where my heart was."

However, if Ben even suspected Brian of cruising another guy, he bristled. "Do you want to fuck him?" he would demand.

But Ben was guilty of a double standard. While he could look, he felt Brian shouldn't.

One weekend, Ben informed Brian of his plans to spend the weekend with some friends. "I stayed home and watched some movies," Brian says. "Later, he told me that he had actually met this guy—Andrew—on Prodigy. They had arranged a rendezvous. Andrew had performed oral sex on him. Finally, I snapped. I just couldn't take it anymore."

However, after several months of a trial separation, Brian and Ben renewed their relationship. "During our separation, I had been able to make several good gay friends, and not worry that these friends wanted to have sex with me," Brian explains. "But when he came back, Ben was always jealous of my friends, no matter their sexual orientation. The distrust factor continued to escalate. He would try to initiate things sexually with me. What turned me on in the past was his nibbling at my ear, but it didn't turn me on anymore. We resumed our normal routines. Admittedly, we shared a lot with each other. Communication *was* better. He was also spending lots of free time with me. We even spent Christmas together, without seeing our parents. Things were getting better. Or so I thought."

Then, on New Year's Eve, Brian and Ben visited a dance club hosting a huge New Year's bash. "I'm a great people-watcher. Naturally, I wanted to sit where I could easily watch the revelers," Brian explains. "When retracted movie screens were lowered, Ben wanted to sit behind the screens. I told him I wanted to find better seats. He got pissed."

"Look, we just had a wonderful Christmas," Brian told him. "Let's not spoil the holidays. Why don't we just go home?"

They did. That same night, after yet another argument, Brian returned to the bar. "The experience was miserable," Brian admits. "I was the only one who had nobody with whom to bring in the New Year. Ben and I ironed things out the next day, but it seemed like we were always griping with one another. Our relationship was becoming so commonplace and tedious. What we had no longer seemed romantic at all. We were just people, keeping each other company. We were safe for each other."

As Brian grew more and more uncertain of the relationship, he felt his students were shortchanged. "Ben and I often stayed up late at night, discussing our problems," he explains. "Often, the next morning, I really felt bad. I wasn't motivated to go to work. The only option I had, for my own survival, was to break things off with him."

Brian told Ben that he couldn't take the way things were anymore. "I was in tears," Brian confides. "As I talked, he sat there like he was in a business meeting or something. I was telling him my deepest feelings, and he didn't seem to care. I needed someone who was supportive, I told him. When my partner says he is somewhere, I added, I need to be sure that he's not meeting another guy in the gay area of town. Ben never expressed any regret or sadness. When we hugged goodbye, he put his hands on either side of my waist, and didn't even squeeze. When I told him I loved him, he didn't say anything. Later, he told me he cried over [our breaking up], but he never cried in front of me."

Though Brian depended heavily on friends for support during his recovery, his parents knew he was gay. "I told them a long time ago that I didn't want to live in secrecy," he explains. "Mom said that she and Dad suspected all along. With her, the biggest thing is that she wants grandchildren. Well, I want children as well, so there's no problem of conflicting ideology. My new partner also wants to have children. Right off the bat, when I came out, I was really worried that I would lose my family. Mom said she and Dad could never kick me out because they loved me; I was their son. That meant a whole lot to me."

However, Ben's family never came close to the level of support Brian enjoyed from his parents. "When he started dating me, Ben showed his sister, who had been initially accepting of our relationship, a birthday card I'd sent. She told him she didn't want to see such filth. To let you know how bad things were with his family, we actually had phone calls blocked from his sister and his parents. We reached the point where we had our number changed, and unlisted. His mom is just a pawn in the whole family ordeal. She regurgitates what his father says. When Ben first came out, his father would actually show up at his job and tell his son that he loved him, but would then shout: 'You're going to hell, and you're gonna get AIDS.' When I bought a used car from Ben's father, he refused to accept a check from me. Eventually, when Ben became extremely depressed over his family situation, we agreed to regard his family as dead. Essentially, we cut off all contact."

The greater our family's acceptance level of our relationship, the more psychologically prepared we are for longevity and continuity. More difficult to ascertain are our individual reactions to families unreceptive to our partnerships. In many instances, we feel torn between commitment to our partner and dedication to our family. When both families accept our relationships, pressure subsides. When our families don't accept our partnerships, we experience a frenetic array of emotions, including depression, anger at both partner and family, and frustration. However, time monopolized by obsessions over familial rejection will take its toll on our partnership. We must be on our guard against animosity toward our family for trying to make us choose, or toward our partner, whom we may subconsciously blame for our alienation from family. When our families are susceptible to homophobia, we cannot experience the fullness of relationship with either our partner or our parents.

Pulled in Two Different Directions

An articulate legal secretary working in New York City, Sam Moore, 31, met Marc through a computer bulletin board. In a week, a face-to-face meeting materialized in a night club. "He was a strikingly beautiful man," says Sam, "and from the beginning, I was inspired by him. You see, Marc is a quadriplegic who lives his life to the utmost. He is quite undaunted by his physical limitations. I was drawn to him on a spiritual level. Of course, I could easily have been inspired by him while not being attracted to him. But I was quite attracted. It was unexpected that I would react in this way."

According to Sam, Marc was drawn to him by his softness and gentleness, his interests and intelligence. For a year and a half, their relationship was smooth sailing—although the expression of their sexuality was something of a problem.

"Marc was not as limited as one would think," Sam says. "He had much sensation in his body; he was able to get erections, but not orgasms—at least, that's what his doctors said. It took us much work to translate desire into action. But the shorthand summary of the sexual component of our relationship was that he taught me what bodies are for. Ours was a very sexual relationship. I learned much about my body, and the purpose of what bodies together are. I just accepted his inability to have an orgasm. I accepted what the doctors said as fact."

Then, one night, the most unexpected of circumstances occurred. "That night, months after we had begun to see each other, Marc actually climaxed," Sam says, in an awed voice. "That was not supposed to happen. It was the most beautiful moment I ever experienced."

However, even such a momentous occurrence could not sustain their relationship. "The problem that marred the relationship in one sense was that I was incredibly fearful of abandonment," Sam explains. "I don't know where that fear came from—perhaps from my family, or from the homophobic impressions I had of homosexual relationships. I simply could not accept that Marc loved me as much as he said he did. I couldn't accept that he wouldn't eventually leave me. After all, I had had two relationships before—one lasted five months, the other a year and a half. Marc and I discussed my insecurities, but communication didn't seem to help. Finally, things began to disassemble. I'm not sure what happened to him. We started to bicker and squabble. The arguments weren't that serious—not to me, not the way I see them."

In fact, much of the arguing tended to revolve around housekeeping. "I'm very much a messy guy, and Marc is quite neat," Sam explains. "Only indirectly did his disability contribute to the breakup. The stuff happening to us was heightened by his condition, but it wasn't caused by it. My feelings, for example, would somewhat influence the care I provided."

Then, Sam recognized another troublesome component of the relationship. "Marc is such a social person, that he would go, go, go," Sam says. "He would often spend hours and hours with friends. Once he came home at the end of the day, I would get the leftovers, so to speak. When it was our time together, he was always exhausted. I started to resent that—although I'm not sure how well I communicated my feelings to him."

Sam admits that a combination of factors contributed to their breakup. "It was just a growing apart, really, and different priorities and an inability to connect," he explains. "Our communication with each other finally revolved exclusively around problem solving within our relationship, and I finally got bored with that. It was my decision that we couldn't go on."

Sam struggles to find yet another way to express his reasons for ending their partnership. "Marc was unable to share with me what he was feeling, unless we were trying to figure out how to fix things within our relationship," he says. "He could say he loved me, but he couldn't express those feelings." Sam sighs. "I don't know whether I would have broken it off more quickly if he had not been a quadriplegic," he says. "I don't *think* that would have any effect on the timing of the breakup. The way he carries on, you almost forget about his handicap."

Time passed, and Sam withdrew. "I was trying desperately to determine whether this relationship was what I wanted," he explains. "I had to withdraw in order to protect my own spaces. Then, a sense of loss really began to affect me. I started to grieve. With Marc, his grieving was really intensified. I could tell. He was alarmed that what we had might be ending, but he couldn't put what he was feeling into words. I could see so much in his face. To be honest, his sadness and confusion intensified my momentum to leave the relationship, because his inability to communicate his feelings was reaffirmed." Sam pauses. It's easy to see that his split with Marc affected him tremendously. "I don't have a healing story to end this with," he says, half-apologetically. "I feel a lot of sadness about that. My superficial contact with Marc all through our relationship really drives me crazy. And still, even now, Marc seems unable to process his feelings. I don't feel very optimistic that our friendship will ever grow from this point, although I'm open to that possibility. It's very hard, but I accept what is."

Sam also accepts the important role that family plays in the quality of a relationship. "Yeah, I fell really hard for this guy," Sam admits. "Our relationship became rocky in terms of fighting and arguing. His brother committed suicide, and a month later, his sister did the same thing. And although I didn't admit it initially, one issue in the breakup was that his family didn't accept his homosexuality. With me, he felt pulled in two different directions. I was even tempted to move to another city to ease the sensation of resisting his family." Sam chuckles. "Perhaps I make a better ex-lover than a lover. But I can't accept the truth of that with Marc. I believe that he and I could have been so much more to each other. I have never loved anyone as deeply as I love him. But if he can't open up, there's really nothing to connect about. We even tried therapy. But Marc was unhappy about going. He just shut right down." Sam chuckles sadly. "Ironically, I'm studying to become a psychotherapist."

Although Sam has been journaling and attending psychotherapy to deal with the break-up, his family also offers a significant amount of support. "To an extreme, my family is very accepting," he explains. "They've been involved in PFLAG for years, along with other activist work. My grandmother found out that I am gay when she was ninety, and had no problem dealing with it. Honestly, I've had to deal with the homophobia of my lovers more so than with my family. My family has always been a refuge from my lovers and boyfriends, and even some of my gay friends. Marc's family, on the other hand, coped with the tragic news of his being gay by not talking about it at all. Silence is a very uncomfortable situation."

Early in their partnership, Sam and Marc planned a covenant ceremony. One reason it never occurred was the resistance of Marc's family. "His family essentially said that they'd accept me into their lives, but they'd be damned if they'd go through a wedding ceremony," he says. "So, we broke up instead."

Magical People

When families are accepting of our homosexuality, and take an actively sympathetic role in the recovery following the termination of our long-term relationships, we are much better grounded and more capable of bouncing back and enjoying our lives once more. One man's parents hosted a dinner party shortly after their son and his partner announced that they were breaking up, and invited relatives of both men to attend. The couple had enjoyed much affection from both sides of the family. News of the split was difficult for everyone. But they managed to waylay their sadness long enough to celebrate the eight years the men had shared their lives. When the evening drew to a close, many tears were shed, but these families communicated to both men their understanding of the nature and meaning of their partnership. Both men knew they could count on their families to lend a listening ear in the tough months ahead.

Engineer Kurt Colborn, who now lives in Ashtabula, Ohio, met his ex-partner at a Pittsburgh Men's Collective meeting, a profeminist men's group. They were members of the same discussion and consciousness-raising groups. This common ground led to their friendship. "His politics were more developed than mine," Kurt admits. "He was very definitely a profeminist.

At that time, I was going to the meetings to meet people as much as anything else. But we clicked in a number of ways. What I miss most about Randall exists on an intellectual level. We had wonderful conversations about philosophy, religion, and politics. We were different enough to learn from each other, yet we complemented each other in community work. He was a visionary and could see connections between other organizations and people. He was a good coalition builder. His practical skills to get work done weren't very good, but mine were. We worked well together, which helped our relationship. He would always come up with new ideas, but to make them happen—well, it took me to do that. Our fathers were both engineers; we both came from middle-class backgrounds. We thought we had a foolproof formula for a successful relationship."

But they didn't. Something was missing in their relationship—namely, emotional intimacy. "When we broke up—yes, he was unfaithful, and I wanted a different kind of relationship than he was willing to provide—I felt a real sense of anger," Kurt explains. "I thought I was going to have a relationship that would last a lifetime. At some point, Randall said, point blank, that wasn't going to happen. Nothing would change. And no change was not acceptable to me."

Kurt feels Randall's inability to be intimate was an inherent part of his personality. "Finally—and some would say too late—he learned how to connect with people better," he says. "But with me, he felt trapped and limited. Those feelings were compounded by a growing recognition of mortality. Our relationship was a limit, not an enhancement, of his life."

During the six years of their relationship, Kurt grew very close to Randall's parents. "They were great," he admits. "I recognized that the first time I ever met them. His parents were big card players. One night, his mother decided I had had too much wine to drink, and shouldn't drive home. Since Randall was legally blind by then, and naturally couldn't drive, she fixed us a bed in the basement. Even now, they refer to me as their adoptive son."

However, Kurt doesn't experience the same level of acceptance from his own parents.

One Thanksgiving, Kurt called his mother to provide their

holiday schedule. "Randall's family does Thanksgiving lunch, so we're going over there first," he told her. "We'll be at your house tonight for dinner."

"No," Kurt's mother said. "Randall's not invited."

"I have trouble remembering why I thought our presence together would be okay," Kurt says. "Randall had never been to their house. That Thanksgiving, I didn't go home. We went to my parents at Christmas, but it was tense and awkward. To be honest, I can't deal with the idea of not visiting my parents over the holidays. Without meaning to sound egotistical, I'm the one who brings some life into the house. Things did eventually get better. Talking about things is not something my family does. Because of their attitude toward my relationship with Randall, my friendship with my parents has suffered. I have not been able to talk about our breakup with them, that's for sure."

How did Kurt deal with the breakup? "It was disorienting for a long time," he admits. "It was somewhat difficult for me to relate sexually to other people because I had become so accustomed to Randall's body. It was his body that turned me on. In my relationships with others—I was handicapped by that discomfort. A friend whose wife died after thirty years of marriage said it was difficult for him to get accustomed to anyone else because it was her body that he related to sexually for so long. I hope I have the patience to get involved in a long-term relationship again. It's very hard to endure the time it takes to cultivate that kind of intimacy again. Randall and I salvaged the best parts of our relationship and put them into something that transcended our friendship. We developed something great from our long history. I feel an impatience, I admit, to have a common history with someone again."

Soon after Kurt and Randall broke up, social activism brought them together once more. "I realized then that neither one of us ever had a better sounding board," Kurt says. "I think he realized that, too. In fact, he asked to be lovers again. It was hard for me to say no."

In June 1996, Randall died. "He bought me a ring shortly before his death," Kurt says quietly. "A Christmas gift. I have it now, and I wear it all the time. I think this gift, really, is an indication of how his HIV status might have contributed to his ability to connect to people more intimately."

Although Jeff, 38, an administrator living in Lexington, Kentucky, isn't out to his parents, he often relies on them for emotional support. He calls his relationship with his family "magical." "They didn't see me for a year after I broke up with Cory," he admits. "But there were a lot of telephone conversations. Honest ones. They know how to be supportive while respecting my space."

When Jeff met Cory, Jeff had been involved in a heterosexual relationship for seven years. "At that time, I didn't put a label on anything," Jeff says. "But through my work with an arts group, I met Cory. He was a performer, and we attended a lot of functions together. As time progressed, we got to know each other. He was also dating a woman I was interested in."

Jeff also heard, through the grapevine, that Cory was essentially gay. One evening, superficial conversation quickly grew meaningful.

"We've known each other quite a while," Jeff said. "You've never talked about your past with other men."

As it happened, Cory had just broken up with Julie. "You know the reason I broke up with her, don't you?"

Jeff shook his head.

"Well, the reason is simple. I want you."

"It's sad that you ended a relationship because of me," Jeff replied. "That makes me feel horrible. I've never even considered having a relationship with a man."

Several days later, Jeff admitted to Cory that he wouldn't object to "an experience." "We wound up in bed together, and we were in bed together for the next five years," Jeff relates. "Cory is both fun and funny. He's childlike in the way he approaches life. He tends to look at life as though it's Romper Room. Our relationship was full of energy. He was incredibly romantic. He was very easy to be with as a man—he was neither extremely masculine or effeminate. There was simply no gender identity about him. I never even thought about the fact that we were two men having a relationship. About a month into the relationship, I regarded my homosexuality as something that was within me that I hadn't experienced. There was no coming-out crisis. I was sexually involved with a woman for seven years, and there was no problem with sexual function. But I was simply in love with Cory.''

Soon, however, Jeff realized that Cory lacked considerable ego strength. ''No matter how he presented himself, there was something missing,'' he explains. ''He emulated the way I dressed, the way I talked. He came from a Puerto Rican family. His father was a violent man. Once, I tried to discuss his father's violence with him. I asked if he was ever sad or depressed—he always pretended to be so cheerful. He would deny it, emphatically. Then, the single time I intervened in a violent altercation between Cory and his father, our relationship changed.''

Part of that change occurred when Jeff realized that he was filling a role for which he had not bargained. ''Like many gay men, Cory had lots of insecurities, and a heavy lack of self-esteem,'' he explains. ''I am not a mental hospital—that's my attitude. Pay for your own therapy. Most gay men I know carry around an impending sense of doom. I have no patience for it.''

Still, Jeff regrets his minimal contact with Cory's mother and siblings. ''His mother is a tremendous human being,'' he says fondly. ''I ran into her about a year and a half ago. She was shopping with Cory's sister, who said she missed me so much. I love them to death.''

But allegiance to the family of one's partner is no reason to prolong a bad relationship. ''On New Year's Day, I went to Mass to get my focus,'' he says. ''I was empty. There were many conversations with Cory when I would say, 'You've got to slow down a little. I have nothing left to give.' Eventually, I became a husk. I became a less-than-nice person. I became rude to my friends—mainly because I was so pissed off at myself because I had nothing. I was depleted.''

After a messy separation, Jeff began therapy, which lasted for three years. ''My counselor is a great lady,'' he says. ''But she was surprised by my refusal to be medicated. I'm going to feel my pain, and I'm going to learn from it. I told her not to give me that bullshit about my mother changing my diapers the wrong way, or that I harbor a latent hatred of my father. Still, I was pretty fucked up.''

At a particularly low point during counseling, Jeff stopped

eating. He would come home, step into the bedroom he once shared with Cory, then lie down on his side of the bed. There, he would fall asleep, get up, then go to work. "Everyone thought I was sick. There were whisperings about some mysterious illness. People even thought I might have AIDS. I didn't answer my door or my phone for the longest time, adding to the suspicions. Eventually, I moved into another apartment."

Jeff's disgust with Cory was equally matched by disgust with himself. "But counseling taught me that my strengths were not lost, just hidden," he says. "I was able to tap back into them. I grew resentful of having had my personal growth interrupted by my relationship with Cory. I bemoaned the fact that I would have been so much further along in my life if it hadn't been for him. My fight for myself accelerated with that realization. I feel now as though I'm finally catching up."

Jeff attributes part of his "catching up" to the support of his family. "I exhibited independence at a young age, and that's the way my parents treated my distancing at the time," Jeff explains. "I also distanced myself from my parents when I hooked up with Cory. This breakup brought me to a reestablishment of my relationship with them."

During a Sunday visit, Jeff asked his mother when he became "my own person."

"At the age of twelve, Jeff, you became an independent person who lived in this house, but regarded himself as separated from the goings-on of the household," his mother replied. "We always respected the fact that you made your own decisions. And we always will."

Jeff was also very close to his grandmother. "She could always sense and say the right things," he says. "I was devastated when she died. She was such a magical person—in so many ways."

Jeff began the exploration of his identity with the support and patience of his parents and his grandmother. "They never initiated conversations," he says. "They never pried. But I knew it was safe to bring up any subject. They respected my space. When I was involved with a woman, they never asked about our relationship. They respected us whether we were simply friends, or lovers. It didn't matter. My personal relationships don't affect who I am to them. It's just me to them."

Jeff feels it's unnecessary to proclaim his homosexuality directly to his parents. "I expect that they suspect," he says. "Besides, mothers always know. If she asked me, I would tell her the truth."

The evening following Jeff's and Cory's breakup, Jeff received an interesting, albeit ironic, phone call from his mother.

"Your father and I have been talking," she said. "We want to apologize if we did anything in your upbringing to make you as sad as you have been lately. We were young, too, when we raised you. We didn't know everything that was best to do. We also want to apologize for raising you to be too nice. We didn't give you the qualities to deal with people who may take advantage of you."

Mirrors

Our families often reflect a variety of our inclinations to respond, as adults, to intimate relationships. As a result, we bear an obligation, both to ourselves and to our partners, to examine patterns of intimacy within our family system. Such an examination may help us to avoid counterproductive patterns of response, and to capitalize on positive patterns integrated into our personalities during childhood.

Identification of our response patterns involves a cultivation of our own observation skills, and a knowledge of what to look for. Here is a list of relationship issues frequently shaped by parental influences.

1. *Level of Commitment.* Did our parents model the kind of partnership where their dedication to their marriage and to each other was unquestionable? Was it obvious to us that their first and foremost allegiance was to each other? Or did their marriage contain elements of emotional distance compelling us to question their level of commitment to one another? Were we, as children living within the family structure, aware of infidelities committed by either or both parents? If we doubted our parents' level of commitment, a resulting cynicism may have caused us to question the value or permanence of romantic relationships. Incumbent

on us is the determination of our own standards, and the awareness of parental influence on those standards.

2. *Expression of Intimacy.* Many men reported loneliness and
disappointment resulting from a partner's inability to communicate his feelings openly and assertively. Others suffering problems
of communication often admitted that their families offered no
models on which to base developing communication skills. Perhaps our parents were uncomfortable with physical displays of
affection in front of the children. Perhaps they infrequently
expressed their feelings for one another. An important way we
learn to be emotionally demonstrative is drawn from the model-
ing our parents provide through affectionate displays to us, their
children. If our parents felt children should be seen and not
heard, or felt an extreme discomfort in expressing affection to
us, then we have been deprived of a most important lesson in
intimacy. However, if our parents were liberal with honest emotions, embraces and other affectionate displays, we were lucky to
have grown up in a fertile training field.

3. *Communication Skills.* Families also provide our most fundamental training for interaction with the world around us. We are
lucky indeed if our parents were assertive communicators—i.e.,
they expressed their thoughts, needs and feelings in ways that
did not incite animosity, defensiveness, aggression or emotional
injury. When our parents did not model effective communication
skills, our schools may have filled part of the gap. But our capacity
for assertive communication is most dynamically influenced by
our parents. "In my mother's eyes, my behavior was never quite
up to snuff," says Bill Salley, 37, a financial planning advisor in
Miami. "She was always extremely critical of me. Maybe because
I'm the oldest of her four offspring, she was under a lot of self-
imposed pressure to make sure I didn't turn out badly. At any
rate, during my first long-term relationship, I became the reincar-
nation of my mother—constantly criticizing my partner, acting
hurt and defensive if he disappointed me, rather than really
expressing what was going on. It was really scary. I spent a few
months in counseling before I realized that, as much as I loved
my mother, she had taught me really lousy communication skills.
I realized that she was doing her best at the time, so I forgave
her, and made the necessary changes in my behavior. I have been

in love with my current partner for almost ten years. Part of the success of our relationship I can attribute to the open way we communicate with each other."

4. *Sexual Values.* Our attitudes toward sexuality and sexual values are also influenced by our parents. In our case, the most damaging stance would be parental condemnation of homosexuality. As children, we are incredibly vulnerable to their influences. We can never fully determine the psychological damage we sustain when our most significant caregivers equate a part of our identity to filth, moral decay, sin, and even the destruction of civilization. However, even if our parents remain silent about homosexuality, we often assimilate at least some of their sexual values. Many parents are too embarrassed to have that chat about the birds and the bees. If they weren't embarrassed, they would probably ignore Nature's variations that are important to us. What does that negligence suggest about sexuality? Perhaps they regard sex from a biblical perspective—a necessary evil visited upon us by God because of our disobedience in the Garden of Eden. Did they blush and avert their eyes whenever adult conversation turned to matters of sex and sexual expression? Were they embarrassed by references to bodily functions, sometimes using cute, infantile expressions to sanitize them? Did they ever openly express sexual desire for one another? Were they rigid in their views of the acceptability of sexual expression— i.e., was there only one way to "do it," with all variant modes of sexual expressions regarded as perversions of what Nature intended? "Although my sexual attitudes weren't the sole cause of my split with Bobby," says Neil Capra, 28, manager of a Las Vegas department store, "they certainly put a lot of pressure on our relationship. I'm originally from the Deep South, and in spite of the southern growth spurt, I think sexual attitudes over there are more medieval than in other parts of the country. My parents never talked about sex. I got the impression that it was a taboo subject—which, to my adolescent mind, made it even more appealing and intriguing. However, I also think their silence exaggerated the importance of sex. If Bobby and I weren't making love almost every night of the week, I was convinced something had gone awry in our relationship."

5. *Environmental Tones.* Because eighteen (or more) years of living with the same people under the same roof creates strong familiarity, we may be strongly inclined to establish a similar experience when we set up housekeeping. However, we must not forget that our partner brings his own familial history into the partnership, as well. He may be just as motivated, consciously or not, to duplicate his own experiences. If both of us have enjoyed childhoods with few rocky patches, understanding parents who always communicated well, and no sibling rivalry, then the environmental tone of our own household might benefit from following a similar pattern. But those of us living in the real world can remember many instances of familial conflict and confusion. Some of us may remember nothing else. In the best interest of our relationship, we should have a powwow early on with our partner about the characteristics of our families of origin. In the long run, we will better understand one another's idiosyncrasies and perceived needs. "Trey and I discovered a big difference in the way our parents operated," says Ed Salomon, 34, a business executive living in Roanoke, Virginia. "While Trey was accustomed to a very quiet family life—he was an only child, too, you see—I came from a very large, noisy family. His parents listened to classical music, read frequently, listened to public radio. My parents wore their emotions on their sleeves—talked first, thought later. My siblings and I all had different interests. Our house always bustled with activity. So, when Trey and I got together, we had a major culture clash. He couldn't stand the volume at which I played the television, and I felt ignored when he wanted to spend an evening quietly reading a book. It took months of talk, exploration, and experimentation before we created a home comfortable to us both."

Even if we never examined our childhoods during our relationship, it is essential to revisit our family histories when our relationships end. Not only do we gain valuable insight into our personalities, we also grow attuned to changes we may need to implement if, or when, we pursue another partnership. Our families are our mirrors. Either we use them to check the way we look, uncritically and superficially, then shrug, turn away, and say to ourselves: "This is the way I am. Take me or leave me."

Or we can take a more insightful look, with strong motivation toward change.

A tilt of the hat forward. A little more emphasis on the smile. Maybe we need to stand a little taller.

Or perhaps we should throw in a dash of mystery.

Family Empathy Quotient (FEQ)

To determine the likelihood of receiving any real help from your family after your partnership ends, mark the following statements "Yes" or "No," based on observations and knowledge of your relatives. Indicate your responses in the chart following the statements.

1. Members of my family are affiliated with a progressive or "affirming" congregation.
2. My partner was always included in holiday activities.
3. My family addressed holiday cards to us collectively, or sent separate cards to both of us.
4. My parents can discuss homosexuality without getting embarrassed.
5. When my ex and I committed to each other, my family seemed very happy for me.
6. I remember my parents saying, "I love you, but I don't approve of your lifestyle."
7. When my ex and I broke up, someone in my family indicated that the divorce was inevitable.
8. My family changes the subject quickly when the subject of homosexuality arises.
9. Members of my family have joined the Christian Coalition, the American Family Association, or some other fundamentalist group.
10. When my ex and I were together, my parents always conveniently "forgot" to introduce my partner to others.
11. My parents always remembered the birthdays of my straight in-laws, but never remembered my ex's birthday.
12. No matter how much literature I give my parents on the topic of homosexuality, they make excuses about not having read it.

13. Family members never liked my ex-partner because of his personality traits, not because of his sexual orientation.
14. Certain members of my family object to homosexuality on religious grounds.
15. I can recall many times that members of my family said cruel things about homosexuality.
16. At least one family member once told me that my ex-partner seemed just like one of the family.
17. Family members called to offer their support and sympathy when they heard of the breakup.
18. Family members have at least one gay or lesbian friend.
19. My family recommends literature about homosexual issues to *me.*
20. Members of my family belong to PFLAG or some other pro-gay group.
21. My parents didn't have a very satisfying partnership.
22. My parents believe in the concept of "hating the sin but loving the sinner" in reference to gays and lesbians.
23. Politically, members of my family equate equal rights for gays to special rights.
24. I came out to my parents only when my ex-partner and I committed to a long-term relationship.
25. My parents didn't ask how my partner was doing.

A	B	C	D	E
1.	6.	11.	16.	21.
2.	7.	12.	17.	22.
3.	8.	13.	18.	23.
4.	9.	14.	19.	24.
5.	10.	15.	20.	25.

For columns A and D, add all "yes" responses.
Place total number of "yes" responses here: _____

For columns B, C, and E, add all "no" responses.
Place total number of "no" responses here: _____

Total the numbers you indicated above, and place that total here. The total is your FEQ: _____

The higher your FEQ, the more likely your family is to help you out.

Key:

0–10: Family is best left out of it.

11–18: Family may be helpful, but don't depend on them as your only parachute.

19 or more: Count on support. Your family will very likely be a port in this storm.

CHAPTER EIGHT

•••••••••••••••••••••

The Urge to Merge

The Circumcision of Souls

We can experience no greater satisfaction than the knowledge that we are part of something greater than ourselves. That feeling applies to our status as an equal partner in a relationship. We feel diminished as individuals once the reality of breaking up sets in. For a long time, many of our activities were both planned and executed as a team. While routine soon settled into our lives, our quickly established traditions provided stability and security. We seldom felt as though fulfilling our roles within the partnership diminished our identities in the least. In fact, we were definitely on a growth track. No longer were we responsible for coming up with ways to avoid feeling alone in the world. We never wondered if we'd ever find someone who would love us enough to want to spend his life with us. Once we hooked up, we felt anchored enough to explore life's offerings, without fear of sailing too far away from the dock. Buoyed by our partner's love, we were empowered to explore parts of our personalities we never even knew existed. In fact, we wonder if we would have ever cultivated our present depth of character without our partner's role in our growth. "A friend once said that he pitied me because of my pathological need to have a partner," says Rick Buergerner, a former New England educator now living in Myrtle Beach, South Carolina. "He said that while our lives together would be exciting for a short and intense period of time, we would eventually grow tired and contemptuous of each other. I reminded him that my life was full of routine before I met Clayton. Actually, meeting Clayton caused me to break up my routines so that I could spend time with him. Yeah, it's true that Clayton and I established some new routines, but we also promised that we wouldn't allow our lives to grow stagnant. What gave me a lot of pleasure was pointing out to my friend the routines in his life that he wasn't even aware of." Rick chuckles. "I get really tired of hearing the same old hype about the limitations partnerships place on us. Yes, they have the potential to do that, but they don't have to."

Much more likely than limiting our lives is the possibility that partnerships establish revolutionary familial links. Upon leaving the nest and the protective arms of Mom and Dad, we long for the same sense of connection we enjoyed while part of a "traditional" family structure. In the early stages of laying the foundation for our lives, we aren't likely to experience such a strong sense of belonging. For a while, we have little opportunity to miss the sensation, since we are forging ahead in our jobs, our personal lives, our very independence. Soon, however, we long to recapture the familiar sensations of family. When we finally hook up with our long-term partner, our sense of detachment from life begins to dissipate. In time, we grow so close to him that his presence provides greater comfort and security than the presence of our biological families ever did. When our relationships gestate over a long period of time, we eventually feel a connection with and knowledge of him that is so deep, everyone will notice our partner's significance. The smells, sights, textures, moods, and sounds of the homes we have made grow even greater in significance than those of the homes where our childhoods were spent. "What was difficult for the both of us," says Rick, "was telling our parents that on occasional holidays, Clayton and I preferred to spend time together, without sharing it with parents or brothers and sisters. Our parents simply didn't want to hear any of that. We tried to be sensitive when explaining our feelings to them. But the fact was that our biological families consisted of people we no longer knew all that well, while the family Clayton and I had created had become the home our parents begged us to visit. It took a couple of years, but we finally created lives which identified us as a family—to our parents, to our friends, to our neighbors. No, we didn't have kids, but neither do my sister and her husband, who have been married ten years. Still, they're regarded as a family, and that's the way Clayton and I felt we should be regarded, too. I'm happy to say that most people we knew felt just that way about us."

However, once breaking up becomes inevitable, our perception of the relationship changes dramatically. In degrees proportionate to the duration of our relationship, we are struck by the perplexed feeling of having wasted a portion of our lives. As a result, we may experience hostility and anger toward our ex-partner—particularly if he initiated the split. After all, we hopped on the relationship wagon for the long haul. We assimilated into our lives Yeats's plans of growing old and gray and nodding by the fire. Now, we're certainly older. Maybe we're a lot grayer. But the fire has been extinguished. In fact, our ex is quite the asshole for misleading us for so long before telling us we couldn't make it as partners. Maybe we're not all *that* old. But we're old enough. Getting someone else interested in us now sure as hell won't be easy. And what of that spare tire we've been wearing around our middle? Quite a challenge losing it will be as we prepare ourselves for dating once again. We have all sorts of work to do before we're willing to be seen even in the subdued lighting of the clubs.

Perhaps such thinking sounds superficial. Perhaps we want credit for more depth than that. But many of us experiencing the shock of breaking up feel severely demoralized before we grapple with more substantive issues. What we want to avoid more than anything else is loneliness. We defeated loneliness in the past with that loving man who packed his bags several weeks ago. Often, we negotiate what we perceive to be the best steps to replace him before we seriously consider the bigger issues of getting our lives back in order.

Another consideration after breaking up revolves around the authenticity of our past relationship. We long to understand its meaning. We want assurance that our relationship was as significant as we thought. Or have we been the victim of wily deception? Our natures often tempt us to think in absolutes, even though our rational mind tells us that nothing is one hundred percent certain. Most relationships were never all good or all bad. Determining the positive and negative components of our relationship is the challenge facing us now. We must resist labeling the relationship as the worst experience of our lives, thereby increasing our bitterness and suffering. We must also resist an unrealistic regard of it as the best thing that ever happened.

In essence, we haven't merely lost the man with whom we thought we'd spend the rest of our lives. We have also lost the connection of family. Life's adventures are much more exciting with the anticipation of hearth and home at the end of the day's odyssey. Now, home seems such a temporary place, and the hearth is always cold. Our experience now isn't just a confrontation of being alone. "That man" has snipped away part of our identity. It's as simple and as maddening as that. Our relationship energized us. Our lives not only were connected, but also assumed greater meaning. What does our life mean now? we wonder. Did it really have meaning before? Or did we confuse feelings of security with meaning and substance?

"I never felt such a sense of floundering as I did when Clayton and I broke up," Rick admits. "I thought way back, to a time before I ever experienced falling in love. I recalled that feeling— of not being in love—and felt it was better than anything I'd ever felt since. I came across to friends and colleagues as self-assured and independent. I had plenty of friends. I had lots of good times. And then I met Clayton. I thought that if you can't *sustain* something in life—even if it's something superficial— then what life boils down to is nothing. And for a long time, that's what I thought we had. Nothing. Everything had been an illusion. I had been duped. I was so stupid! Several months passed before I was able to salvage something of value from the relationship. Guess you can say I'm still in the process of salvaging. Periodically, I will review what Clayton and I had, and I will grasp something else that makes me feel better—something that reminds me of what my life means. For example, I was a very selfish person before I met Clayton. He taught me what it means to be a giving person. I realized that I may have lost Clayton, but I haven't lost my capacity to be unselfish. That quality will be very beneficial as I establish new relationships in the future—a future I'm gradually beginning to regard as very, very bright."

As Rick implies, our self-esteem inevitably takes a beating once our partnership dissolves. The wholeness defining our identity gradually fades, and some of our connections short-circuit. The certainty of self-knowledge dissipates. We feel there's no way to survive. The circumstances constituting our life's most defining moments have come to an end. "I have searched and searched for a metaphor to describe what it's like," says Rick. "I don't want to imply that my whole sense of self was destroyed by breaking up with Clayton. But he was an essential part of me in a meaningful, spiritual way. I used to apologize for the use of that word, *spiritual.* Not now. I can separate my use of the word from what the fundies mean. To me, spiritual means mysterious—a mystery that's impossible to solve. So yes, Clayton was attached to me spiritually. We were two souls joined. And when we decided we couldn't go on as a couple anymore, I experienced what I refer to as the circumcision of our souls. Yeah, the core of us remains. But part of us is missing—a significant part that causes pain and longing. Healing occurs. Of course it does. But even the most complete healing leaves a scar."

Single Again

One of the strangest sensations we'll ever experience occurs when we find ourselves single again. It's like walking into an unfamiliar setting, with no guide map. Any familiarity with the place has to be obtained through trial-and-error. A piece of furniture here, a strange painting over there, doors leading into rooms we never imagined, unfamiliar sounds emanating from somewhere behind those walls—there's something enticing about the exploration, but something frightening, too. We aren't capable of knowing, without intense inspection, the implications of discovery. After breaking up, our psychic interiors become fragmented, even frightening. We are forced to participate in a search of marvelous magnitude, but not without the trepidation and the fright typifying any foray into the unknown. For what we have become to ourselves are strangers searching for redefinition. As we continue the search, we feel as strangers to ourselves, uncertain, fearing the wrong moves, self-censoring so that we don't say or do the wrong things.

Again, Rick recalls his experience. "It would have been easier for me to latch on to a new guy right after Clayton and I split up than at any other time in my life," he says. "My ego had been depleted. My self-confidence was shaken. I felt an urge to attach myself to another person right away, as though such a merger would have reestablished my sense of self. My house felt as though it didn't belong to me. My friends weren't completely mine. Even my car seemed to belong to someone else. When the phone rang, I wondered whether the caller would want to speak to me, or to Clayton. This was so weird, you know? It wasn't exactly an emptiness inside, but that was part of it. I felt optimistic about my future. I was mature enough to realize that I would grow beyond the pain. But so much had to be done for my full recovery. I wanted to hook up with another man right away. I was blind, then, to the qualities I wanted in another partner. I was susceptible to anyone who might find me attractive, personable, worthwhile. I was ready to try on almost any identity anyone wanted to provide for me."

Quickly, Rick moved beyond this dependence. "I decided to embrace the uncomfortable quality of strangeness in my life. I would be patient as I got to know myself again, and my surroundings grew familiar once more. It was hard, to be sure, because I had to confront and experience feelings that followed the split. However, I also had to keep in touch with my rational side. Otherwise, my feelings would have directed me toward some pretty damned big mistakes."

Besides feeling as strangers to ourselves, we are likely to experience an even more bizarre sensation. Even close friends and colleagues suddenly assume a Chagallian quality once our relationship dissolves. Who are these people? we wonder. How did we come to know them? In our minds, we see them staring at us with expressions of perplexity. Sometimes, they may even appear to be amused by us. When they speak, the quality of their voices seems alien to us. We feel we have heard them for the first time. Sometimes, what they say makes little sense. We also notice their tiresome fuck-up of mentioning our ex-partner each time they visit.

Once, we regarded these people as friends. We still do, but now, we're no longer sure what we have in common. Maybe we're just paranoid, but we're certain they're entertaining the same doubts. Their facial expressions convey that they don't know who we are anymore. Well, we concede, the feeling is mutual. When they speak of personal aspects of our lives, we experience a sense of violation, as though strangers have stolen our diary. Yet, we recognize them as friends. We care about each other, but don't quite trust each other. Our feelings are crazy, but how can our friends know us now when we don't even know ourselves? We're determined to open lines of communication, but how much time must pass before we can really *talk* with each other again? How long will it be before anyone understands what we're saying?

Once more, we rely on our friend, Rick, to clarify the experience. "I spent a lot of time with friends after Clayton and I split up," he says. "There were times when I know I looked a little crazy to them. I felt a little crazy to myself. Once, I had to stop myself from saying: 'Who *are* you, for goodness' sake?' When a foundation as solid as the one Clayton and I had turns out to be situated on mud, I think it's to be expected that after the mudslide, life will be a little different. We must give ourselves time to recognize that the world is still the same. We have to put up with a little dust and debris during reconstruction. Eventually, we'll be able to spot a familiar environment. The worst thing to do is run away, searching for a prettier landscape and a sturdier foundation, when all we're doing, really, is running away from ourselves."

Loneliness is inevitable when we're living in a world turned upside down. Like earthquakes, tornadoes, and hurricanes, the disaster in our life weakened us before we could gain strength. We are left with no connections in the world. If we have connections, they feel tenuous, at best. Our best efforts to strengthen those connections often backfire. We renew an old friendship after breaking up, only to lose the old friend to cancer just months after the renewal began. We seek empathy from our family, only to realize they have unresolved homophobic attitudes we never suspected before. We seek companionship and clarity from our current friends, only to recognize that they are also mourning the dissolution of our relationship. They have no idea how to relate to us as a single man. At times, we float from one event in our lives to another; there is no solid ground on which to place our feet. More than ever, we understand that to experience true freedom, we need to be tied to something that elevates our lives. We're tied to nothing right now. We know what it means to be without direction. And God knows what it means to be without the man who knew us almost as well as we knew ourselves. Our lack of connection reminds us of the fog that drifts in after smoking a joint. This time, we have no guarantee of awakening to a clear morning. God knows our loneliness feels more like a prison sentence, and less like a growth experience. We don't care what the *Psychology Today* article says about breaking up. We don't watch the afternoon talk shows, either. The only good advice remains the most painful: Suffer, suffer, endure, endure. The only good advice has become our mantra.

Maybe some higher purpose is served by this test of endurance. Only, we feel like frauds. If we want to save face, we are probably walking through life wearing a smile. Who do we think we're fooling? We're smiling only because we don't want to bring anyone else down. As observers of our new but painful lives—we're not really capable of *living* them yet—we know that wherever we are beneath this veneer of hypocrisy, we don't care about *their* feelings. Hell, we don't even care all that much about life. Which is a far cry from our first experiences of being single. We once equated singlehood with independence. Now, independence feels a lot like desperation. Once, the world was our oyster and the clubs were orchards in which to locate the apple of our eye. Once, our lives blossomed with possibilities. We met the world head-on. We gave life one hundred percent. We gave it all. We felt no detachment because our lives were open books. We were empowered authors ready to fill each page with our poignant adventures. The smiles on our faces each morning weren't painted on; they were the genuine article. Now, fear is our dominant experience.

Predictably, Rick has a few observations about being single again. "Shortly after Clayton packed his bags and moved away, I recognized the power potential in being single. I recognized it intellectually, but didn't really feel it—not deep in my gut, where it would mean something. Here's new life again, I thought. But the minute I felt the energy from that viewpoint, I was struck by the sensation that I would, in a way, have to start certain components of my life all over again. For quite some time, I vacillated between optimism that I could create so many changes in my life and pessimism that, somehow, I had relinquished the best qualities of my life. Life felt shabby and cheap. Not quite my own. I was living a predictable virtual reality, but I was growing increasingly impatient for my life's true reality. It took a while to understand that rekindling the fire of one's life—the fire in the belly, to steal a phrase from the men's movement—didn't mean that my first priority was to find another man.''

Junctures

Once we accept—*really accept*—that we are single again, our lives are poised at several very important junctures. First and foremost, we must decide whether we are brave enough to face our vulnerabilities. We should not succumb to temptations that seem, upon first examination, to be our best options. It would be easy to regard our efforts at healing as a waste of time, the obsession of the introvert who postpones living fully while he analyzes his life *ad nauseam*. Real commitment to recovery compels us to take action. When we are committed to recovery, we examine forthrightly what has weakened us, dimmed our vision, and changed our taste for life; such examination occurs only when we segue into thoughtful introspection. We can choose to play only the games with familiar rules, but those games are merely the anesthetic, not the cure. "Yeah, I turned into quite the little whore once we broke up," Rick admits. "That lasted about three months, then I got really tired of it. There is one thing you can say about casual sex, though, and no one can argue with you. Finding it takes a lot of energy. Fighting the emotions that occasionally creep into even casual relationships finally exhausts you. Of course, you have to fill your life with activity, or you'll go nuts. But it's often not growth-oriented activity. Soon, I grew very numb. I stopped all the screwing around. When I faced my pain, rather than covering it up with my capacity for orgasm, doing the required work on myself became so much easier. Maybe my promiscuous period was something I had to experience. Maybe many of us have to experience it. But it's really naïve to try to

convince ourselves that sex is a substitute for, or even comple-
ments, what we have to experience before becoming functional
human beings again."

Just as capricious as hopping from bedroom to bedroom is
the proclivity some of us feel to rush headlong into another
partnership. The proverbial "urge to merge" is an incredible
trickster; we might feel the new man we've met is The One. How
could we possibly be mistaken? No other man is as magnificent.
He understands us. He worships us. He is hot in bed. He can
intrigue us with conversation all hours of the day or night. Our ex
pales by comparison. How, we wonder, could we have sentenced
ourselves to the mediocrity of the man who recently drove away
behind the United Van Lines truck? Soon—much *too* soon, actually—we're thinking commitment. He's talking it. That silver-
tongued little devil, we think, while melting in our shoes. What
he says is precisely what we want to hear. Before long, we're
sharing the same underwear, the same towels, the same bed, the
same address. Then, one morning, we wake up before he does,
take a quick look at the snoring man beside us, and wonder what
we've gotten ourselves into. We don't want to admit our error
when we told him we had eyes for no other man, so we say—
nothing. At least, we *verbalize* nothing. But we start to give all
kinds of signals that we've made One Big Mistake.

If we didn't have to account for another man's feelings, experimentation with a new partnership wouldn't be such a big deal.
But we're still close to breaking up. How can we inflict such pain?
We're better than that—better than our ex. Besides, what do we
say? "You know, I realize now that I said 'I do' because I was
feeling terribly lonely, but maybe being single isn't such a bad
idea for a while." Then, we push him gently out the back door.
We even pack his belongings into the trunk of his car. We kiss
him goodbye, and tell him we'll see him later. We know, however,
we've had our fill of him. As he drives away, we tell ourselves
that he's a grown man; he'll get over it.

But grown men can be hurt, too. Many of us are afraid of
commitment simply because we've been hurt far too often. We
were taught that a man is as good as his word—particularly a
man who means everything to us. Upon discovering that what
he says has no more substance than the stream of air on which

the words were uttered, we suffer because of his breach of our faith. When we move too fast into a new relationship, we risk eroding our confidence in our own ability to make good decisions. We also risk inflicting deep emotional scars on someone else. No matter how well he seems to take our change of heart, somewhere beneath the veneer of confidence lies pain. "The minute you feel you can confidently say, 'I'm ready for a new relationship,' chances are you need to wait another six months before you're *really* ready," advises Rick. "Besides, if you have established a good relationship with another man, you can wait a little while longer before you exchange rings and pick out china patterns. Our craving for happiness, just like our inclination to avoid pain, sometimes makes us do foolish things."

Pain avoidance also entices us to steer away from solitude. Chances are, after a couple of years with the ex, we grew comfortable enough to cherish our times alone. We could be ourselves more fully because of the liberating qualities of his presence. How easy it was to enjoy being alone, when we knew it was only a temporary condition. However, knowing the other side of the bed is perpetually empty, and the dog's barking signals the arrival of neighbors, not our lover, makes solitude no longer satisfying, but awkward. Where solitude once provided space for mental and spiritual growth, now we find the experience toxic and fear-provoking. *Who is this man with whom we're spending so much time alone?* we wonder. *Can he be trusted? Does he have something edifying to tell us?* Perhaps the most disturbing revelation of solitude is the potential discovery that we have no answers for the questions plaguing us. Sometimes, we discover we don't have access to the right questions. Languishing in personal confusion, we feel diminished, as though our identities are being funneled away. Whereas solitude once provided space for introspection and intonation, now that space is consumed by disharmony, perplexity, and discord. The more important our questions, the more elusive the answers seem to be. The experience provokes frustration, not amplification.

Still, if recovery is indeed our goal, solitude must become a positive experience for us. Sometimes, we confuse loneliness and aloneness. Loneliness is an emotional state that must be escaped. It is the awareness of a nagging, parasitic ache, a void receptive only to the negative emotions of self-pity and self-doubt. Loneliness leads us to mistake illusions for reality, like fleeting sexual gratification for fulfillment, like thinking a man who enjoys our company is in love with us. Loneliness gives us the capacity to fill up quickly, but the process of emptying out is twice as fast. Loneliness tricks us into doing nothing, accepting defeat when life requires much more of us if we want to feel alive again. Loneliness is counting a million sheep at night when we could be watching the stars. Loneliness is staying at home when we could attend a concert with friends. "Loneliness," Rick says, "was my punishment for accepting defeat. When I started fighting again, loneliness abandoned me."

Aloneness, however, is quite a different experience. It is our ability to converse with ourselves, without the incumbent feeling of going crazy. Aloneness is the conviction that we are our own best company, a sensation influencing the quality of our friendships because self-assurance adds pleasure to our companionship. Aloneness is the willingness to turn off the television and the stereo so that we can get in touch with our sadness. Aloneness is, above all, patience. Patience while we redefine our life. Patience like the predator while waiting for life we want to seize, to tear into, to savor and consume. Aloneness is the only experience allowing us to hear the lyrics of our lives.

But above all, aloneness is the joint act of clarification and purification. In the solitary state, we push forward in our quest to purge our spirits of life's toxins. Our success depends on our ability to identify what impedes our happiness, what stumps our mobility, what breeds the debilitation of loneliness. After clarification, we purge life of its poisons. Purification leaves room for self-knowledge. When we live with self-knowledge, we can act without second-guessing ourselves, and without self-absorption. "After getting sex out of my system," says Rick, "I allowed myself the experience of solitude. I explored several types of meditation and some yoga techniques. I even saw a spiritualist once a week. Soon, I stopped being so uncomfortable with myself. I was able to see that my relationship didn't fail. The end of it wasn't something 'bad' that happened. Our breakup was yet another passage in my journey through life—a journey which, if you are true to it, does nothing to devalue a man's existence."

However, the rediscovery of solitude should never replace the renewal of friendships. Rather, growth through solitude should complement our growth through social interaction and public interface. Despite our temptation to withdraw socially, we should resist by reestablishing old friendships and pursuing new ones. We know ourselves more moderately when we surround ourselves with friends, family, and associates. But what happens to our growth as a result of such interaction? As social beings, we don't experience spiritual growth solely through the contemplation of our navels. In some ways, we're similar to the Borg in *Star Trek.* We assimilate.

Martha, a lesbian neighbor, tells us how she got even with Gwen, her ex-lover. Our memory catalogs her tale—not because we want to emulate her behavior, but because her story is proof that revenge breeds bitterness. Upon meeting a philosophy professor after a lecture we attend with Damon, our new boyfriend who is pursuing his doctorate, we learn of a revolutionary way to view God and the Universe. In fact, his lecture inspires us. We are intrigued by his concepts. As a result, our skirmishes with depression are less severe. How nice it is, after a romance dissolves, to be capable of falling in love with ideas—and yes, maybe just a little with the man of ideas. In fact, we've surrounded ourselves with stimulating people—people who enlighten and intrigue us. As a result, we're getting to know ourselves all over again. Not only do we recall many interesting things we'd forgotten—so many activities that once energized us—we are also cultivating new personality traits. Temporarily blinded by embarrassing flashes of self-recognition, we expand our capacities and broaden our knowledge. We keep adding to the structure of our identity until it grows beyond recognition, except by loving people who encourage our growth. In fact, we wonder why, during the time we spent with our ex-partner, we never indulged in such daring exploration.

"I got involved in so many new things after we broke up, I sometimes felt as though I were dressing another man every morning," Rick explains. "But a crazy thing happened. Instead of seeing a stranger in the mirror, or feeling that the more I learned, the further I left the old me behind, the more comfortable I became with myself. Finally, I pledged myself to my true nature as a learner. To be honest, I think everyone who breaks up after a long-term relationship should get involved with new activities that will challenge his brain, his attitudes, his intellect, even his emotions. If you remain static, I'm not sure you'll ever establish distance between your sorrow over the old relationship and where you are now. What choice do you have but to push yourself spiritually, emotionally, and intellectually? In a way, new learning is like creating a new man. How can you not feel comfortable with something you've created?''

With Rick's encouragement to get in touch with ourselves, to create new men out of the old ones, and to enjoy solitude, we might be inclined to swear off dating for years. For most of us, however, such an extreme step would be a big mistake. We need romance to balance our intellectual, spiritual, and emotional growth. However, we can't allow ourselves to become fused with the men we are dating. Emotional dependence at this stage of recovery would impair our progress. We have to be up front, too. We must tell each man that, for right now, we will be seeing other men as well—that is, if we can find 'em. In fact, it's probably not a bad idea to let our boyfriend know that we are recovering from a broken relationship, then hope he doesn't haul ass.

"The first weekend after Clayton left, I went out to the bar,'' Rick relates. "I remember feeling very vulnerable, very lonely. Since I wasn't a frequent customer—I mean, I didn't need to go out that much before; I had what I needed at home—I received a lot of attention. A new face, you know? Well, the first guy who came up to me was a very handsome man, around thirty-five. We talked for about fifteen minutes. A very good first impression, you know? Not to mention he owned a very lucrative business. At any rate, when I casually mentioned that my ex and I had just parted company, he wasted no time. He patted me on the shoulder, told me that everything would work out, and headed toward the other side of the club. I didn't see him for the rest of the evening.''

Still, Rick feels it's important to let potential boyfriends know the truth. "I'm convinced that men are just as vulnerable—perhaps even more—as women are in matters of the heart. So, even though it's a big risk to tell guys we're on the rebound, we have an ethical obligation to do that. Of course, the dynamics are different in casual sex, when we can damn well choose to disclose absolutely nothing about ourselves. But we're relationship-oriented creatures. Although we may deny it all the way across the dance floor, when we meet someone at the bar, expectation begins to blossom. So, we tell the guy that we're not looking for a husband—not yet, at least. Then, the ball is in his court. If he wants nothing else to do with you, it's probably for the best. He would have turned out to be a clinging vine. But if he's not bothered by your rebound status, by all means try to cultivate a friendship, if you like the man at all. The most important thing to remember is that when you tell the guy about having broken up, tell him matter-of-factly, and possibly with a little humor. Otherwise, you'll come across like a pathetic little torch-carrier."

The Dating Game Rules

The first and most important rule of thumb once we resume dating is to take things slowly. When we consider our feelings of loneliness, vulnerability, and confusion, it's not surprising that once another cute guy shows interest, a little voice inside tries to convince us that he's our next husband. We'll listen to almost any delusion as long as we don't have to keep coming home to an empty house.

"The house that Clayton and I lived in for more than ten years," Rick pipes in, "suddenly lost the comforting familiarity it once had before he moved away. When he left, I couldn't stand being there alone—even though my dog made very good company. I planned escapes almost daily. Sometimes, I even worked long shifts—just to avoid looking at myself in the mirror, or facing my loneliness and isolation. It amazed and shocked me that my house felt as though it belonged to a stranger, and I had trespassed with impunity. I could admire the way it looked, just as I might when I visit a neighbor's house. I could appreciate its potential, but nothing about it made me want to continue living there."

Because of the uniqueness of our new single status, it's inadvisable to let our emotions take control of our lives. While enjoying the dating circuit, we become easy prey to the pleasure we feel when someone else sees value in us, so soon after we began to question our value. But we're still working on recovery. Because his attention and affection feel so damned good, we're likely to fall in love with him—if we're not careful. Perhaps we should adopt yet another mantra: "Take it slow. Take it slow." Otherwise, as time places even greater distance between us and the breakup, enabling us to look more objectively at our lives, we may see certain flaws in the new man we're dating—flaws invisible to us while our egos were stroked and our libidos inflamed.

Precisely because we are easy victims of our emotions, we should be honest with our dates during the post-divorce period. We can tell him how close we feel to him. No harm in that. We can describe how our heart flutters when he's next to us. That's just stoking passion's fires. But we should also inform him of the confusion and fear we're experiencing. If our rebound status is not a secret, and if he is a sensible and a sensitive man, he'll understand the necessity of taking slow, baby steps. Those fifteen-hundred- dollar engagement rings can wait. Even if we are determined to build a substantial relationship, it's best to let him know just how simultaneously ebullient and confused we feel. If we commit the sin of omission, and neglect to tell him that we're on the rebound, we risk hurting him and, by extension, ourselves.

"I told you earlier about the guy who ran in the opposite direction when I informed him that I had just split up with my ex-partner," Rick says. "At first, I thought that I had made the biggest mistake in the whole world—although I toyed with the idea of using this tactic to get rid of the unappealing men who hit on me. So, for a while, I didn't tell anyone about my recent past. The rationalization? I didn't consider it any of their business. But I soon realized that if you're going to keep a relationship cooking, you'll eventually have to tell the guy the truth. When you wait, and he realizes how deceptive you've been, he'll find trusting you more and more difficult. To save myself the trouble and the time involved in constantly analyzing my actions, I decided to change my approach. I decided to approach everything in my life with the utmost honesty. If you don't lie about anything, I decided, you don't have to waste energy coming up with excuses and cover-ups."

Any time the topic of past romances arises, Rick comes clean

in a most tactful way. "If I honestly believe this,
I feel very deeply about him, and that I want t
possibilities of a future together," he explains. "Bι
him that in spite of my strong feelings for him, I
process my feelings about the separation. I need
Generally, as long as I am rational, he will accept what I'm saying,
and continue to see me. It's obvious that my honesty is appreciated. I think all of us, in romantic situations, are tempted to be
dishonest—or at least clandestine—because we want to present
ourselves in the best possible light. We simply don't think ahead
to those times when intimacy will require a recanting. What will
he think of us then?"

In fact, if disaster is our goal, we can follow a simple recipe
that works almost every time. If we paint a rosy picture of ourselves
with little consideration of the truth, we'll find ourselves twice
as lonely when our new boyfriend breaks up with us. Recovery
is all about reestablishing the certainty of our identity. This particular task embraces the challenge that we can't really reclaim our
full individuality without actively pursuing relationships. Perhaps
we *can* feel comfortable about living our lives without the old
ball and chain. Perhaps we *can* compartmentalize our lives to
work on recovery and healing first, then save romance until last.
Yet, even with that kind of structure, the joke's often on us,
particularly when the emotional intensity of dating throws us
into seizures of confusion about our ex-partner. We wonder: Did
we do the right thing? Should we attempt a reconciliation? Were
we wrong not to overlook his affair that lasted only six months?
To avoid dealing with multiple issues, it's best to commit to
rediscovering ourselves *while* we're dating. However, we must be
willing to let the man know about the journey we're taking, and
share with him our insights along the way.

"When I met Brent, I told him that while I was about as nice
a guy as anyone could meet," Rick relates, "I was, right then,
pretty messed up because Clayton had recently left me. Fortunately, it hadn't been all that long since Brent broke up with his
partner after about four years of a very turbulent relationship.
Much of our time together—at least, at first—we devoted to
reviewing components of our old relationships. As we laughed
and cried about our lives, we also found ourselves growing closer

..d closer. We were more than willing to open up, to help each other in discovering what each wanted from his life—and what we wanted from a new relationship. Soon, we had to face the wonderful, but frightening realization that we were falling in love.''

Despite that revelation, Rick and Brent waited a year before committing to a monogamous relationship. "Both of us felt very sure that each of us fit the bill of what the other wanted," Rick continues. "But for the sake of our own sanity, and to make sure we had given our wounds time enough to heal, we decided to wait until we could stand to wait no longer. It amazed me how easy it was for us to move in together, and after that, how natural it was for us to get along. We already knew one another well enough to read moods, and even to anticipate how we might react to certain situations. This experience was such a contrast to the beginning of my relationship with Clayton. Clayton and I met one Saturday night. Then, two weeks later, we had set up housekeeping together.''

But before Rick and Brent explored the potential of a long-term partnership, they made certain they understood, and accepted, each man's personal philosophy. Before committing to the relationship, they committed themselves to an idea. After extraordinarily painful separations from their ex-partners, they determined that whatever they ultimately decided as their future roles in one another's life, there would simply be no more pain. Both of them had had enough of that.

No More Pain

Myrtle Beach, South Carolina, despite its recent ability to attract several world-class entertainment venues, can hardly be regarded as a first-class vacation destination. In fact, until 1997, references to Myrtle Beach's entertainment values as aligned with "family values" would have struck most people familiar with the ocean resort as comical. During the summer, sunbathers flock by the thousands to its sandy white beaches, known as the Grand Strand. They come from all over the United States. In the evenings, when the amusement parks, bars, clubs, and roadside attractions light up like Walt Disney World on amphetamines, the kind of "family values" for which Myrtle Beach has long been known becomes obvious.

Forget driving your car along Ocean Boulevard, known as The Strip, unless you're wasting your fuel for the same reasons the rest of the jammed motorists are. Even gay cruisers on their worst behavior are no match for these heterosexual motorists of all ages. For what happens after dark at South Carolina's most popular tourist destination is a transformation of a vacation resort into the world's largest pickup strip for straight men and women.

Little wonder that even the most incurable heterosexuals snickered when Myrtle Beach's oldest family of entrepreneurs, who also happen to own a large percentage of the city's business real estate, blasted South Carolina's Gay Pride Committee when it announced that the South Carolina Gay and Lesbian Pride Movement March, the nation's first gay liberation celebration to be held each year, would occur in Myrtle Beach. The reason? Homosexuality was not compatible with Myrtle Beach's "family image." Under pressure from Burroughs & Chapin Company, Inc., the region's biggest developer east of the Intracoastal Waterway, several businesses already committed to hosting various events during the celebration withdrew their support, including an auditorium where the Village People had been scheduled to perform. When that happened, local interest news suddenly became national, the city council denounced Burroughs and Chapin's tactics, and a conservative mayor who won the election by the seat of his pants found himself in the middle of a controversy. In fact, the controversy promised to grow even bigger as gay rights groups from San Francisco, Atlanta, Washington, D.C., and New York pledged to make South Carolina's festivities not only the first annual Pride event in the country, but also one of 1998's biggest.

From this setting Rick's story unfolds. Rick, a former high school teacher who moved to the Grand Strand from Connecticut, now runs a surf shop close to The Strip. His current partner, Brent, owns a kite shop that is quite a lucrative business during the busy spring and summer months. "When Clayton and I got together back in 1985, I thought he was the man with whom I'd spend the rest of my life," Rick says pensively. "I never thought

I would hook up with a man like Clayton—a blond surfer, actually, that I met when I was walking my dog along the beach. I always thought I would hook up with a corporate suit." He chuckles. "Well, I don't guess it's fair to identify him as a surfer. He is a career man, after all. Surfing is what he does for recreation. Actually, he runs a nightclub on Kings Highway."

Rick and Clayton were very deeply in love for more than six years. "Hell, we were so wrapped up in each other that we didn't even go to the local gay bar but once in a blue moon," he admits. "We'd rather stay at home together and watch something silly on television. That might sound superficial, but actually, Clayton and I delved into a lot of things—like different religions, philosophies, recreational interests, travel. You name it. So, our relationship was very vibrant. We weren't two old sisters who sat around and drank coffee all the time. It's just that we both found the bars pretty boring. In South Carolina, at least, you go to the bars when you want to be a slut, or you've been unlucky in establishing a relationship."

Rick continued to teach in South Carolina's schools during most of the years he spent with Clayton, though he was not out to other teachers, and "never to my students. I've met other teachers in states like California, Washington, and Rhode Island who can be themselves and it doesn't matter. I envy their being able to offer support and guidance to gay and lesbian youth. But South Carolina isn't like that at all. If it isn't *the* most repressed state in the country, it certainly ranks among the top three."

Rick thinks it was his position as a teacher that contributed to the dissolution of his relationship with Clayton. "Indirectly, at least," he concedes. "You see, a former student of mine, who had graduated three years earlier and had gone to college in North Carolina, wanted to come to Myrtle Beach during the summer to earn some extra money. However, he didn't have a place to stay. Since rental rates are pretty steep here during the summer, Clayton and I decided we'd let him live with us for cheap. After all, it would be for only three or four months. There was no need for rent to drain such a large percentage of his earnings."

Rick smiles coyly. "I didn't realize, then, what his living with us would ultimately mean."

As far as Rick knew, Christopher was straight. In high school, he always dated one young woman in particular. So, when Christopher told Clayton and Rick that he was bisexual, and found himself attracted to "older men," they were blown away. "We simply acknowledged the information, accepted it, then went on our way," Rick explained. "Over dinner, while Christopher was working, Clayton and I discussed the possible implications of his disclosure. Clayton predicted that, eventually, Christopher would make a pass at one or both of us. Later, I discovered that Christopher had already hit on Clayton, and that Clayton had scored with the young man—as an 'experiment'."

This "experiment" was the beginning of the end of Rick and Clayton's relationship. "Both of us became very attached to Christopher," Rick said. "He was a very charming young man. And the fact that he was 'attracted' to us, as older men, was a big ego boost. Before long, we were all engaged in a *ménage à trois*. That was fine, until both Clayton and I developed a crush on Christopher." He laughs. "Can you believe it? Here we were, men in our mid-thirties, falling head over heels in love with a kid only twenty-four years old."

Rick arranged to see a counselor. Clayton didn't see the need. He thought the affair would pass, and they would resume their relationship as before. But Rick discovered, during counseling, that Christopher was merely a symptom of what had become a dysfunctional relationship. "It was, in the end, my honesty that broke us up," Rick says sadly. "I told him that I felt our relationship had become static, that it wasn't fulfilling either of us anymore. I remember that Clayton cried when I told him that. Well, the long and the short of it is that Christopher went back to school, and several months later, Clayton informed me that he had met another man, seven years older than I, with whom he'd fallen in love. He intended to move with him to Atlanta."

Rick was devastated, but since Clayton had refused to attend counseling sessions with him, he figured Clayton felt their relationship was doomed. So, after a six-year absence, Rick began to visit the local gay bar. "It was there I met Brent," he says. "He was—and still is—sort of a hippie type. Very intelligent, he knows a lot about many things, but his appearance belies his intelligence. I found that quite appealing. He's almost ten years younger than I, but we have so much in common. I mean, the way we think about things. When I met Brent, he was very unhappy with his current relationship, but had not yet made the break."

And he didn't, for quite some time. "His reticence to tell Alex that he wanted out of the relationship drove me crazy for a while," Rick admits. "I wanted to move faster than he did. My relationship with Clayton was my second long-term relationship. Brent had already been involved with four men. His longest relationship lasted only three years. He was scared to break up with Alex because he had this craving to *know* that our partnership would last forever. He was afraid of getting hurt again."

Meanwhile, Clayton began calling Rick from Atlanta, confiding that he was very unhappy with his decision to leave Myrtle Beach, and Rick. "I felt a lot of sympathy for him," says Rick. "I mean, I could tell he was miserable. He said his partnership just lacked the vibrancy ours had. Soon, he was singing the tune that maybe we should hook up again. Although he had met Brent, and liked him, he started calling me when he knew Brent would be working, rather than visiting me."

The difficulties lay in the fact that Rick still loved Clayton, even if he didn't feel the sexual passion for him he once did. Furthermore, Brent still vacillated about tying the knot. "Although Brent had technically broken up with Alex, they were still living together, and that drove me crazy," Rick said. "Alex felt that he still had a chance, and did every fucking thing he possibly could to get between us. I tell you, Alex didn't back off for many months. During those months I was more than a little tempted to call Clayton and say, 'Hey, guy, let's do it!' But my shrink had asked me one very important question: 'Do you really want to go back to the way things were?' Well, I knew I didn't. As much as I loved Clayton, and still do, I can't be his lover anymore. There's too much uncertainty involved. Besides, we're just not sexually attracted to one another anymore, and we both have to have that."

Finally, Rick told Brent of Clayton's frequent phone calls, and his pressuring of Rick to get back together.

"Look, Rick, you do what you have to do," Brent told him. "But I don't want to lose you. I *think* I want to sign up with you.

I *think* you're the one. But I want to be sure. Do you understand? As sure as two people can be. I don't want any more pain. No more pain. Okay? There's been too much of that."

"So that became our theme," Rick laughs. "No more pain. Our dating intensified. We spent more nights together than before, once we had that conversation. But we still didn't move in together for another eight months. Although I was the impatient one, I'm glad we waited. We gave ourselves the chance to know one another better, and to know that living together was really what we both wanted."

And what of Clayton and Alex? "Well, Alex moved away, and left no forwarding address," Rick says, then shrugs. "Which is all right with the both of us. He had become incredibly codependent, and was just bad news all around. On the other hand, Clayton still keeps in touch. He's still not happy with his partner, but he's coping. And I don't feel quite as guilt-stricken as I used to about his unhappiness."

Red Flags

That Chicago resident Brin Adams and his ex-partner are roommates may provide Brin a perspective that allows him to move slowly with the dating situation in which he finds himself now. As he explores the possibilities of another long-term relationship, he grapples with issues inherent in both relationships past and present. He is determined to give himself time to deal with each and every question. "What holds me back is the fact that there's never been a time when Cal and I stopped loving each other very much," he explains. "Sex was the only way to express that love, even when we broke up. I was completely taken by surprise by so many things once we separated."

During their two-year partnership, Brin noticed several warning signs, but didn't think they were such a big deal. "We had heated arguments that I quickly forgot," Brin says. "Both of us said some pretty cold, cruel things. When we broke up, we had no choice but to continue living together because of financial reasons. We were forced to come to some sort of reconciliation, or we'd end up killing each other when we passed in the room."

For a while, Brin refused to accept the termination of their partnership. "I spent a couple of months trying to make things happen again," he says. "I made many attempts to communicate options—options that would enable us to continue being lovers. But Cal persisted in telling me why those options weren't correct, and why he wasn't willing to take those risks again. He had simply been too hurt to feel confident enough for reconciliation to occur. I didn't understand the degree of his hurt, since neither of us had been sexually unfaithful. I learned there are other ways to betray one's partner than sleeping with another man."

As Brin and Cal established some emotional distance, Brin's respect for his ex-partner deepened. "We broke up because Cal didn't want to participate in something that wasn't making him happy," Brin explains. "I still love him deeply; no question about that. Our separation made me understand that I didn't need this relationship to survive—nor did I need any, quite frankly. This was a realization that I hadn't had before."

The continuation of their sexual relationship even after they had broken up made things "somewhat more difficult, but I don't regret that involvement," Brin continues. "It extended the healing process, and made it harder for me to reconcile myself to the fact that things had indeed changed. What painfully reminded me of the changes were the other men we dated. Also, I was stage manager for a production of *Who's Afraid of Virginia Woolf?* Working on this drama was, understandably, quite difficult for me. But it might have been the most important force in motivating me to see other men romantically."

Lately, Brin has been dating another man exclusively. He admits that he hasn't been totally honest about his relationship with Cal. "At this point, since Cal still lives with me, I refer to him as my best friend and roommate. Nothing else is information he needs—not at this point. The rest will come along, but it will come along as history. Besides, Cal and I have become family. It's hard to imagine we are former lovers. We spend every Christmas together in Chicago."

Still, the new man has been good for Brin. "I'm far, far more stable. I don't break into tears at the drop of a hat. On a larger scale, I've become more confident, and more capable of functioning effectively in a relationship. After two and a half months of dating, things are very strong. Now, I am capable of honest communication. I actually understand what honest communication means. More than simply saying what's on your mind, it also means saying certain things to significant people that aren't always going to be taken well."

According to Brin, monogamy is one of the most difficult issues in his new relationship. Just when, he wonders, is the right time to make a decision? "I don't think there's any absolute rule about monogamy," he says. "Different things work for different people, and at different times. The man I'm seeing now and I haven't made any absolute decisions. We haven't nailed it down in either direction."

But Brin would be hurt if his current boyfriend dated another man. "The implication is that we are still in a holding pattern," he explains. "But I will be honest. I'm not sure whether our relationship could withstand our dating other men. It could more easily withstand casual sex, but date? I don't know. Dating would be trickier. Dating other guys would certainly bring us to the brink of a decision. Of that, I'm sure. I would probably at the very least feel some jealousy, despite the fact that jealousy's not a very valuable reaction to anything."

Although Les Wright admits that he will never completely get over his former relationship, he has managed to filter intellectually the differences between sexual passion and more substantial commitment. In Les's opinion, commitment based on sexual passion is not as important as "finding the surefooted component of a relationship."

Les thought he had found that kind of relationship when he met Jason. "At the time, my situation was somewhat tenuous," Les explains. "I was in graduate school, and living on very little money. Things were rough all over. When I placed a personal ad in the *San Francisco Gay Times*, I wanted to meet someone not involved in recovery. You see, I had been involved in Alcoholics Anonymous. I knew tons and tons of people, but I wanted to connect with someone 'normal.' Specifically, I was looking for a relationship with someone who would not be unstable."

Les and Jason arranged a coffee house rendezvous in the Castro. "So I arrived first, and ordered coffee," he says. "Then, this guy walked through the door. I never had this experience before. The moment I laid eyes on him, I was in love. I never had this experience since."

Their commitment permitted sexual involvement with other men, but no emotional involvement. "One morning, Jason came home after having been out all night. He told me he had spent the night with someone else," Les explains. "At that time, for all I knew, this guy might have been a new acquaintance from the bar. I found out pretty quickly that wasn't the case. In fact, I discovered that the guy Jason was involved with was a man I had been attracted to earlier, but I had not acted on my attraction. Jason is still involved with the same man."

Possibly, their living arrangements contributed to the rough patches in their relationship. "I was living with my ex while Jason and I were lovers," Les says. "Still, we spent five out of seven nights together. Ultimately, my ex died of lung cancer. After his death, I suggested moving in with Jason. His answer was that his apartment was one room too small for two people. It was another one of those red flags that I didn't read correctly."

Monogamy was also an issue. "You know, this relationship was the one where I got clear about monogamy," Les explains. "I have tried both open and closed relationships. What I experienced with Jason was that even though we had, formally, an open relationship, it was the first relationship, out of three, when I *chose* to be monogamous. I realized that monogamy works only when the partners have a choice. And that's the way my current partner and I regard sexual fidelity."

Once it was clear that Jason and Les would separate, "it was as though Jason flipped a switch. After confrontations, we would sit down to have further discussions and evaluations. Soon, I realized he was simply getting rid of me. It took him another six months to actually close things. He really strung me along. The gaps in his divergence, his play-acting, and his true feelings widened more and more; he became a stranger. Generally, the men I've dated, or have been in love with, and I have become very close friends. I never had the experience of someone turning himself into a stranger. Yeah, it was his decision to create distance between us. I realize that much of his relationship with me was predicated on nonreality. As he began to see who I was, he realized that I was someone he didn't want in his life."

One disturbing component of their breakup sticks out in Les's mind. "I did something I never did before," he admits. "I never raised a hand to him in violence. But on several nights, I left my house and walked the night away. Sometimes, I would hide behind shrubs close to the house of the man he was seeing, waiting for him to come out. I did that three times. It really scared me. I mean, I had no conscious control over it."

Finally, Jason confronted him. "You're stalking me," he told Les.

Les looked away in embarrassment. "Yes, I guess I am."

"Well, for God's sake, stop it!"

Les clears his throat. "And so I did."

After the split, Les didn't want to see other men. "This is interesting," he says. "It was the first time I lost interest in other guys. I didn't want to be sexual at all. After the fourth month following the separation, someone made a pass at me. I told him I couldn't be sexually intimate, but we could sleep together. It was a full year after the breakup before I could stand to be touched by someone else."

Finally, Les met Bruce, and things changed. "I chilled out a lot. I'm involved with Bruce now. We're very happily married. The relationship with Jason was a major turning point. The whole texture of my relationship with Bruce is very different from my relationships in the past. We definitely have a partnership. Bruce and I are very much friends. Sex is very low-key. Having or not having sex is not an issue. Technically, we have an open relationship, but neither of us has a desire to be with other men. While there's a good deal of romance on his part, for me, it's a marriage more than a romance. He knows how I feel. He appreciates our sense of family, connection, and compatibility. Our relationship is much more sober than others have been."

Les separates their relationship from others by denying that it has elements of a "romantic fantasy." "We are building a life together," he explains. "We have made some financial commitments together. We are nurturing our dreams; we support each other in our professional development. We have a very quiet life. We have a home together with two children." He pauses—for effect. "Actually, they're cats. Bruce and I are doing things we have not done in the past—the main things we both wanted to do. In fact, when I start feeling that romantic stuff, a red flag rises. I know that my vision is clouding up when I feel like that."

Les emphasizes the value and nobility of their partnership. "Slowly but surely, we nurture our relationship, and we nurture each other," he says. "We have been together for three years. I love him more and more every day. What we have is low key and surefooted. He is every bit as honest with me as I *thought* Jason was. Even though we have a sexually open relationship, we are completely emotionally faithful to each other. I've had a couple of sexual contacts, but literally, only a couple. It makes a difference now that I'm in rural New England, rather than in the Castro. Sure, I miss San Francisco. But I don't miss the availability of casual sex, and I don't miss all the craziness of that city."

Despite Les's high regard of his current relationship, his romance with Jason reached storybook proportions. "And that's the hardest part," he says. "It's one of the reasons I wanted to talk about this particular relationship. It's unfortunate that Jason and I have nothing to do with each other. Because I would say that our relationship was the kind of thing one sees in a novel, or in a movie. He was the one great love of my life. I'll never forget him. Not one day has gone by that I don't think of him."

Loneliness and Insecurity Quotient (LIQ)

In this activity, you will calculate your Loneliness and Insecurity Quotient, or LIQ. Your LIQ will establish the depth of your loneliness and insecurity so that you're more self-aware. Through self-awareness, you will be able to address and rectify deficiencies in your self-confidence.

Begin this activity by rating each of the twenty-four statements below with a value from the following table. Remember to be honest. No one else will see your responses, and self-deception here will interfere with moving on toward recovery.

5—This is always true of me.
4—This is often true of me.
3—This is occasionally true of me.
2—This is seldom true of me.
1—This is never true of me.

1. I tend to latch on to one friend, then cling.
2. I look for people who need me as a caretaker. If they depend on me, they're not likely to abandon me.
3. I have a big streak of jealousy.
4. Frequently, I am fearful that bad things will happen to me.
5. I twist my hair, bite my nails, or exhibit other obsessive behaviors because of a low-grade, ill-defined anxiety.
6. At work, colleagues tend to maintain a distance. I feel as though I'm walking on eggshells.
7. I search for excuses to avoid social interaction, even with my closest friends.
8. I prefer staying at home to going out.
9. I sense that people are avoiding me.
10. Because of breaking up with my ex-partner, I am *really scared* to start over.
11. When I meet a new man, I extend a great deal of effort to hide personal traits that I think might be a turnoff.
12. I am awkward in social situations.
13. I can't stand to be alone in my house.
14. I keep replaying in my memory entire conversations my ex and I once had.
15. I find myself frequently bursting into tears.
16. Frequently, I dial in to phone-sex lines.
17. I feel a sense of desperation to start a new relationship.
18. After one date with a man, I begin to entertain fantasies of setting up housekeeping with him.
19. I've realized that I can't shop without someone else.
20. I keep playing the same sad songs over and over again.
21. Day after day, everything in my house stays so untouched, so unmoved, I wonder if this is how it feels inside a tomb.
22. The phone rings and I'm crushed when I discover it's only a wrong number.
23. Occasionally, I feel strong urges to contact my ex-partner and beg for us to get back together.
24. I find myself thinking of what my life will be like if I have to spend the rest of it alone.

1.	7.	13.	19.
2.	8.	14.	20.
3.	9.	15.	21.
4.	10.	16.	22.
5.	11.	17.	23.
6.	12.	18.	24.

To compute your LIQ, add the values you assigned to statements 1–12, and place that number in this blank.

IF (Insecurity Factor): _____

Then, add the values you assigned to statements 13–24 and place that number in this blank.

LF (Loneliness Factor): _____

What the numbers mean:

I. Insecurity Factor (IF)

41–60: Dangerously insecure. Don't worry. Everything's going to be all right. Pull yourself together. Things aren't *that* bad.

31–40: Room for improvement. This is normal after a break-up. You've probably come a long way from where you were at ground zero. But there's more you need to do. Keep plugging away!

21–30: Almost there! This is where many of us are. We're pretty secure, but then, we worry about various issues bringing us down.

12–20: Close enough! This is where we want to be. Nobody's perfect, but this is secure enough for most of us.

II. Loneliness Factor (LF)

41–60: Do something! There's got to be someone out there to hang with. Just find a friend, and don't be alone.

21–40: Things will be all right! As the days go by, things will feel more and more normal. Maybe when you're ready, you'll meet a new guy.

12–20: Keep it up! Having fun and getting on with your life, either with friends or comfortably alone, you're doing great.

III. Putting the Numbers Together

Create a fraction by putting the LF above your IF, like this:

Interpretation:

Low LF/Low IF: Great! You must decide yourself whether anything needs touching up. If so, have at it, but you're probably pretty close to okay.

Low LF/High IF: Although you're not especially lonely, you're insecure. Think of steps you can take to facilitate change in your life, and to feel as though you're in control.

High LF/Low IF: Although secure, you're feeling a little lonely. Get out there and mingle, for heaven's sake! Find something (or someone) to take your mind off being alone.

High LF/High IF: You're lonely and insecure. You just have to take a leap of faith that things will work out. Swallow your fear of failure, and push on in a quest for companionship, or whatever you seek to cure loneliness. Come on. You can do it!

If both your LF and IF are in the middle of the scale, you're in fairly good shape. However, to determine which area needs the *most* work, consider the numbers in relation to one another. A lower IF, although it still rests in the median area, calls for a little work on security issues—though you won't have to bust your chops to implement improvements.

CHAPTER NINE

Getting to Know Ourselves All Over Again

Putting Two and Two Together

In 1994, a program coordinator for a New York state service provider to the aging, Gene Gilfus, 44, not only found his relationship of eight years ending, but a three-year chapter of darkness beginning. "It was not until a year before our breakup that I was aware that something was wrong, and really, that realization was in retrospect," Gene explains. "Our relationship was simply falling apart. The year prior to that, my mother had a massive stroke. Caring for her consumed a lot of my weekend time. So, I'll admit, I was somewhat preoccupied, and ill-prepared to notice anything amiss. Well, Lance came home from a vacation with his son, and told me then that he was leaving me. He said we didn't have the same hobbies. He said I didn't respect his profession. He said I seldom did things with him. And he said that he had to move on with his life. Later, I discovered that he was having an affair with someone we'd both met about three weeks earlier. When he moved out, he moved into another apartment with the new man in his life."

It was an ugly ending to a relationship that began so well. Gene's romantic involvement with Lance began at work. They ran into each other for the first time at the copy machine. "I was immediately attracted to his intelligence," Gene says. "Once we moved in together, we had a monogamous relationship. God knows, I admired his sensitivity, as well as his generosity. Besides, he was very, very sexy. He was also quiet, and naïve. You see, this was his first gay relationship. He had been married for eight years before we got together. He had one son, to whom he was very close, although he and his wife couldn't stand each other. Lance told me that he had been forthcoming to his son about our relationship from the beginning. However, his son was quite leery of me. From his perspective, I was the guy responsible for his father not being involved with his mother anymore. After all, he was only twelve years old, and he couldn't comprehend exactly what our relationship meant. He was most comfortable thinking that I was his father's roommate."

Willingly, Gene bears part of the responsibility for the end of his partnership. "I wasn't giving Lance the attention he needed," he explains. "Many things were happening in my life. My father was diagnosed with cancer while we were together, in addition to my mother's medical problems. In looking back, I can also see that Lance needed to have gay friends, which he never sought out before. He read gay-themed books, which was wonderful. At least, he had begun reading for a change. But for the longest time, I was not only his gay lover, but also his only gay friend."

Not that Lance didn't try to establish some autonomy—at least at work. "Shortly after we became partners, he moved from my department, and transferred to the Department of Health," Gene says. "He received no more money, and no advancement for the move. He just wanted to become a bit more independent."

However, the transfer was the classic tale of too little, too late. Lance felt smothered by the partnership in all kinds of ways.

When they split, Gene never ventured from the apartment for a month. "I was very hurt," Gene says, "and I didn't want him to bring men home. It hurt me very much when he did that. We were also having sex with each other about twice a week, despite the fact that we'd broken up. It was hell, living with him. It was traumatic. I was hurting. He wasn't, because he had somebody. Jesus! We had just met this guy at the bar. Those fuckers always move in at the bar, don't they?"

When Lance broke the news, he was cool and calm. "On the other hand, I didn't even try to hide my tears," Gene continues. "I was very angry and depressed. I tried desperately to negotiate his staying. He said he would always love me, but we couldn't continue to be partners. I talked to him about going to counseling. He said no. I told him *I* would go through counseling. He said there was no need. I suggested that we try separating, then trying it again after a few months. He said our partnership had ended." Gene chuckles. "I had a hard time putting two and two together."

Despite Lance's unwillingness to attend counseling, Gene hired a psychiatrist anyway. "And I'm still going, God damn it," he says, with a bitter laugh. "He told me that time heals all wounds—the kind of bullshit I didn't want to hear when I first started therapy. He provided fairly useful ways of handling my situational depression, but I sank into a clinical depression. He prescribed various medications, but he couldn't find antidepressants that worked very well for me. Finally, I was diagnosed as having bipolar manic depression."

After the diagnosis, Gene increasingly withdrew from friends. In fact, his withdrawal was an extension of isolation that began at the start of his involvement with Lance. "Most of my friends are in Buffalo and New Jersey anyway," he explains. "I moved to Albany to be with Lance. My straight friends—and most of my friends are straight—thought I would get over this in time. It wasn't very much understood among them that two men could really love each other. My one close gay friend thought that I would go from one guy to the next—you know, casual sexual encounters—but he just didn't understand that depth of our relationship. And I guess [our involvement] wasn't all that apparent when Lance and I were in public. We weren't very touchy-touchy all the time. At night we cuddled. I never talked a hell of a lot about him in public. I didn't say to people how wonderful he was. I never did that. Our intimacy wasn't continuously displayed in front of everyone. Maybe that was a mistake."

Gene acknowledges the possibility that social pressures contributed at least partially to their breakup. "Neither of us wanted to be considered effeminate in the least," he proffers. "We succeeded in not coming across as two stereotypical gay men. I enjoy straight people. I never wanted to be caught in this narrow path of being gay, gay, gay. Y'know, what I've discovered is that many gay men are caught up in their sexuality. The straight people I know don't seem to have constant conversations about sex. That distinction might have contributed to our not having—or wanting—a lot of gay friends during our relationship. Our neighborhood restricted our gay social contacts as well. Don't misunderstand. Our neighbors were nice. They knew we were gay, and appreciated the fact that we were low-key. I've always respected people for their values, and don't inflict my values on anyone."

Predictably, the dissolution of their partnership took its toll on Gene's work performance. "My shrink took me out of work for the four months," he explains. "When I returned, colleagues wanted to know why I'd been out. I didn't want to tell them the truth, but I didn't have any scars to prove that I had been in surgery, either. Yeah, my absence had an effect, all right. I worked for the [New York] state government and directed programs that were nationally recognized. When I returned, I was assigned to a position with fewer gutsy responsibilities. They weren't challenging to me at all. Then, when my father died, I had to take even more time off. Many times I wish someone could have supported me emotionally. I mean, Lance's parents were always very supportive. I would love to see them again, even after our split. But I would feel two-faced if I tried to re-establish a relationship with them. I'm afraid of saying something nasty—like asking them how they could raise a son-of-a-bitch like their son. Besides, there are other issues. Like Lance, his parents felt that we would always be very good friends, even after we broke up. To be frank, not maintaining a friendship was my decision. I couldn't handle it."

Once Lance moved out, Gene attempted to see other men. "But no one seemed to interest me that much," he says. "I tried tricking around; that was no good. This time, something had changed. Maybe I would get to the point of going to bed with someone—then decide not to. I haven't seen many men I would be interested in. I know it's going to happen. I *want* it to happen. Falling in love is the most beautiful thing, but while on lithium, even something as simple as getting an erection can be a problem. So I have to establish some honesty with a man before I get to the point of sleeping with him. Once a man proves to me that he understands a relationship is a two-way street, then I can pursue romance with him."

As Gene's therapist continues to treat his manic depression, agoraphobia, and mood disorders, Gene has found some degree of solace in solitude. "I love solitude," he admits. "For a couple of months, so many things in this house reminded me of him, and I would cry. I got over that phase of hating to be by myself. A while back, I started crying because I had lost not only him, but also what went with the person—someone touching you, loving you, having sex with you. I started feeling bad for myself. I have pictures of Lance here, which I took down for a while. Now they're back up on the walls. I wish the best for him. But I miss our wonderful times."

Right now, Gene isn't sure of his capacity to make another partnership work. "I don't feel I have anything to offer anyone right now," he says candidly. "I don't even have my job. I will have to file for bankruptcy soon. My home is such a beautiful place, but I may have to give it up. So what do *I* have to offer another man? God, there must be *something* I have to offer." He pauses to consider. "Companionship, I have that to offer. I'm better looking than ever before. Hell, I'm forty pounds lighter. So yeah, I'm working on myself."

Gene concedes his therapist is right about one thing. "Time *does* heal all wounds," he says. "You have to give the grieving process some time. Still, I know that in the back of my mind, there will always be a special place for Lance. I will always love those years. Yeah, I have a few scars to show. But I'm not defeated, no matter how bad it sounds. I *still* cherish and value a committed relationship. It's the only way. I don't see how two people can go through life without that. It's not the sex. It's the beauty of two people together. I'll have that again someday."

Regaining Clarity

When experiencing a relationship's end, many of us don't suffer the severity of grief that Gene experienced. But despite the fact that some of Gene's issues are related to organic mental health conditions, we *can* relate to his loss of self-esteem, identity, well-being, and focus. Most of us find that, within weeks or perhaps months, we are functional enough to examine our life's values. Fortunately, we will be able to make adjustments to aid us in our quest for healthy living.

To improve the quality of our lives, we must reexamine and fine-tune three types of values as quickly as possible after breaking up. First, we should assess those emotional values we cherish, to determine our capacity for establishing those values in our lives. Shortly after he walked out on us, we felt an erosion of self-confidence, and probably wondered whether we'd ever regain sufficient bravery to face life again. With self-awareness, we can determine those areas of life where we are the shakiest, and work toward building strength. After suffering paralysis, we are satisfied with a twitch of the finger or toe before moving on to bend our arms and legs. It's hard, but our vision of a life during which we operate at full capacity keeps us going. Without self-confidence, the new guy we're seeing (or will eventually see), might spend an evening with us, but once perceiving that our lack of courage isn't merely the dating jitters, he'll buck like a horse at the sight of a snake.

Another important emotional value to cultivate is the deepening of our ability to love. We hope our past relationship has taught us intricate meanings of love and romance. However, the ability to love deeply won't expand without cultivating a more loving view of the world around us. Like the old man who advises the boy in Carson McCullers's short story, "A Tree, a Rock, a Cloud," we should strive to love the *idea* of life itself. It's easy to love those who listen easily, who meet our ego needs—not so easy to love nature "in the raw," or to wake up eagerly to another day. In our progression toward what the old man says will take most people a lifetime to achieve, we find that all our relationships expand and embrace our lives in ways we never thought possible.

Yet another emotional value that creeps into our frame of reference after breaking up is a capacity for vulnerability. Willingly, we relinquish our tendency to hold feelings in check, to act as though emotions should always fall neatly into place. Instead, we stop playing those roles that lead others into believing that we have it all together. Surprisingly, after breaking up, we often lose that self-consciousness which keeps us from embracing our human fragility. Not only do we discover that vulnerability strengthens friendships, but it also makes us attractive to others searching for love. As gay men, we are accustomed to our sexual orientation being equated to moral and personal weakness. More than likely, we have taken compensatory steps to appear strong, unconcerned about the attitudes of others, perhaps even arrogant. But the dichotomy of vulnerability lies in its capacity to build strength while allowing us to admit weakness. Holding fast to facades alienates people. They will avoid those who lack authenticity. Yet they are attracted by the substance that vulnerability builds.

"There were times when something inside warned me not to let others know exactly how I was feeling," says Sean Mauldin, 47, a salesman in Tacoma, Washington. "Particularly when friends wanted to know how I was dealing with my breakup. But I swallowed my pride, and resisted any show of false strength. I found that my friends seemed more closely drawn to me. Also, as a result, I started to see humor in all sorts of situations. When you're willing to admit you're hurting, you also become willing to laugh at yourself. For the first time in my life, I noticed that, when meeting a new guy, I could ask personal questions without putting him on the defensive. I accomplished this feat by coming across as a little flippant about my own emotions and vulnerabilities. To put it in Lenny Bruce's terms, I recognized that we're all the same *schmuck*. That recognition enabled me to drop all my pretensions."

A final step in clarifying emotional values requires the surrender of absolutes. Some of our sentiments and attitudes, whether deeply held or expressed through our emotional pain, imply that all people respond to common crises in the same way. Yet there is no standard way to deal with the bullshit that is an inevitable part of life. We may be tempted to draw conclusions about all men based on the characteristics of the one we just left, even though we know (hope?) such conclusions aren't true. We may be inclined to believe that the guy we just dumped—or who just dumped us—was the one great love of our lives, the like of whom we'll never see again. The law of probabilities would indicate that we have been misled. Or we may nurse our pain for an inordinate amount of time. We hurt so badly, we're convinced the pain will never go away. We think deeply and frequently, and analyze our plight continuously, but the pain seldom subsides. How do we grow beyond this hurtful tendency to obsess? We know, after all, that the very nature of life is change. As Gene's therapist commented, "Time heals all wounds." It will also heal ours. Once our friends, family, and dates see that we embrace the dynamic nature of life, and are willing to relinquish our tendency to think in boxes, they perceive our willingness to tap into our humanity. We become more capable of tapping into theirs.

Intellectual values also play a significant role in our quest to regain clarity. Soon after breaking up, not only do we deal with evolving, new emotions, but our intellect is changing as well. If we are constricted by ideas that confine us, or stunt our growth, we should examine our bitterness quotient. Perhaps we can put bitterness in reverse. Most of us, once we have survived the initial burst of pain, discover an eagerness to examine new ideas. As we fill our own prescriptions for healing, we understand the necessity to slow down, kick back, enjoy what we can. Usually, we find new ways of joining the human race—or rat race—once more. We read books, newspapers, and magazines with more attentiveness. Other people and their ideas attain more importance; hence, our regard of them increases. As we grow accustomed to new landscapes and new lives, we become seekers. In our search for happiness and contentment, we welcome new ideas with the capacity of bringing those qualities once more into our lives. If we reject movement, novelty, and adventure, we risk living a retroactive life. How can we possibly get over the love of our past if we are afraid of moving on?

As we entertain revolutionary ideas, we also experience a sharpening of our analytical skills. We don't assimilate new ideas into our intellect unless we can pull them apart, see how they work, perhaps even tinker with them. In fact, we may discover that during the final phase of our previous relationship, we entered an intellectual stasis. We became much too willing to accept the standards of the status quo without critical examination. "Looking back, I'm amazed at how intellectually boring I had become," Sean says. "I don't know the reasons for that. Troy was a very intelligent person. I think that we had grown *too* complacent in our relationship—perhaps *too* happy. The security of our partnership made us passive. Why did we need the stimulation of new ideas when we had this wonderful thing with each other? And maybe our willingness to accept mental atrophy contributed to the death of our partnership. I can't say for sure. But I know one thing. If we had committed not only to each other, but also to our own consciousness and intellectual growth, I'm sure we would have been better equipped to deal with what happened to us when our lives began to unravel.''

Sean's uncertainty about the impact of intellectual growth on the health of a relationship leads to a consideration of yet another important value. As the longevity of our partnership increases, many of us lose touch with ourselves—with who we are. Why focus attention on personal growth when we enjoy the security of this relationship? We have devoted much of our lives to finding the one man whose love and commitment would pave the way to happiness. Our earlier personal growth—the growth of our formative years—culminated with this relationship. Our growth path led to our partnership. Perhaps our identity as part of this unique union was enough for us. We saw little need to sharpen our perceptions of ourselves as individuals. Regardless of our present self-awareness, we must look inside ourselves once more. Our appreciation and knowledge of our early identities no longer serve us. As we clarify emotions and explore new ideas, we cultivate qualities of insightfulness and perception. What do these new components of our lives mean? How have we expanded? Into what new breed of individual are we evolving? In fact, if we intend to establish lives offering us happiness and satisfaction once again, we have to use the experience of breaking up as an opportunity for intellectual growth. We owe it to ourselves to read new books, meet new people, watch movies we would never have chosen before—perhaps even enroll in university or community classes. Even if we possess the highest degree attainable, new knowledge and new talents can be cultivated. As the old man assimilates with the new, pain subsides. Energy expands. We feel a renewed sense of empowerment.

As we clarify emotional and intellectual values, we can't ignore the spiritual component of our lives, which is closely related to romantic love. An earlier literary allusion bears expansion. Great romantic poetry asserts that to fall in love is to taste eternity. When we fall in love, we can't conceive the relationship, or our love for our partner, will ever end. The emotional components of our lives, together with the intellectual and erotic elements, all converge into our spiritual natures. Not only do we possess cosmological, even mystical, insights about the nature of life, but we also have some understanding of how our relationships interface with our spirituality. Even if we reject the idea that our consciousness thrives in a corporeal body after death, the most spiritually jaded of us accept that the memory of us lives on in the minds and spirits of the people we've touched. The men who lost their partners to death agreed to interviews because of their wish to contribute to the legacy of those they loved. A danger of breaking up lies in our temptation to refute the idea that life possesses a single everlasting component. Those of us who handle breakups best regard endings as transitions, as part of a growth process. We reject the temptation to hate our ex-partner. Hatred destroys the dynamism of spirituality and stops the flow of creativity into our lives. Spirituality demands that we live our lives on a human scale. Even if we can't produce a coherent image on a canvas, or produce a pleasant sound from the simplest of musical instruments, we can certainly bring a unique creative flair to our lives. Creativity is the ultimate involvement in life. The true artist isn't the man who can make his violin sing, or his canvas explode in vibrant, provocative colors. The true artist is capable of bringing something of an eternal nature to his life.

Meeting People at a Distance, but Not Down the Street

When library director Dustin Whitworth met Mike at a gay student alliance in college, he regarded Mike as a father figure. After all, he was almost ten years older than Dustin, and an instructor at the university. Despite the difference in their ages, the relationship worked—that is, for twenty years.

"We moved in together after dating for almost a year," Dustin relates. "After I graduated from college, when one of us got a job, the other would follow. We moved around all over the Northeast. Eventually, we ended up in New York City."

Seventeen years into the relationship—one marked by frequent moves—Dustin realized the relationship was in trouble. "We had a monogamous relationship for the entire twenty years we were together," he explains. "But I developed a crush on someone else. It was the first time this had happened to me since

Mike and I had committed to each other. I tried to have sex with Mike, to prove to myself that our relationship wasn't over. But he wasn't the least bit interested. Without confronting him directly, I tried to drop hints that it was over. I finally spelled it out to him. He started crying. God, he must have known, but just wasn't recognizing it. So, to placate him, I suggested we go to couples counseling. We did, and a whole mess of stuff came out."

The "mess" included the disclosure that Mike was an alcoholic. "Mike also suffered from major depression," Dustin continues. "That illness had more to do with his father being an alcoholic than with his own alcoholism. In fact, Mike never drank while we were together."

For Dustin, Mike's most shocking disclosure was that he perceived himself as transgendered. "He's still working through that," Dustin says. "But with that information, I saw no future in our relationship. We had done everything we could to stay together. We both recognized that fact—finally."

Were there other warning signs? "We had arguments, of course," he says. "All couples do. But after moving in together, we had a commitment ceremony. We regarded ourselves as married, just like straight people do. If we got mad at each other, we handled it just like married people do."

But once their partnership dissolved, Mike had nothing at all to do with Dustin. "I would e-mail him. There was no response. That went on for almost a year. It's only been in the past nine months that we've met a few times. Then, it was at my initiative. I think this dissociation was his way of saying that he has a new life. I guess, maybe, I was hoping that I would find some possibility of getting back together. Last year, he even suggested it. But last year, he was also considering gender reassignment surgery."

Through therapy, Dustin realized that he was part of a seriously codependent relationship. "Whenever we went on a trip, I had to do all the math, the directions, the navigation," he explains. "I would also have to drive. If I screwed up, he would make nasty, insulting, personal remarks. Then, when I got upset, he would say he was just joking. I realized that he had been psychologically abusing me. Obviously, some masochistic tendency inside me wanted that. From his point of view, the verbal abuse was his way of distancing himself from me."

Still, Dustin had a hard time getting over the realization that Mike wasn't his soulmate. "To be honest, I would probably consider getting back together if he said he was over the transgender stuff," Dustin admits. "He wasn't verbally abusive to me in college. He was my mentor then. I have to think that a lot of his behavior is attributable to his alcoholism."

Dustin and Mike's relationship excluded friendships with other gay men. "We were divorced from the gay community," he says. "When I knew it was over, I started making new friends. I even counted on friends for sex. But to be honest, Mike forced me to give up my gay friends while we were together. So I did. I felt he was the person I was living my life with, and I didn't need anyone else. Now, I've noticed the most well-adjusted gay couples seem to be those who have gay friends."

For five years, both Dustin and Mike shared the same workplace. "Not very many people were out at work in those days (1979-1984)," says Dustin. "We acted like we were mild acquaintances. When I returned to that business two years ago, I was in for a shock. Everyone had known about us all along! They really liked Mike then, and wanted to know about him. One colleague was surprised that we had split up. She said we were one of the stablest couples she knew. It was really funny, how we were trying to hide our relationship, and no one even cared."

Now that the possibility of getting back together has grown even more remote, Dustin has placed himself into the dating scene, but says everything has changed. "I just didn't know how to date, or what was expected of me, or what to do or not to do," he explains. "It's a totally different world. Finding sex is as easy as it's always been. Finding someone who really cares—well, I haven't found that yet. I find it remarkable that there aren't many people at the bars who are my age or older. I'm attracted to older guys, and now I'm forty-four. My therapist thinks I'm looking for men who look like Mike—the same age, the same physique. I think she's wrong. I think I've gotten over that. Now, I really want a deep, psychological relationship—an intimate relationship. It's funny how I miss it, although, according to my therapist, I never had it. I come from a good Catholic family, and I think people should be partnered. I've met people in open relationships, and I don't understand that concept. I don't think you can have an 'understanding,' and realistically think you can have a long-term relationship. It makes no sense. The happiest people I know are those in a monogamous relationship. And that's what I want for myself.''

Dustin hopes to find intimacy again, but he is somewhat cynical. ''I feel more confident now, and more in control of my life,'' he says. ''I know now not to look for a mother or father figure, but for someone who is my equal. I've learned from this experience. I know lots of people who have a different 'partner' every month. And that just isn't me. My therapist says I'm still attracted to unattainable people—people who will treat me the same way Mike did. I think she's mistaken about that now. I'm being selective. America Online helps. I've been meeting people all over the place. Sometimes, though, it seems I just can't meet people living down the street.''

Practicalities

Now it's time to fine-tune our identities.

Our first chore is to determine both the positive and negative characteristics of our former relationship. Similar to a yard sale, we get rid of the shoddy material, so that the good stuff looks even better on display. Through introspection, we manifest new insights about our lives. Maybe the old relationship injected lots of passion and spark into our life. Maybe we experienced a strong sense of belonging and security. Perhaps the relationship gave us the respect of friends and family for making a commitment. Then, despite our unfathomable love for another human being, we confront the awful truth that we never really trusted each other, so we felt a lot of jealousy. He was unfaithful, both physically and emotionally, to the partnership. He insisted we give up most of our friends. Our sense of security in the relationship became an excuse for closing doors to all kinds of opportunities for personal growth.

Customarily, we don't disassemble the engines of our lives, but after *this* crisis, an overhaul provides not only goals, but also an appreciation for who we are now and who we are becoming. Logically, after circumstances during which we continually lost power, it's neither unreasonable nor futile to stop for repairs. What might we discover about ourselves? A tendency to be insecure. A tendency not to trust people. An embarrassing jealous nature. God, were we really *that* controlling? How can *anyone* like such a scruff? How do we even like ourselves? Shocked by these characteristics, we're tempted to total our lives and start all over. However, our purpose is to grow awareness. If we see our faults clearly, then we can work to minimize them. Besides, let's look at the positives. We have an ability to commit to people and ideas. What about that winning smile? Every boss we've had says we're hardworking and goal-oriented. Now, we don't look quite as bad.

Next, we take a close look at our goals, desires, and needs. Obviously, all three have changed now that we're single again. We ask ourselves what we really want now that the parameters of our lives have changed. Our personal goals might include establishing new hobbies. God knows we need to get in shape. Is it time to move into a new place? Would our thoughts of the ex diminish if we did? Perhaps we need to filter more money into our savings account and pay off a few debts. What about work? How satisfied are we in our current position? Is it time for a change?

What about our social lives? Have we reestablished old friendships? Have we made new friends? We need to stop sitting home alone on the weekends. Let's throw more dinner parties. We need to make changes! We must create momentum!

Upon closer examination of our lives, we may discover residual desires that linger from our old partnership. That's okay. Unachieved desires, no matter how dusty they are, don't necessarily lose their validity. For example, we may think of things we've always wanted to do—like skydiving, parasailing, mountain climbing, or spending a week in Key West. Perhaps we wish to examine important characteristics of a successful relationship. Maybe we will settle only for a new man who is a suit in a major corporation. Maybe we will insist that he believes in sexual monogamy. Maybe he has to be willing to move into the house we've owned for over ten years, since we love the house and refuse to sell. It's essential that we clarify our desires for a new relationship *before* falling in love. Once our emotions overpower reason, we become willing to make considerable compromises. Later, we may discover we were never really amenable to them.

Our deep longings also qualify as desires worth pursuing. If we have always wanted to be a professional cellist in a major symphony orchestra, we may have to make some major sacrifices. But inner longings, with their undeniable knack for goading us, can shape our relationships, and affect the quality of our lives. Now is the time to recognize those longings, spell them out, and do something about them. While people don't always attain their strongest dreams, working toward them provides contentment and satisfaction. As a result, we experience spiritual, emotional, and intellectual growth. People are attracted to us. As Langston Hughes's famous poem states, a dream deferred shrivels like a raisin in the sun. Dreams are important in our creative approach to living. To diminish ourselves by not working toward them ensures our ineptitude as friends or lovers.

However, a fine line exists between needs and desires. Needs are those qualities and components of our lives that we cannot live without. How many relationships have fallen apart because the partners were not sexually compatible? We may need sex only once a week, while our partner has a libido that rages out of control. To what extent are we willing to compromise? We also have specific material needs. We may never be happy living in a home furnished with sixties vintage Sears furniture. If that's true, then it would be far better to live a Spartan existence while we save for more expensive items. Or maybe we can't be truly happy unless we're earning an exorbitant income. In that case, we should actively pursue another job or profession. Otherwise, what we want to accomplish in our lives will never happen because we don't have the means. Perhaps we are more susceptible to American consumerism than many straight men, but if we're incurable shoppers, we should stop the guilt and find the means to shop. Each of us has social needs as well—needs that often affect the quality of our romantic relationships. If we need daily contact with friends, we have to find time to "work them in" regularly. However, if we enjoy solitude, with only weekly forays into society's jungle, to force ourselves into taking more frequent excursions will create undue pressure and dissatisfaction. Going into a new relationship, we should clarify our needs so that acceptable accommodations and compromises can be made.

It's essential to discover what effects the old relationship has had on our character and personality—possibly long-term effects that we may need to address. If we blindly go into another relationship, stubbornly refusing to examine our earlier attitudes and behaviors, we run a strong risk of making the same mistakes as before. Unless we latched on to Evil Incarnate when we tied the marital knot, we must accept the fact that our own shortcomings partially contributed to the dissolution of our partnership. We set ourselves up for another failure if we stubbornly adhere to the same old patterns.

Important questions to ask ourselves now are: What did we relinquish during the old relationship? What compromises did we make? Compromise is an element crucial to every relationship. Any man who says he makes no compromises when he hitches up with someone is a liar. Essentially, compromise means making concessions, altering our needs or desires, in order to meet someone halfway. We *could* argue the philosophical questions over the degree of independence we surrender when establishing a relationship. Some of us may feel we relinquished quite a lot. Others will retort that through our romantic connection, we became even more independent-minded. The truth probably lies somewhere between the two schools of thought. Let's take a look at what we gave up because we thought our partner was "worth it."

Many of us surrendered the excitement of exploring our sexuality with multiple partners. In fact, many men agree—though, as we've already discovered, certainly not all—that sexual infidelity often guarantees unpleasant closure of our relationship. Furthermore, considering the temporal limitations of a day, we probably curtailed the amount of time spent with friends so we could shower our partner with attention. That's not to imply we spent time with our partner because of coercion. Most likely, we often *preferred* his company. He was new, and the friends so familiar.

Establishing relationships is hard work. Even the most compulsive among us will find his time management system has run amuck. Although each of us can recall specific compromises we made once the past relationship began, the most fundamental compromise consisted of compacting the elements of our lives into a smaller time frame. Most of us had to relinquish some elements to ensure the survival of our romance. The challenge we face now is to decide which compromises are worth making, and which ones aren't. That decision isn't easy once our lives have accelerated, along with our beating hearts, once we've met the new man of our dreams.

In reviewing our past, we discover we abandoned some interests, and cultivated new ones. The decision we have to make now is simple—at least, on the surface. Would we like to rekindle any of the old interests we once relinquished for love? One man not only resigned from his position in the community orchestra once he committed to his partner—not enough time, he said—but also stopped playing his trumpet altogether. Once they broke up, he realized how much he'd missed the instrument. Although he had to wait six months for a vacancy in the organization, he used that time to work on his technique and build up his lip.

In the past, maybe we cultivated some interests solely to humor our partner. Time to give them up, right? Certainly. If we haven't found intrinsic value in a hobby or pastime, it only reminds us of our ex-partner and prolongs our recovery. We never actually *enjoyed* archery, but pursuing the sport allowed us even more time with the expert archer we married. Our biggest challenge during a crisis, when we are unlikely to find interest in anything, is to determine which activities can energize us. Likewise, we must determine which personal attributes define us best as human beings, and which ones have impaired our personal growth, our friendships, and our romances. What we dislike about ourselves, we should take steps to overcome. If that means hiring a therapist—or getting one free from the state or local mental health clinic—then that's what we have to do. By extension, we should also examine attributes of our past relationship that we admire. If we feel that our relationship grew because of spending Friday evenings alone with our partner, then we probably want to keep a similar tradition alive when we hook up again. But if we gave each other the silent treatment for two days after major arguments, we probably remember how completely abandoned we felt as a result. Perhaps we want to establish new ground rules for fighting. The bottom line is simple, really. We examine our past lives closely, both as individuals and as part of a team, and determine what we like and dislike.

The potential questions to help us determine the quality of our lives in the future are endless. Do I want to continue living where I am now; maybe Key West would be a better place? Are there areas of my sensuality I did not explore with my old partner; how about that thing with honey I read about? How did I repress my identity in the convenience of a partnered relationship; how many times did I refer to the old ball and chain as my roommate, rather than my partner or spouse? Did I give up some of my friends in the passion of romance? What kinds of friends do I want now? What are the qualities of the partner I want now (if, indeed, I am interested in another partnered relationship)? What were some of my ex-partner's habits that really annoyed me (by God, the next guy will not trim his toenails in bed)? What interests, hobbies, and activities did I give up as a result of that relationship; dare I take up cross-stitching again? Do I want to reestablish those activities in my life; can my eyes and hands handle the thread and those tiny squares? As we candidly respond to our questions, we become more effectively focused on who we have become. Now, we are capable of moving into a new relationship with a stronger character, and a more securely anchored sense of ourselves. In fact, some men reported that, a few months after their breakup, they were told they looked younger—younger, because they had more self-confidence. Or maybe it was because of their perpetual smile. Once they responded to the questions that had to be answered—once they were honest about who they wanted to be, now that this unique opportunity was afforded them—they were much more cheerful than they had been in a long, long time. They experienced this elevation in mood precisely because they were willing to ask the hard-hitting questions.

"My friends told me that I had really come into my own after Joey and I split," says Doug Chambers, 35, a city council member in Fort Lauderdale, Florida. "I laughed when they made that comment, only half-believing it. Then, I began to take a close look at myself. I had become less willing to take bullshit from the homophobes here, and I had closely examined how I could be an even better partner to another man. Not that I was a bad spouse for Joey. But most importantly, I examined how I could be a better friend to myself by clarifying my feelings, what I wanted from my life, and what love really means to me. I think those things increased my value as a human being. Finally, I understood what my friends must have meant."

No Regrets at Taking Risks

After twenty-three years, Los Angeles stage actor and director Richard Epstein broke up with his partner, Louis. There is no better way to determine a man's identity than comparing his sensibilities as a partner to those as a single man. His confidence, insight, and spirit determine the level of difficulty in recovery.

"Louis and I met at an audition, and ended up in the same show together," says Richard. "We became intimate, and began our relationship maybe two or three weeks into our association with the show. We knew we shared a lot of common interests. However, we didn't live in the same town for a while, and he was also married—although his wife knew he was gay. His marriage, the way I understood it, had more to do with his political aspirations. After a while, I got to know his wife, and she welcomed me into the family. And right up to the breakup, there seemed to be no problem."

Although the men couldn't live together, they arranged their schedules so that they spent at least a week together per month. Often, however, Richard felt that he would prefer living with someone. "At the end of our relationship, he was saying, a lot: 'Just commit to me, and we'll be all right.' Finally, he wanted to live with me, and for me to take care of him and support him. He was in a state. He couldn't take care of himself. Latterly, I think that if I had ever seen some evidence that he could be independent, and make a positive effort to look after himself in the good sense of self-loving, I probably would have said, 'Okay, we'll try again.' All I could see was that he was going from one caretaking situation to another. His wife had always been quite the nurturing one, and now I was at risk of filling her role."

Richard, a survivor of child sexual abuse and incest, had dealt with many of his personal issues—except one—and felt "better able to give more to the relationship. Even though I was giving as much as I could before, there was always the thought that I might be abandoned, and there was always the fear of being hurt. There might have been all kinds of problems coming to the fore living with someone—like dealing with personal boundaries—but they didn't come up with me because we had this relationship from a distance. We always wanted to make our time together really good—really special. By being at a distance, we didn't have to deal with a lot of domestic things. We heightened the good parts of our relationship when we were together."

However, just as Richard began to deal with past sexual abuse, Louis was coming apart at the seams. "At that point, I couldn't share the rediscovery of myself with him," he explains. "That was very frustrating. Also frustrating was the fact that, as an alcoholic, he would pay lip service to Alcoholics Anonymous's steps of recovery and other counseling, but he rejected facing some essential issues directly. It was very hard watching him because I had experienced the benefits of finally facing things and he seemed stuck at avoiding, rejecting, and manipulating. Don't get me wrong. I am not on any kind of therapy or counseling bandwagon. I recognize that everyone will have his own way of handling particular issues in his life. But I think that one can at least recognize a healthy approach to personal problems and issues, even though it may be a very different journey for the other person."

Despite these problems, sexual intimacy was not affected—at least, not strongly. "I would tend to be more concerned about making sure he had pleasure than myself," Richard explains. "It meant more to me that he was satisfied than my having an orgasm. And from that point of view, it was very difficult for me just to lie back and enjoy his giving me pleasure—like if he were going down on me or something. That was something that I really had to overcome. I think he also worried that I might be with someone else when we weren't together. Yes, it's true, in the theatre we have very intense work relationships. But there was never anything to threaten our relationship. This issue [of sexual fidelity] was directly affected by our living apart."

When Richard and Louis *did* get together, they were often joined by Louis's wife. As the relationship lost its momentum, Louis's wife dropped almost completely out of the picture. "However, I noticed a certain pattern where suddenly, he would be off with little advance warning," Richard says. "I didn't even get a chance to say I might be able to join them on the trip. He tended to gloss these trips over as being a reward to his wife for 'putting up with him.' I suppose I interpreted it as the cost of her accepting our 'arrangement.' In any case, I would never have imposed myself. Eventually, I came to recognize this, rightly or wrongly, as his essential choice of wife-and-family over a gay relationship with me. I also think there were more ambiguous motives, like concern for his outward appearance and control over others. Early on, I discovered how controlling he was. I used to observe it happening with his wife. It was quite ugly how he manipulated her in domestic affairs. With myself, I observed his same efforts, but I rationalized that if I recognized it when he is doing it, even if I go along with what he wants, he is not quite controlling me because I'm aware of it. You might recognize there the typical accommodation of an abuse survivor, or perhaps a codependent."

Richard thinks Louis's wife accepted their arrangement because "we had a stable relationship. I was obviously no threat to the family, and she always knew where he was. In other words, he wasn't out in some park picking up strangers." Richard pauses. "And then, eventually, the big thing was . . ." His voice trails off. "He is an alcoholic, and he managed to keep this information from me for all these years. He's had to deal with it. He became quite unmanageable. I was really devastated that he had never revealed even the hint of a problem to me before. Well, I did stick by him through numerous attempts at rehabilitation. Supposedly, he was really working hard. But in fact, he wasn't. We had a couple of trial times just coming back to my place. He claimed he was the happiest ever staying with me. He said he was comfortable living with me. All the stressors were gone, and yet, he was still drinking. In the end, he almost burned the house down through some alcoholic negligence. The house was a total mess when the flames stopped."

"Leave things alone!" Louis screamed at Richard as he cleaned the house. "I'll take care of it."

"Good," Richard thought. "You take responsibility to clean up after yourself for a change."

"But all day, he sat in the same place, and didn't do a thing," Richard says. "Eventually, I had to start cleaning up a little, but instead of being apologetic about what had happened, and his subsequent inaction, he went to the bedroom to lie down and let me finish the job."

Shortly after that incident, Richard insisted Louis's key to Richard's house be returned. "We went through a year of a lot of talking," Richard says. "He tried to persuade me to take him back."

"I'm not looking for perfection," Richard said to him. "But I'm healing from my sexual abuse, and you from your alcoholism. I want to be reasonably assured that we are two healing, positive people coming together. Not that we are crutches for each other; not that we have to caretake for each other."

Richard hoped his proposal would be acceptable, but he saw no signs of improvement in Louis's behavior. "I was fearful that if he came to live with me at this point, I would end up the victim of the same lack of responsibility as I'd seen in him in the fire incident," Richard explains. "He kept saying to me, 'Alcoholics can't promise anything.' I know his vocabulary very well indeed. He skirts around the truth. He says things in an ambiguous way so that later he can technically deny them. So when I heard this, I heard myself thinking: 'Yeah, you're just giving yourself that excuse so you won't have to work at our relationship.' "

There has been no contact between Richard and Louis since this episode. "Right before this altercation, there were a few, rather pained phone calls," Richard qualifies. "Then, a couple of periods when he would inundate me with calls demanding for me to commit to him, but in a voice and style which I recognized as one when he was drinking. Now, there is no contact."

When they broke up, Richard shut down emotionally. "I cried a lot," he says. "I felt really devastated. I kept imagining: Here I am, throwing away the one big relationship in my life. I wondered if I would have another. Would I end up a lonely old man, never having a relationship again? That was the sharpest feeling I had. At the same time, I felt an immense relief that I had stood up for myself."

Still, Richard feels he made the healthy choice. "At the same time, in typical fashion, I did not make a decisive break at first:

I left things open to the possibility of our getting back together—really together, no longer with some arrangement," he explains. "This prolonged the breakup and had me on a bit of a roller-coaster ride for at least a couple of years. But I had put so much and so many years into this relationship, I just couldn't discard it out of hand. Is that another sexual abuse survivor's abandonment issue? I wonder. And of course I still held out faint hope deep down inside because we really had been compatible in many ways, and were a good match for intellect and interests. I think another issue is that one hates to feel or admit that he has failed in a really important relationship, and perhaps not recognized it in time and, therefore, wasted a good life."

Complicating the issue was the "horrible timing," as Richard characterizes his decision to call the relationship off. "I was suffering a lot of pain and angst due to the realizations connected to the sexual abuse," he explains. "My sexual abusers were my mother, over a long period of time; my father, briefly, but he was also aware of the maternal situation; and a cousin, when we were in our teens. I was also gang-raped as a youth. Most of the work, both in coming to terms with my sexual abuse and in dealing with the breakup, I did by myself. I was, however, part of a male support group. It was my only resource, other than myself. I did a lot of work and thinking on my own, and journaling. Even through my worst nights, I had always been able to pull out of myself enough to see if there was anything I could do for my lover. I can't think of a single time when he asked what he could do for me. Many, many years ago, he and my father had gotten quite drunk on a fishing trip. Although I had no intention of prying into their conversation, I wanted to know if Father said anything I should know. Louis said there was nothing. Only years later, when I finally broached the details of what I remembered about the sexual abuse, did he inform me that my father told him about the incest and the abuse. Although I welcomed the news as validation of my struggles over the accuracy of my memories, I always wondered why Louis kept the secret."

By then, too many promises had been broken for the relationship to survive. "One aspect of my abuse background is that if someone says he will do something, it's a big deal to me that I not be betrayed—even in trivial things," Richard explains. "In fact, with Louis, there were promises about buying a house together, and an implied promise of living together, which ended up with my buying the house while he did nothing. And the pattern still holds. In the middle of our relationship, I tried to tell myself that I was being petty by putting too much significance on these matters. Still, I would be hurt, and would feel that maybe he didn't think I deserved anything. That was a big threat, because I would worry that he didn't love me enough, even to keep one of these insignificant, trivial promises. Maybe that meant the relationship was ending. I couldn't stand that thought, that eventuality, so I tried to convince myself that I should be looking for something else—something deeper and more elusive—in the relationship. I got to the point that I knew I couldn't count on him to keep his word. I couldn't count on anyone else to get what I wanted or needed. I always had to take care of myself. This realization made me strong and independent, but there are times when you want to be taken care of. That would feel really nice, even in small ways. I certainly wasn't looking for a sugar daddy, or to be kept, but just once in a while, you like to just let go and be taken care of. For a moment. A little respite.''

Despite Richard's frustrations over the dynamics of their relationship, Richard and Louis still enjoyed many happy times. ''There were many ways that we were compatible, and complemented one another,'' he explains. ''Early on, there were some areas where I grew because of the relationship. For one thing, I became much more confident as a gay man. It felt good to be in a stable relationship, rather than pursuing promiscuous, anonymous encounters. Because I had to do a lot of managing and arranging our time together, and I attempted to make my house a special home away from home for my lover, I gained a foothold on self-confidence. Later, the major efforts and growth and risk taking in development were, however, my own.''

Though Richard currently has a friend with whom he's sexual, he hasn't pursued romantic relationships. ''I guess I'm open for anything,'' he says, ''but I'm not desperately seeking a romantic relationship. I'm not quite sure what people do at my age. I think it's easier for heterosexuals of any age. There is that big social imperative that they're going to join households, even though straight, mature individuals may have some of the same questions about being lonely and the risk of trying another relationship. What does a commitment mean for me now, with the complications of being set in one's ways and having a lot at stake in joining households at this stage of the game—especially with no guarantee that this one will last either? Still, the support that goes with being a legally recognized couple is a big advantage. I am, however, encouraged by meeting more and more openly gay couples."

Now, Richard lives by himself, and doesn't mind it— "although I sometimes feel lonely," he says. "I have made particular efforts these days to make sure I get out and associate with colleagues in the theatre. Actually, because of the very jealous imperative of my ex-lover to have an exclusive relationship, and his intolerance of any friendship he thought threatening, I find that I am quite naturally more friendly toward people nowadays. I find myself much freer, and more open, and even confiding in them. Because of what I've been through, I am very respectful of other people's issues and their boundaries. I recognize the importance of being able to talk about feelings and expectations, and have perceptions validated or corrected so that one isn't second-guessing the other person. I am much less afraid of risking honesty with others, and expressing myself."

Richard's openness did, in fact, inspire his meeting one person with whom he thought something romantic might develop. "It was quite lovely to feel wanted, and to enjoy the new freedom of being able to talk and exchange thoughts and share feelings," he says. "In the end, although I enjoyed the togetherness, I discovered we weren't that compatible sexually. I was disappointed, but not shattered. I did not regret having risked getting to know the chap, even if nothing came of the experience."

Still, Richard looks to the future both optimistically and realistically. "Superficially, I look older than I actually am, and definitely much older than I feel," he explains. "I regret that I don't have the youthful, buffed exterior to attract people to get to know the much better man I am now. But I'm not despairing. I know there are people who put more store in the person than just the exterior. It may take a little time to find them, and connect—I doubt they are in the bars or on the meat racks— but I guess that's life. I just hope I recognize the right person when he comes along—and that I have the courage to go for him.''

Making Changes

In this activity, you will indicate changes you've already made, or are in the process of making, in three areas of your life—lifestyle, personality, and values. To get you started, several subcategories have been listed. For example, ''My life at home'' would address changes that have occurred on the home front, while ''Attitude toward trying new things'' would refer to your sense of adventure during your recovery process.

Lifestyle Changes—changes in the way I live my life	
My life at home	
How I dress	
The car I drive	
Money matters	
Feelings about work	
Social life	
(Other categories)	

Personality Changes—changes in my personality and disposition	
How outgoing I am	
My ability to analyze feelings and motives	
Attitudes toward friends	
Attitude toward ex-partner	
Attitude toward trying new things	
Value Changes—changes in values, standards, and morals	
Romance	
Family	
Religion	
Politics	
Finances	
Love	
Relationships	

Now, in the chart below, you'll take a subjective look at the changes presently occurring in your life. In the first column, list the changes in your life you like. In the second, list those changes you could do without—those that get in the way of recovery.

Changes I Like	Changes I Don't Like

Finally, using the "Changes I Like" category, write a description of the person you'd like to become by the time you've achieved full recovery.

My Ideal Self

CHAPTER TEN
• • • • • • • • • • • • • • • • • • • •
Celebration!

Friendly Terms

A significant stretch of time has passed since we said our goodbyes
to our ex-partner. We never thought we would make it this far,
but we're amazingly close to recovery. We have identified new
interests, hobbies, and activities to energize our lives and reactivate our spirits. We gave up cross-stitch for skydiving. We reestablished old friendships, and initiated new ones. Our bodies are
tighter and sexier than they've been in years. After painful deliberation, some of us decided that our work preserved the legacy
of our past relationship at the expense of doing what fulfills us.
How could we have been willing to neglect all the important
things life had to offer? Finally, we feel it in our bones—there
is no better time for change than Now, when we've established
a newfound independence and friendlier terms with ourselves.

We will never forget our journey toward courage. We learned
so much from the pain and suffering that resulted from falling
out of love and the subsequent breaking up. At times, we thought
the sheer loneliness and desperation of it all would ultimately
swallow us up, but we were persistent enough, if not brave
enough, to stick with life's challenges. We knew we'd eventually
heal. We knew we'd feel comfortable living in the world once
more. We even knew that we would get to know ourselves all
over again, even though we often thought we would forever
remain strangers to ourselves. It was an arduous journey we took,
but we became real again. "Real isn't how you are made," says
the Skin Horse to the Rabbit in Margery Williams's *The Velveteen*

Rabbit. "It's a thing that happens to you. . . . It takes a long time. That's why it doesn't often happen to people who break easily, or have sharp edges, or who have to be carefully kept. Generally, by the time you are Real, most of your hair has been loved off, and your eyes drop out and you get loose in the joints and very shabby. But these things don't matter at all, because once you are Real you can't be ugly, except to people who don't understand."

The End of Anger

When Duane Sharp met Charles, he sensed that Charles was a mature individual with a good sense of what he wanted from life. "He seemed to be stable and even-keeled," says Duane. "He articulated his desire to be in a long-term, monogamous relationship. That's what both of us wanted."

But things turned sour quickly. At the time, Charles was 34, but he hadn't been out very long. When he and Duane moved to Hollywood, Florida, Duane realized that Charles still had oats to sow. "He even thought of becoming a porn star," says Duane. "He started doing drugs. He began going to the gay clubs frequently. In short order, Charles was spending very little time with me."

For a while, Duane passively endured the pain. "Then, I realized how angry I had become. In many ways, I was not ready to examine the situation in terms of what was really happening. At one point during the summer, Charles went into a week-long group therapy session. He was really upset when he returned. He tried to explain how torn he felt—about being in our relationship, and exploring his sexuality, as well. I suggested that we separate for four months; then, we would come back together and see what we wanted to do. It took him only a month to decide he didn't want to continue our relationship, because it was within the course of a month that he met another man."

Once Charles expressed his desire to end the relationship permanently, Duane was upset, but relieved. "I was glad to have my life back again," he explains. "I felt very sorry for him. I realized that what was happening to him, in terms of his promiscuity and indecision, had to do with his coming out. He was having one hell of a difficult time."

Upon recognizing the inevitability of their separation, Duane felt extremely angry. "At first, I was angry at myself—to the extent to which I denied what was happening. I was angry at him for telling me one thing, and doing another. I expressed my anger to my friends, who didn't give any advice—thankfully—but realized the best they could do was to listen."

Once the break was final, Duane found it very difficult to be sexual with anyone else in a romantic, or even semi-romantic, way. "Part of me didn't want to connect with another person on anything other than skin level," he says. "I got burned real bad, and I needed time to heal. Sometimes, even now, I go out by myself. I don't see that kind of solitude as bad. I don't see it as permanent, either. God, I certainly hope not. Besides, I've noticed a change. I've begun to look at all the pretty faces and buff bodies in South Florida. I'm starting to pay attention."

Duane is finally coming to the end of the hostility he felt for so long, once he discovered his victimization by a repressed gay man trying his homosexuality on for size. "I'm beginning to think about dating again. I'm a little uncomfortable, certainly. But I'm slowly regaining my confidence. Emotionally, I'm not nearly as raw as I was four months ago. For a long time, I couldn't see what I wanted with my life because Charles was obscuring that vision."

One of Duane's desires is to establish another relationship. "I would be able to offer experience, maturity, self-awareness, and self-knowledge to another man," he says. "Also, I would bring a real bottom-line, no-bullshit attitude to the relationship. It's that attitude that makes me laugh when I see, in the personals, some guy wanting to find someone with whom to enjoy romantic walks along the beach at sunset. It's such an unrealistic attitude. At forty-six, I feel time's passage deep in my gut. In one sense, I feel my options aren't as large as they once were. Lately, they're balanced by the awareness that I can survive—and live—without a relationship. The good thing is that I really have a firm idea of what I want in a relationship. I don't experience this tremendous urge to get involved again, although, you know, it would be so nice."

Duane compares his feelings now with those he experienced when an earlier relationship ended. "That was a really profound experience and it took me three years to recover," he says. "The problem was me. I wasn't involved in the relationship totally. This time, I feel more confident of my ability to survive, and to thrive, now that it's over. Now, the emotions are nowhere near as intense. When I broke up earlier, I had only a vague sense of who I was. It just shattered me. But I had a strong self-awareness when I broke up with Charles that made things a little easier."

After fifteen years, Bill Van Patten, a professor in Champagne, Illinois, told his partner: "Let's not kid each other, Karl. It's over. Do me a favor, and don't hang around."

The problem was simple. With Karl's midlife crisis came a proclivity to pursue partners almost half his age. Bill had definitely had more than enough. "Besides, I was bogged down in depression," he says. "My mother's cancer had returned, and it was terminal. A good friend committed suicide. And both dogs we owned for a very long time had to be put to sleep. All I can say, Prozac is wonderful. I recommend drugs to anyone dealing with a breakup."

At work, Bill pasted a smile on his face and pretended that everything was okay. "I just don't bring that stuff to work," he explains. "In my department, I would solve people's problems for them, then go into my office and collapse. I had two countenances—one in public, and one behind my office door."

Bill began dating other men several months after splitting up with Karl. "I haven't been all that successful yet," he says. "I don't pursue people. I'm not a sleep-around type, or a date-around type, for that matter. I *am* seeing someone regularly now. We've been hitting it off. We were supposed to see each other on the weekend, but he called on Wednesday. He needed a couple days of solitude because he ran into his ex, who had been leaving hateful messages on his answering machine. The argument between them had played a number on him."

Bill and Karl might still be together had Karl been able to express his feelings openly. "It would have given us something concrete to work on," he explains. "If you can identify the problem, it gives a couple common ground, and common goals. I could have tried to understand his routine of having to sleep with younger guys. I could have attempted to understand the pathology there. But I was tired of being the only one working on the partnership. Even if he had felt he had to go away to work things out, fine. Over the last year, I spent a lot of time hurting for him. Trying to figure out if there was something I could do for him. But I let him go. I realized that I couldn't be the one who solves his problems. It's got to be him."

Once Bill was able to let go of the relationship, he noticed quite a few changes in himself. "There had been so many things I repressed," he says. "That included making my own friends. I didn't realize how popular I could be. I came bounding out of that old marriage closet. I got back into being physically fit. In the past, I was into aerobics, then got out of it, partially because of Karl. Then, about a year ago, I started doing a little drag. Now, people come from miles away to see LaBette. The first time I performed, I got a standing ovation. I opened up all of my dormant talents once again. One thing that often happens in a long-term relationship is that you don't devote enough time to yourself."

What about a new relationship? "Oh, yes, I would be interested," Bill says. "But one thing I would make absolutely clear is that my partner has to take me as I am. I'm very giving. Very loving. Very attentive. But I have to be who I am. I have a tremendous strength to hold people up, and help them through challenges. I have a great sense of humor. Hell, I spend half my time laughing. But I have learned something through my healing. I've learned to be more self-reflective. We have to be courageous enough to ask ourselves the hard questions, then find the real answers. If we don't, we're just walking through life—not living it. I also insist that people are honest with me. I have no patience with people who don't say what they're really feeling. I hope to take the new discoveries about myself into a new relationship and push any new partner to be just as open. Actually, I would never get involved with someone who hasn't reached this level of honesty."

The Most Amazing Men

The most important lesson we can learn before reaching the point of celebration is how to make our peace with the relationship that ended. As long as we mourn for the loss of our ex-partner, or of our partnered status, happiness will elude us. The most amazing men among us will find a way to move on. We can accept that we're usually better off as a result of change, no matter how uncomfortable it makes us. Moving on is an experience of freedom, of self-actualization and of celebration. Moving on invites the admiration of friends, of family, of colleagues—and yes, it even invites the attention of the eligible bachelors in our midst.

John Politis, 52, a librarian in Philadelphia, is ready—though hardly desperate—for another relationship. After all, he's had two partnerships of long duration—the first lasted ten years, the second more than fifteen—and he learned a lot about making a relationship work. "I was only twenty-one years old when the first relationship began," he explains. "I met Bob at some college function. We became roommates, but we were both really naïve at the time. One night, we finally had a discussion during which we told each other we were gay. Right then, we made a commitment to stay together. And we did—for a decade. However, Bob said he felt really tied down throughout the relationship."

One night, over dinner, Stan, John's second partner, was direct enough to ask if he could move in. "I said okay," John continues. "We had an open relationship—an arrangement with which I was always uncomfortable. I just bought into that philosophy at the time. It wasn't as though I really *felt* its credibility."

With Bob, John didn't know for almost nine years that anything was wrong. "He thought promiscuity was growth," John explains. "But it was just growth away from me. Finally, he left a note, saying he was gone. I saw the note when I got home from work. I didn't even get to say goodbye. It was the most cowardly way to handle things."

With Stan, the problem was his manic-depression. "I knew about his illness before we started the relationship, but I thought I could live with it. He took lithium, but he wasn't responsive. Once, out of the blue, he actually left me for someone else—a really manic act. Once he was gone, I got used to not having him around. My sentiment was he would come back when he came back. And he did. We agreed to stay in counseling for a while, but it didn't help. He left after a turbulent eight months."

When John and Bob broke up, John felt depressed and bitter. "The depression and bitterness manifested themselves behaviorally," John says. "Basically, I'm a stay-at-home person, but when we broke up, I went out a lot. Still I faced the difficult challenge of readjusting socially. People had been used to us as a couple. So, for about five years, people tried to be equally friendly to us both. Ultimately, they gravitated to one or the other of us. When Stan and I broke up, it wasn't as big a deal. Actually, I felt some relief that I was rid of a few major problems. Besides, while we were together, I had my own social life. I had been through a breakup before; I didn't feel it was the end of the world."

Even so, John found the second relationship more fulfilling. "I think, with Bob, I was really too young and naïve to understand what a relationship was all about," John admits. "I was just glad to find someone else who was gay—someone with whom I shared common ground. Some of the closeness I felt at first was definitely artificial. It would be fair to say that part of the reason we got together was that we had found somebody 'like us.' Back then, I saw most gay people in terms of stereotypes; they didn't seem like me. Fortunately, now I've found a circle of friends who are much like me."

Finally, John feels stronger and more capable of doing things on his own. "When I broke up with Bob, I had never been alone before. I really needed to be with people—almost all the time. Now, I'm very independent. Some guy has invited me to go out with him next week. Also, I answered a personal ad several days ago. It looks as though we'll get together. Now, I look at any encounter as an adventure. I have no idea whether I'll like either of these men. But I know one thing. I won't be looking for ways in which we're similar. What two guys have in common means less than what I thought in the past. Sometimes, opposites click, and things work out beautifully. But there is one big warning sign that I will respect more than any other. I don't think I'll ever go into an open relationship again. At the time, my agreement was more experimental. I was buying into current trends. I feel I was right in the first place; I've got to learn to stick with what I feel. That's a problem I have, and I'm working on it."

Another man living in Portland, Maine, found that learning to acknowledge his feelings to family and friends was more difficult than he imagined. However, if he continued to conceal them, his feelings would forever be undermined by the people he was trying to protect. In a letter to relatives and friends, he wrote: "Two weeks ago, Stuart moved out of our house. And with him went seven years of visible and undeniable evidence that I am a gay man. I am writing to you all today because I don't for a minute want you to confuse my living alone with the possibility that I am a 'confirmed bachelor,' or that I am waiting for the right woman to come along.

"Being a gay man in our family has not been hell. Unless one considers forty years of denial and silence hell. Unless hearing your father call some men fairies and knowing you're one hurts. Unless all the adulation from engagements and weddings and births and christenings seems isolating. Unless trying to drink and drug away all of the feelings from age fourteen on seems like suicide.

"Today (October 11) is National Coming Out Day. A day set aside for each gay man and lesbian to go one step further in coming out of the closet. A day to further educate the rest of the world that we are everywhere. We are your sons and brothers and brothers-in-law and uncles. Our sexual [orientation] is as natural and God-given as yours.

"I have always handled the 'gay issue' with kid gloves. I have tried to protect you and save you from the pain of having a gay brother, brother-in-law, son, or uncle. But I will no longer attempt to do that.

"From today forward, when you ask me what I'm up to, I intend to tell you. And let me begin by telling you that last night, I volunteered to chair a fundraiser for the Bowdoin Gay and Lesbian Alumni Association. We just received approval to establish an endowment which will fund semiannual speakers on gay issues. And this year, I will continue to serve as the Maine contact for the Chiltern Mountain Club, a gay and lesbian outdoor club.

"From today forward, when you ask me how I feel, I intend to tell you. And let me begin by telling you that it hurts like hell to have my partner and lover of seven years leave. It especially hurts when you pretend to the straight world that it's a roommate who has moved out. Or some insensitive person reminds you that 'we told you gay life is unstable.'

"From today forward, I anticipate telling you that when I climbed Katahdin, it was with eighteen other gay men, many of whom were recovering alcoholics. I look forward to telling you that the Bowdoin fundraiser is going well, and who our next speaker will be. And I look forward to someday telling you that I have just met the most amazing man in Maine, and that he has swept me off my feet."

And that's what it boils down to, really, for all of us, this moving on with our lives when we have fallen out of love. We want to be swept off our feet. We want to sweep someone else off his. What we mourn, more than anything else, is the realization that our ex-partner no longer has the ability to sweep us off our feet. We have lost our touch as well. As long as we have the potential to excite someone, to make him feel passionate about life, to feel the certainty of love and acceptance no matter how much we bare our souls, we live a life full of celebration, confetti, and fireworks. But when the songs end, the fireworks fade into darkness, and the party never resumes, we're not living anymore. We're merely surviving—paying homage to the memory of living. We must find something to compel us to claim ownership of our lives again—something to make us feel our lives aren't merely tests of endurance. "My self-direction had a lot to do with the relationship ending," says Jeremy Richards. "He complained he needed more space. I told him, at first, that was ridiculous. We'd have these ferocious arguments; he'd bring it up again. We need our own space, he would repeat, over and over again. When he first said that, my father had just died. I wasn't ready to hear what he was saying, much less to deal with it. For God's sake, I told him. Let me deal with one thing at a time."

Finally, Jeremy conceded that his ex-partner might be right. "He'd gone back to school to study architecture," he explains. "I knew what I wanted to do. I knew some of my choices had gotten in the way. I hadn't put enough energy into my acting career. So we decided to get separate apartments and maintain the relationship."

During those months of separate living arrangements, Jeremy decided he wanted to end the partnership, but not the friendship. "There was no turning back for me," he says. "When he suggested getting a larger apartment and moving back in together, I told him it wouldn't work for me. I was having serious doubts about the relationship. It had taken me a long time to decide whether to tell him, but it wasn't fair to string him along. I knew I had made the right decision, but it hurt me to hurt him so much. We talked and talked and talked, and talked some more. After I reassured him that our divorce wasn't attributable to anything he was doing, but to something I felt I had lost along the way, he said he understood. We still talk, but for a while, we couldn't. It hurt too much. Then, I told myself to try. I could try to talk, because I care about him. Perhaps we could stay friends. I love him deeply. I don't ever *not* want him in my life. I just can't be with him romantically."

It's been nice, Jeremy says, this being alone. "It's a chance to get centered. That's part of it, isn't it? So, once I started seeing other people, I wasn't going out and getting hurt. I didn't feel I was running away from anything."

Solitude helped Jeremy sort out another issue. "It was hard not to feel responsibility for helping him get over the breakup," he explains. "I knew that was part of his process. I had to do what was good for me. Sometimes I had to say: 'I'm sorry you feel the way you do. But that's the way things are. There's nothing I can do.' "

Several months later, Jeremy submits this update. "Clint and I are still on amicable terms and we talk often," he says. "After being together for a little over six years, it took the breakup of our relationship to enable us to have the most open, frank and honest conversation we've ever had. We talked about how our needs weren't met. I felt he was too overbearing at times, and too possessive. He mentioned that I was closed off to him—especially in the last two years—and told him only what I felt he needed to know. Interestingly enough, it was in the last two years that I began to feel that I really needed to be out of the relationship. I also learned that he slept with other men on two occasions—both when he had traveled to San Francisco. He claims it happened because our relationship was in limbo. I see now that our relationship was in bigger trouble than I thought. I always felt that if anyone would cheat in this relationship, it would be me. I was shocked to hear of his infidelities. It makes sense, however. His infidelity was just another symptom of our failing relationship. I often wonder if we had sought out couples therapy, would things be different? I think we still would have separated, but it would have happened sooner. I have no regrets, though. Things happen for good reasons, and we both continue to discover the lessons we need to learn. He says he misses me. He says he is still in love with me. He still hopes we will get together again. As time goes on, I see the chances of that happening getting slimmer and slimmer."

"Where am I now?" Jeremy asks himself. It is the same question we must ask ourselves. "I enjoy having the freedom to share physical relations with another man I find attractive, but I'm not looking for another husband," he says. "This is the happiest I've ever been."

If not now, then soon, we must be able to make the same assessment of our happiness. If our happiness includes the presence of another man in our lives, we must move slowly, but with clarity and sensitivity. We don't want to close the spaces between us too quickly, or we might overlook the caution signs. We keep the questions coming. Is he the kind of person with whom we can see ourselves for a long period of time? Does he have habits we can't stand? Are our interests, if not alike, at least compatible? Are his unique interests stimulating to us? Do we like his friends, and does he like ours? Are we both willing to give each other space to grow, both as individuals and as a couple?

Regardless of our romantic status, however, the time has never been better to celebrate the man we've become. Like Jeremy, we should, with gratitude, acknowledge the contributions of our previous partnership to our capacity for celebration. We could never be in the place we stand now if we had not met our previous spouse, loved him, broken up with him, and then possessed the courage to carry on.

What do we do now? The answer is simple. We thank our ex-partner for what he helped us accomplish. Then, we move on with our new, exciting lives.

Recovery Zone

The following activity will determine whether you've entered the Recovery Zone, as well as determining your readiness to enter another relationship with open eyes. Most likely, no statement will qualify for an exclusive "yes" or "no" response. Using the evaluative guidelines below, determine the extent to which each statement is true at the present time. You will find completing this activity even more beneficial if you return to it several times until you have achieved what you feel is your highest possible score. Once you've made it to the Recovery Zone, you have, indeed, moved on with your life.

5—I always feel this way.
4—I feel this way most of the time.
3—I feel this way more and more.
2—From time to time, I feel like this.
1—This is rarely the way I feel.

1. When spending time alone, I am very comfortable with myself.
2. I think of my ex-partner less than ten percent of the day.
3. Even if I'm not already doing it, I know what I want to do with my life.
4. Although I genuinely like people, I don't consider myself someone who follows the crowd.
5. I view each new day of my life as an opportunity for new discoveries about myself.
6. I can see the humor in most situations I encounter daily.
7. My attitude toward life and living is very positive.
8. I have a positive attitude toward the work I do.
9. Friends seek me out for social activities, advice, and parties.
10. I am comfortable confronting and expressing my true feelings.
11. I can identify my feelings very clearly.
12. I have taken steps to improve my appearance since breaking up.
13. I am acutely aware when other men find me attractive.
14. I face dating situations with confidence and humor.

15. I possess the attitude that life doesn't create problems; instead, it creates opportunities.
16. I can intuitively sense how those people who are close to me feel.
17. I seek ways to connect to other people, rather than avoiding connections.
18. I fully understand how and why other men might find me sexually appealing.
19. I feel less willing to apologize for being gay.
20. Breaking up has made me braver and more confident to face life's challenges.
21. I find pleasure in the "little things" of life.
22. I can hear my ex-partner's name without slipping into a bad mood.
23. I am willing to try new things in my life.
24. I have made lifestyle changes that will ensure better health for me.
25. I am very self-aware, and can tell when I need to make changes in my behaviors.
26. I avoid experiences and situations that will bring me down.
27. I have examined my history, including my childhood, and understand how that history has influenced my identity.
28. I maintain steady contact with my friends to let them know they are cherished.
29. I communicate assertively and honestly with others, even if the topic of communication is unpleasant.
30. I stand up for myself when anyone makes a remark that disparages my sexual orientation, or homosexuals generally.
31. I am strong enough to demand equal respect from my family. If they aren't willing to extend that respect, I am strong enough to walk away.
32. With other men, I never hide traits of my personality.
33. I feel no urgency to set up housekeeping with somebody new.
34. I am willing to be a friend to my ex-partner.
35. I can take constructive criticism without growing defensive.
36. I feel a sense of gratitude for my past experiences, including breaking up with my ex-partner.

1.	7.	13.	19.	25.	31.	
2.	8.	14.	20.	26.	32.	
3.	9.	15.	21.	27.	33.	
4.	10.	16.	22.	28.	34.	**GRAND**
5.	11.	17.	23.	29.	35.	**TOTAL**
6.	12.	18.	24.	30.	36.	

Add the numbers in each vertical column, and place the sums in the bottom row. Then, add all sums in the six bottom compartments to calculate your Grand Total. Place that total in the box to the far right of the chart.

What the Numbers Mean:

72–107: Danger Zone. You'll manage to enter the Recovery Zone eventually, but much work is needed before it happens.

108–143: Discovery Zone. You are well on your way to finding positive elements in your life to propel you to the Recovery Zone.

144–180: Recovery Zone. You have done well in moving on with your life. Congratulations! May you continue to experience contentment, fulfillment, and happiness.

Conclusion

For a long time, we hear his voice, see his face, revere all the good memories. We think they will never fade into the past. We smell his fragrance on another man, and our heart skips a beat. We speak fondly of him, as though we were still lovers, while our friends surreptitiously glance at one another with a worried expression. We caress the phone as we ponder whether to give him a call. Maybe he's experienced a change of heart, and he's just too embarrassed to call—too proud to admit the mistake he's made. Perhaps if we just make it easy for him . . .

Realizing the futility of phone calls and flashbacks, we step into the crisp night air, breathe in, and take a tentative step forward. We should probably be in bed now, but sleep, like contentment, eludes us. So we walk. And walk. The moonlight bathes over us, reminding us of our ex's constancy in a past we remember much too well. How difficult it is to forget. How difficult it is to know whether we even *want* to forget.

"I feel what I went through was sort of a test run," says James McKeon from his Miami home. "I'm in a pretty good space now. It's been a long healing process, but I'm happy. Yes, I want to be in an honest relationship. I don't want one where each man has his own agenda, and we are never on the same frequency. Now, I am more reflective, more introspective. I look for warning signs. I approach my life differently. I lay it out, you see. I want it to be more real."

As in James's case, moving on provides each of us with an opportunity for reflection. Early in my relationship with Robert, I was often insecure and petty. I could never trust his love. But he stuck by me as I grappled with the internalized message that the love one man has for another cannot last, cannot endure, cannot sustain—until I finally understood how much he cared for me. How Robert would describe his personal growth during our relationship, I do not presume to know. Perhaps he would not choose to mention how I failed to nurture him when he needed it most. Perhaps he would spare me the criticism that often I didn't greet him affectionately when he came home from work. Perhaps he would be silent about my failure to recognize how much his parents meant to him, or my lack of sensitivity in a thousand situations. Luckily, for our peace of mind, we have talked frequently since we broke up. We have made our peace with ourselves, and with our shortcomings. And we have become the friends we couldn't be to one another for the two lonely years that preceded our decision to go our separate ways.

Now that we're moving on with our life, we're able to identify our shortcomings and our flaws, face them, take steps to transform them, without being defeated by them, or attempting to shift the blame onto someone else. When Kurt Colborn hears the phrase "moving on," he thinks of "all the words that I hate hearing. But it means an ability to identify and express my feelings, needs, and wants. It means being able to identify what really belongs in each of those categories. It means cultivating a certain patience to deal with relationship issues."

And it means persistence in our adventurous search to discover what we want next. A self-help book can provide guidance in our search; it can even provide motivation. But the real work has to come from within our hearts and minds. Ultimately, all of us have to take charge of our own lives, and move on in ways that are most harmonious to our needs, desires, and dreams. "Since my ex-partner is no longer part of my life," says John Eastwood, "I've become increasingly disheartened by what it feels like when the party ends, the bar closes, the personal ad fails to garner any serious response. In some ways, I'm becoming desperate to find someone who is real. I want to know that genuine, caring people still exist—people whose first interest is friendship. It is not wrong to want a relationship with someone I can cherish above everyone else, whose life I would protect with my own, who is capable of returning a deep abiding love. I've been there once. I know it can happen again."

"Are you a taker?" John asks. "If you are, maybe things will work out. You don't know until you take that step forward."

And that's what I hope for you: that you are a taker. That you are willing to take not just one step forward, but many. That you are willing to take a close look at what was wrong—and what was right—about your former relationship. That you are able to indulge in such painful yet crucial self-examination without guilt, animosity, or blame. That moving on ultimately prepares you for an even greater love of life—and perhaps of another man—than you've ever experienced before.

Contact the Author

Via letter:
Dann Hazel
PO Box 781
Summerville, SC 29484-0781

Via e-mail:
dannh54@dannhazel.com